First World War
and Army of Occupation
War Diary
France, Belgium and Germany

24 DIVISION
17 Infantry Brigade
Royal Fusiliers (City of London Regiment)
12th Battalion
21 August 1915 - 13 February 1918

WO95/2208/1

The Naval & Military Press Ltd
www.nmarchive.com
Published in association with The National Archives

Published by

The Naval & Military Press Ltd

Unit 10 Ridgewood Industrial Park,

Uckfield, East Sussex,

TN22 5QE England

Tel: +44 (0) 1825 749494

www.naval-military-press.com

www.nmarchive.com

This diary has been reprinted in facsimile from the original. Any imperfections are inevitably reproduced and the quality may fall short of modern type and cartographic standards.

© **Crown Copyright**
Images reproduced by permission of The National Archives, London, England, 2015.

Contents

Document type	Place/Title	Date From	Date To
Heading	WO95/2208 12 Btn Royal Fusiliers Aue 1915-Feb 1918		
Heading	24th Division 17th Infy Bde 12th Bn Royal Fus. Aug 1915-Feb 1918		
Heading	73rd Inf. Bde. 24th Div. Battn. Disembarked Boulogne From England 2.9.15. 12th Battn. The Royal Fusiliers. August And September (21.8.15 to 30.9.15) 1915 Oct 1915		
War Diary	Perbright Camp	21/08/1915	21/08/1915
War Diary	Perbright	22/08/1915	01/09/1915
War Diary	Boulogne	02/09/1915	03/09/1915
War Diary	Maresquel	03/09/1915	03/09/1915
War Diary	Embry	04/09/1915	21/09/1915
War Diary	Beaumetz	22/08/1915	22/08/1915
War Diary	Busnes	23/09/1915	24/09/1915
War Diary	Beuvry	25/09/1915	25/09/1915
War Diary	In Action N.E. Of Vermelles	25/09/1915	28/09/1915
War Diary	Fontes.	29/09/1915	30/09/1915
War Diary	24th Division 73rd Infy Bde. 12th Bn Roy Fusiliers Sep 1915-Oct 1915		
Heading	24th Division. 12th Royal Fusiliers Vol 2 Oct 15		
War Diary	Fontes.	01/10/1915	02/10/1915
War Diary	Herzeele	03/10/1915	05/10/1915
War Diary	Proven	06/10/1915	10/10/1915
War Diary	Reninghelst	11/10/1915	14/10/1915
War Diary	Near Voormezeele	15/10/1915	19/10/1915
War Diary	Hubertus Hoek	20/10/1915	25/10/1915
War Diary	St Hubertushoek	26/10/1915	31/10/1915
Heading	24th Division. 12th Roy Fus. Vol. 3		
War Diary	Reninghelst	01/11/1915	02/11/1915
War Diary	Voormezeele Sector	03/11/1915	07/11/1915
War Diary	Verbranden Molen	08/11/1915	10/11/1915
War Diary	Renninghelst	11/11/1915	14/11/1915
War Diary	St Hubertus Hoek	15/11/1915	15/11/1915
War Diary	St Hubertushoek Camp A	16/11/1915	21/11/1915
War Diary	Poperinghe	22/11/1915	22/11/1915
War Diary	Eecke	23/11/1915	23/11/1915
War Diary	Arneke	24/11/1915	24/11/1915
War Diary	Wattin	25/11/1915	25/11/1915
War Diary	Est Mont	26/11/1915	30/11/1915
Heading	24th Div 12/Roy. Fusrs. Vol 4 December 1915		
War Diary	Estmont	01/12/1915	31/12/1915
Heading	17th Brigade. 24th Division. 12th Battalion Royal Fusiliers. January 1916 Feb 18		
Heading	12th Roy Fus. Vol 5		
War Diary	Esmont	01/01/1916	04/01/1916
War Diary	Poperinghe	05/01/1916	05/01/1916
War Diary	Guderdons	05/01/1916	05/01/1916
War Diary	H Trenches	06/01/1916	13/01/1916
War Diary	Camp. H 13 D 91	14/01/1916	16/01/1916
War Diary	Camp H 13 D 91 (Ouderdom)	17/01/1916	29/01/1916

War Diary	B 7 to C.3	30/01/1916	31/01/1916
Heading	17th Brigade. 24th Division. 12th Battalion Royal Fusiliers. February 1916		
Heading	12th R. Fus Vol 6		
War Diary	B 7 to C 3	01/02/1916	05/02/1916
War Diary	Zillebeke Dugouts	06/02/1916	10/02/1916
War Diary	C 3 B 7	11/02/1916	15/02/1916
War Diary	Camp. D	16/02/1916	29/02/1916
Heading	17th Brigade. 24th Division. 12th Battalion Royal Fusiliers. March 1916		
Miscellaneous	12 R Fus Vol 7		
War Diary	Camp D Ouderdom Vlamertinghe	01/03/1916	07/03/1916
War Diary	Sanctuary Wood	08/03/1916	08/03/1916
War Diary	Warrington Avenue	09/03/1916	09/03/1916
War Diary	Trenches B1 to B 4	10/03/1916	18/03/1916
War Diary	Camp C	19/03/1916	20/03/1916
War Diary	Camp F Ouderdom	21/03/1916	23/03/1916
War Diary	Godwerrevelde	24/03/1916	31/03/1916
Heading	17th Brigade. 24th Division 12th Battalion Royal Fusiliers April 1916		
War Diary	Ploegsteert (Vicinity) Trenches 132-133 Hill 63	01/04/1916	05/04/1916
War Diary	Bulford Camp.	06/04/1916	11/04/1916
War Diary	Trenches 132 to 135 Hill 63	12/04/1916	17/04/1916
War Diary	Grand Mungue Farm.	18/04/1916	18/04/1916
War Diary	Grand Mungue	19/04/1916	23/04/1916
War Diary	Trenches 132 to 135 Hill 63	24/04/1916	29/04/1916
War Diary	Bulford Camp.	30/04/1916	30/04/1916
Heading	17th Brigade. 24th Division 12th Battalion Royal Fusiliers May 1916		
War Diary	Fulford Camp	01/05/1916	04/05/1916
War Diary	Trenches 132-135 Hill 63	05/05/1916	11/05/1916
War Diary	Grand Mauque Farm.	12/05/1916	17/05/1916
War Diary	Trenches 132-135 Hill 63	18/05/1916	25/05/1916
War Diary	Bulford Camp.	26/05/1916	31/05/1916
Heading	17th Brigade. 24th Division. 12th Battalion Royal Fusiliers June 1916		
War Diary	Bulford Camp.	01/05/1916	02/06/1916
War Diary	Trenches 132 to 135 Hill 63	03/06/1916	10/06/1916
War Diary	Grand Munque	11/06/1916	18/06/1916
War Diary	Trenches 132-135 To Hill 63	19/06/1916	23/06/1916
War Diary	Map. Ref. X4.C.4.4	24/06/1916	24/06/1916
War Diary	X.4.C.4.4	25/06/1916	27/06/1916
War Diary	Badajos Hots.	28/06/1916	30/06/1916
Heading	17th Inf. Bde. 24th Div. 12th Battn. The Royal Fusiliers. July 1916		
War Diary	Dranoutre (Billets)	01/07/1916	08/07/1916
War Diary	Trenches C4 To D4	09/07/1916	11/07/1916
War Diary	Wakefield Huts.	12/07/1916	13/07/1916
War Diary	Trenches E2-F5	14/07/1916	19/07/1916
War Diary	Wakefield Huts.	20/07/1916	20/07/1916
War Diary	Billets Near Metenew	21/07/1916	24/07/1916
War Diary	Billets SE Piere-a-Gorey	25/07/1916	31/07/1916
Heading	17th Brigade. 24th Division. 12th Battalion Royal Fusiliers August 1916		
Miscellaneous	Headquarters 24th Division.	09/09/1916	09/09/1916
War Diary	Bois Des Tailles.	01/08/1916	01/08/1916

War Diary	Sand Pits.	02/08/1916	07/08/1916
War Diary	The Craters Carnoy	08/08/1916	09/08/1916
War Diary	Bernafay Wood	10/08/1916	11/08/1916
War Diary	Crater Trenches Carnoy	12/08/1916	13/08/1916
War Diary	Trenches Between Delville Wood & Guillemont	14/08/1916	17/08/1916
War Diary	Craters Carnoy	18/08/1916	18/08/1916
War Diary	Bernafay Wood	19/08/1916	21/08/1916
War Diary	Near Trenches To Guillemont.	22/08/1916	22/08/1916
War Diary	Happy Valley	23/08/1916	25/08/1916
War Diary	Dernancourt Vicinity	26/08/1916	30/08/1916
War Diary	Fricourt Vicinity	31/08/1916	31/08/1916
Heading	17th Brigade. 24th Division. 12th Battalion Royal Fusiliers. September 1916		
War Diary	Carlton Trench Between High Wood & Delville Wood	01/09/1916	01/09/1916
War Diary	Orchard Trench Chesney Walk Water Lane	02/09/1916	04/09/1916
War Diary	Camp Nr Fricourt	05/09/1916	05/09/1916
War Diary	Camp Nr Dernancourt.	06/09/1916	06/09/1916
War Diary	Billets Nr Bussus	07/09/1916	19/09/1916
War Diary	Cauchy A La Tour	20/09/1916	23/09/1916
War Diary	Bruay	24/09/1916	24/09/1916
War Diary	Estree Cauchie	25/09/1916	25/09/1916
War Diary	Trenches Alhambra & Coliseum & Dugouts Cabaret Rouge	26/09/1916	30/09/1916
Miscellaneous	To D.A.G. 3rd Echelon.	01/06/1916	01/06/1916
Miscellaneous	Casualties. Sept. 25th-28th 1915		
Heading	17th Brigade. 24th Division. 12th Battalion Royal Fusiliers October 1916		
War Diary	Trenches Alhambra Coliseum Cabaret Rouge	01/10/1916	02/10/1916
War Diary	Camblain L'Abbe & Villers Au Bois.	03/10/1916	09/10/1916
War Diary	Carency Sub-Sector	10/10/1916	18/10/1916
War Diary	Villers Au Bois.	19/10/1916	25/10/1916
War Diary	Estree Cauchie	26/10/1916	26/10/1916
War Diary	Mazingarbe	27/10/1916	27/10/1916
War Diary	14 Bus Sector	28/10/1916	31/10/1916
Heading	17th Brigade. 24th Division. 12th Battalion Royal Fusiliers November 1916		
War Diary	Trenches Near Loos Sub. Section 14 Bis	01/11/1916	02/11/1916
War Diary	Village Line	03/11/1916	10/11/1916
War Diary	Trenches 14 Bis	11/11/1916	16/11/1916
War Diary	Mazingarbe Northern Huts.	17/11/1916	22/11/1916
War Diary	Trenches 14 Bis.	23/11/1916	28/11/1916
War Diary	Village Line	29/11/1916	30/11/1916
Miscellaneous	Corrections in Casualties from Sept. 29th/1915 to Nov. 28th-1915		
Heading	17th Brigade. 24th Division. 12th Battalion Royal Fusiliers December 1916		
War Diary	Village Line	01/12/1916	03/12/1916
War Diary	Trenches 14 Bis	04/12/1916	10/12/1916
War Diary	Northern Huts Mazingarbe	11/12/1916	15/12/1916
War Diary	Trenches 14 Bis.	16/12/1916	22/12/1916
War Diary	Village Line	23/12/1916	28/12/1916
War Diary	Trenches 14 Bis	29/12/1916	31/12/1916
War Diary	Trenches 14 Bis	01/01/1917	03/01/1917
War Diary	Northern Huts Mazingarbe	04/01/1917	07/01/1917
War Diary	Trenches 14 Bis	08/01/1917	16/01/1917
War Diary	Village Lines	17/01/1917	23/01/1917

War Diary	Trenches 14 Bis.	24/01/1917	30/01/1917
War Diary	Northern Huts Mazingarbe	31/01/1917	05/02/1917
War Diary	Trenches 14 Bis	06/02/1917	13/02/1917
War Diary	Billets Mazingarbe	14/02/1917	14/02/1917
War Diary	Huts Noeux Les Mines	15/02/1917	28/02/1917
War Diary	Noeux Les Mines	01/03/1917	04/03/1917
War Diary	Bully Grenay	05/03/1917	09/03/1917
War Diary	Trenches Angres Section	10/03/1917	15/03/1917
War Diary	Fosse 10	16/03/1917	24/03/1917
War Diary	Trenches Ancres Sector	25/03/1917	27/03/1917
War Diary	Bully Grenay	28/03/1917	31/03/1917
Heading	12th Royal Fusiliers 17th Infantry Brigade 24th Division April 1917		
War Diary	Bully Grenay	01/04/1917	01/04/1917
War Diary	Trenches (Angres Sect)	02/04/1917	07/04/1917
War Diary	Marque Affeda Farm	08/04/1917	18/04/1917
War Diary	Marqueffles Farm.	19/04/1917	19/04/1917
War Diary	Marles Les Mines.	20/04/1917	20/04/1917
War Diary	Ecquedecques	21/04/1917	24/04/1917
War Diary	Lisbourg	25/04/1917	27/04/1917
War Diary	Bethune	28/04/1917	29/04/1917
War Diary	Allouagne	30/04/1917	30/04/1917
Miscellaneous	Officer Commanding 12th Royal Fusiliers.	05/04/1917	05/04/1917
Operation(al) Order(s)	Operation Orders No.100	27/04/1917	27/04/1917
Heading			
Heading	War Diary Of 12th Battalion Royal Fusiliers For May 1917 Vol 21		
War Diary	Allouagne	01/05/1917	09/05/1917
War Diary	St Floris	10/05/1917	11/05/1917
War Diary	Hazebrouck	12/05/1917	12/05/1917
War Diary	Steenvoorde	13/05/1917	15/05/1917
War Diary	St Laurent	16/05/1917	26/05/1917
War Diary	Camp S. Of Poperinghe	27/05/1917	28/05/1917
War Diary	Dickebush Huts.	29/05/1917	31/05/1917
Miscellaneous	Operation Orders By Lt-Col. H.W. Compton, Commanding 12th. Battalion Royal Fusiliers.	09/05/1917	09/05/1917
Operation(al) Order(s)	Operation Orders No. 104 By Lt-Col. H.W. Compton, Commanding 12th. Battalion Royal Fusiliers.	10/05/1917	10/05/1917
Heading	12th Royal Fusiliers. War Diary For June 1917 Volume No. 22		
War Diary	Camp S Of Poperinghe	01/06/1917	02/06/1917
War Diary	N. Of Steenvoorde	03/06/1917	04/06/1917
War Diary	Heksken	05/06/1917	06/06/1917
War Diary	Alberta Camp Reninghels	07/06/1917	07/06/1917
War Diary	Dammstrasse	08/06/1917	10/06/1917
War Diary	Micmac Camp South	11/06/1917	12/06/1917
War Diary	Impartial Trench	13/06/1917	15/06/1917
War Diary	Micmac Camp South	16/06/1917	19/06/1917
War Diary	Hill 60 Area	20/06/1917	27/06/1917
War Diary	Micmac Camp South	28/06/1917	29/06/1917
War Diary	Lumbres	30/06/1917	30/06/1917
Miscellaneous	A Form. Messages And Signals.		
Heading	12th Battalion Royal Fusiliers. War Diary For Month Of July 1917. Volume No. 23		
War Diary	Henneveux	01/07/1917	17/07/1917
War Diary	Fromentel	18/07/1917	18/07/1917

Type	Description	Start	End
War Diary	Bayenghem	19/07/1917	19/07/1917
War Diary	Renescure	20/07/1917	20/07/1917
War Diary	Chestre	21/07/1917	21/07/1917
War Diary	Eecke	22/07/1917	22/07/1917
War Diary	Steenvoorde	23/07/1917	25/07/1917
War Diary	Micmac Camp	26/07/1917	31/07/1917
Miscellaneous	Report On Attack On July 31st, 1917		
Miscellaneous	Remarks.		
Miscellaneous	Casualties.		
Miscellaneous	17th Infantry Brigade.		
Miscellaneous	12th Battalion Royal Fusiliers. Operation Order No. 1 by Lt. Col. H.M. Hope-Johnstone M.C.		
Miscellaneous	12th (S) Battalion The Royal Fusiliers. War Diary For the Month of August 1917		
War Diary	Canada St Tunnels	01/08/1917	02/08/1917
War Diary	Echeux Trench	03/08/1917	03/08/1917
War Diary	Micmac Camp	04/08/1917	06/08/1917
War Diary	Larch Wood Trenches	07/08/1917	11/08/1917
War Diary	Micmac Camp	12/08/1917	13/08/1917
War Diary	Micmac 5th Camp.	14/08/1917	15/08/1917
War Diary	Camp H Dickebusch	16/08/1917	19/08/1917
War Diary	Canada St Tunnels	19/08/1917	23/08/1917
War Diary	Micmac Camp 5th	24/08/1917	27/08/1917
War Diary	Dickebusch Camp H	28/08/1917	31/08/1917
Heading	To Headquarters, 17th Infantry Brigade. War Diary No. 25 For The Month of September 1917		
War Diary	Canada St Tunnels	31/08/1917	02/09/1917
War Diary	Accot Camp	02/09/1917	02/09/1917
War Diary	Micmac	03/09/1917	06/09/1917
War Diary	T Camp Dickeybush	07/09/1917	11/09/1917
War Diary	Trenches.	12/09/1917	15/09/1917
War Diary	Camp J Dickeybusch	16/09/1917	16/09/1917
War Diary	Outersteene	17/09/1917	21/09/1917
War Diary	Valluart Wood Camp.	22/09/1917	25/09/1917
War Diary	Vadencourt	25/09/1917	30/09/1917
Heading	To Headquarters, 17th Infantry Brigade. War Diary No. 26. For the Month Of October 1917		
War Diary	Vadencourt 62 Sheet R 17a	01/10/1917	04/10/1917
War Diary	Vadencourt	05/10/1917	06/10/1917
War Diary	Sheet 65 B Nun Al Sub Sector From Lomignonther To G 26000	07/10/1917	09/10/1917
War Diary	AI Sub Sector	10/10/1917	13/10/1917
War Diary	Vadencourt	14/10/1917	15/10/1917
War Diary	Busnes	16/10/1917	24/10/1917
War Diary	Ai Sub Sector	25/10/1917	31/10/1917
Operation(al) Order(s)	Operation Orders. By Major J.O. Hartley. Commanding 12th. Battalion Royal Fusiliers. Appendix I	06/10/1917	06/10/1917
Miscellaneous	Operation Orders. By Major J.O. Hartley. Commanding 12th. Battalion Royal Fusiliers. Appendix II	15/10/1917	15/10/1917
Miscellaneous	Appreciation. Appendix III		
Operation(al) Order(s)	Operation Orders. by Lt. Colonel F.R. Day. Commanding 12th. Battalion Royal Fusiliers. App 4	22/10/1917	22/10/1917
Miscellaneous	Relief Orders. by Lt. Colonel F.R. Day. Commanding 12th. Battalion Royal Fusiliers. App 5	30/10/1917	30/10/1917
Miscellaneous			
Miscellaneous	Defence Of Somerville Wood	30/10/1917	30/10/1917

Miscellaneous	To Headquarters-17th Infantry Brigade.	29/10/1917	29/10/1917
Miscellaneous	To Adjt 12th R.F. Report On German Raid		
Miscellaneous	Report On Enemy Raid on Sommerville Wood		
Heading	War Diary Of 12th. (S) Battalion Royal Fusiliers. From 1/11/1917 To 30/11/1917. (Volume No. 27)		
War Diary	Vadencourt (Bde Supports) Sheet 62 C SE R. 17a	01/11/1917	07/11/1917
War Diary	In The Line Sheet 62 B S.W	08/11/1917	09/11/1917
War Diary	In The Field	10/11/1917	11/11/1917
War Diary	Sheet 62 B N.W. G 33.b	12/11/1917	12/11/1917
War Diary	Sheet 62 B S.W M 2.d 60.40	13/11/1917	13/11/1917
War Diary	Sheet 62 B N.W. G. 32 C.d	14/11/1917	14/11/1917
War Diary	In The Line G 33 C	14/11/1917	14/11/1917
War Diary	Sheet 62 B S.W. And 62 B N.W.	15/11/1917	16/11/1917
War Diary	Bernes	17/11/1917	23/11/1917
War Diary	In The Line	24/11/1917	24/11/1917
War Diary	Sheet 62 B NW G 31.d	25/11/1917	25/11/1917
War Diary	Sheet 62 B SW M 2	26/11/1917	26/11/1917
War Diary	In The Line	27/11/1917	30/11/1917
Miscellaneous	Operation Orders. by Lt. Colonel. F.R. Day. Commanding 12th Batt. Royal Fusiliers. Appendix I	08/11/1917	08/11/1917
Miscellaneous	Operation Orders. by Lt. Colonel F.R. Day. Commanding 12th Battalion Royal Fusiliers. Appendix II	23/11/1917	23/11/1917
Miscellaneous	(Unit). 12th (S) Battalion Royal Fusiliers. War Diary For The Month Of December 1917		
War Diary	In The Line	01/12/1917	03/12/1917
War Diary	Bernes	04/12/1917	17/12/1917
War Diary	BM. reserve	18/12/1917	19/12/1917
War Diary	Centre Sub Sector	20/12/1917	24/12/1917
War Diary	BM. reserve	25/12/1917	27/12/1917
War Diary	Bernes	28/12/1917	31/12/1917
Operation(al) Order(s)	Operation Order No 75 by Lt. Col F.R. Day. Commanding 12th Battalion. Royal Fusiliers. Appendix II	19/12/1917	19/12/1917
Miscellaneous	Report on Minor Operation on front of 12th Bn RF which took place at 2.35 a.m. on 20.12.17 Appendix III	20/12/1917	20/12/1917
Miscellaneous	O.O No 76 Col Lt Col F.R. Day Commanding 12th Bn Royal Fusiliers Appendix IV		
Miscellaneous	Operation Order No 77 by Lt Col. F.R. Day Commanding 12th Royal Fusiliers.		
Miscellaneous	O.O. 77	26/12/1917	26/12/1917
Miscellaneous	Appendix I		
Miscellaneous	To 17th Infantry Brigade. Appendix V	24/12/1917	24/12/1917
Heading	(Unit) 12th. (S) Battalion The Royal Fusiliers. War Diary For the month of January 1918		
War Diary	Bernes	01/01/1918	01/01/1918
War Diary	Vraignes (Div Res)	03/01/1918	14/01/1918
War Diary	BM. reserve	15/01/1918	15/01/1918
War Diary	Centre Sub Sector	16/01/1918	20/01/1918
War Diary	Vraignes (Sheet 62 C N.E)	21/01/1918	26/01/1918
War Diary	Vraignes	28/01/1918	31/01/1918
Miscellaneous	Dear Colonel Day.	25/01/1918	25/01/1918
Miscellaneous	General Headquarters, British Armies In France Appendix II	20/01/1918	20/01/1918
Miscellaneous	H.Q. Dv A.	17/02/1918	17/02/1918
Miscellaneous	To Headquarters, 17th Infantry Brigade.	16/02/1918	16/02/1918

Heading	Unit. 12th. Batt The Royal Fusiliers. War Diary for the Month of February 1918 Vol 30		
War Diary	Vraignes	01/02/1918	13/02/1918
Miscellaneous	Appendix I War Diary RE Disbanding Of Battalions		
Miscellaneous	Special Divisional Routine Order by Major General A.C. Daly C.B. Commanding 24th. Division.	03/02/1918	03/02/1918

WO 95/2208

12 BTN ROYAL FUSILIERS
AUG 1915 - FEB 1918

24TH DIVISION
17TH INFY BDE

12TH BN ROYAL FUS.
AUG 1915 - FEB 1918

DISBANDED

73rd Inf.Bde.
24th Div.

Battn. disembarked
Boulogne from
England 2.9.15.

WAR DIARY

12th BATTN. THE ROYAL FUSILIERS.

AUGUST AND SEPTEMBER

(21.8.15 to 30.9.15)

1 9 1 5

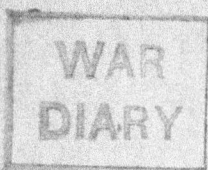

Oct 1915

Army Form C. 2118.

WAR DIARY
INTELLIGENCE SUMMARY.
(Erase heading not required.)

Instructions regarding War Diaries and Intelligence Summaries are contained in F. S. Regs., Part II. and the Staff Manual respectively. Title pages will be prepared in manuscript.

Place	Date	Hour	Summary of Events and Information	Remarks and references to Appendices
Pirbright Camp	21 Aug		First day of mobilization. 2/Lt Ventress having been posted to the Battn. is posted to 3 Coy.	
Pirbright	22 Aug		Capt. Dick Cleland with his servant proceeds to France	
"	23	7.30 a.m.	Battn. proceeds to Chobham Common to carry out an interesting scheme and bivouacked there for the night – Weather fine – 10 men transferred from 7th Northants Regt.	
"	24	6.30 p.m.	Battn. returned to Pirbright Camp after practising advancing trench. Lieut Nelson appointed to command the details left behind. The following Officers being temporary will be left: 2/Lt Andrews, Vandyck, Cook, Krug, Hatcher, Fitt, Meade-Smith, Butterworth.	
"	25	7 a.m.	Nos 1 & 3 Coys proceeds to CHOBHAM COMMON to fill in the trenches dug by the Battn. Nos 2 & 4 Coy relieves them at 1 p.m. Weather hot and dry many officers and men on leave.	
		2 p.m.	Draft of 880 men arrive from 5th Battn. R.F. to complete this Battn. to war strength. Amongst the number were one or two of the undesirables & weaklings which had previously been transferred from this Battn. to the 5th. Last such is the System military.	

Army Form C. 2118.

WAR DIARY
INTELLIGENCE SUMMARY.
(Erase heading not required.)

Place	Date	Hour	Summary of Events and Information	Remarks and references to Appendices
Pirbright	26 Aug		Three fatigue parties from Each Coy proceed to CHOBHAM COMMON to complete yesterdays work. Weather hot & dry. Many men away on Embarkation leave.	
Pirbright	27 Aug		Embarkation leave expired — over 100 men still absent. Weather hot and dry. 2/Lt BETTESWORTH posted on the list of	
Pirbright	28 Aug		Births and yet more births!! 2/Lt HOME-GALL detailed to accompany the Battn in place of Lieut HOME-GALL. Attestations also	
Pirbright	29		Route 70. Weather hot. F.S. Casualty Forms Checks.	
			Checks and packs up.	
Pirbright	30 Au		Absentees 19 — much better. Weather fine but extra.	
Pirbright	31 Aug 12.30am		Transport of the Battn under Lieut RIDGER with machine gun section under Lieut TANNER — 72 horses and 108 rank & file marched to WOKING Station for Embarkation for HAVRE	
Pirbright	1 Sept 3 p.m.		Remainder of Battn paraded under Col C.J. STANTON and marched to BROOKWOOD Station where they entrained in two trains for FOLKESTONE en route for BOULOGNE. Lt Col GARNONS-WILLIAMS commanded the second train. The first took the 73 Bde Head quarters, the Batt." Head quarters, and N°1 and 2 Coys. The second took N° 3 & 4 Coys. The whole Battn has safely on the last Channel boat "Queen" by 9 p.m. which was escorted across by Destroyers. The Officers & 19 men were attached as details.	N.N.

Army Form C. 2118.

WAR DIARY
INTELLIGENCE SUMMARY.
(Erase heading not required)

Instructions regarding War Diaries and Intelligence Summaries are contained in F.S. Regs., Part II. and the Staff Manual respectively. Title pages will be prepared in manuscript.

Place	Date	Hour	Summary of Events and Information	Remarks and references to Appendices
Boulogne	2 Sept	12.30 am	The Boat was met by the embarkation staff — rather a fussy staff — and by the Camp Commandant who was both clear headed and obliging. The Colonel and the Quarter master proceeded up to Camp — a distance some two miles — whilst the Batt'n was assembled and marched up through the sleeping streets with drums a-beating to remind the inhabitants that a war was on. On arrival at Camp tents were found ready pitched and every man was present with one blanket. Luckily it was a beautiful night. We therefore slept in tiers to sleep till 1 a.m. after which we spent a quiet day confined to Camp. About 7.30 p.m. it began to rain. Two men to Hospital at BOULOGNE	
Boulogne	3 Sep	3 a.m.	We paraded and marched with much banging of tins to the GARE CENTRALE where we entrained the whole Batt'n less the transport into one long train and received orders to go to MONTREUIL. About 5.30 a.m. we arrived there, when a private soldier thrust his head into the Headquarter Carriage and asked for the "Ordre de Mouvement". This was shown to him. He took it, and vanished up the platform, only to return a minute later bringing it back with the destination MONTREUIL changed to MARESQUEL	N.M.

2353 Wt. W3544/1454. 700,000 9/15 D.D. & L. A.D.S.S./Forms/C. 2118.

WAR DIARY
INTELLIGENCE SUMMARY.
(Erase heading not required.)

Army Form C. 2118.

Place	Date	Hour	Summary of Events and Information	Remarks and references to Appendices
MARESQUEL	3 Sept	6 a.m.	We struck his orders and went to MARESQUEL where we were pumped. The Bde Major of the 73 Bde met us. It was pouring in torrents and there was no shelter. Our transport Officer also met us with the Batt" transport, but as he had been marching first of all down to MONTREUIL to meet us and had afterwards received orders to come to MARESQUEL his horses were too tired to move for at least 3 hours. We therefore quickly knocked open a few ration boxes, issued some "bully" to the men, and started to march to our Billeting area EMBRY — a distance of some 9 miles. The way to the village meant retracing our steps towards MONTREUIL for some distance, which suggested we thought that it might have been better of the Private Soldier at that Spot had not changed our original orders. The tramp to EMBRY was a mighty wet one. It poured the whole way. 50 men fell out, dead beat with carrying their packs and their "rain-soaked great coats", and 23 went sick in consequence. Reached EMBRY about 11 p.m. H.Q. of the Battn at the Chateau.	
EMBRY	4 Sept		A quiet day — raining hard. Busy pulling our selves together. Batt" grounds fixed at ½ a mile from EMBRY Church. Notice to go beyond this limit without Co's Permission. 2 men of Hospital ETAPLES. A bright fine day. F. Drummond Pierrepont was killed in a field ½ a mile N of the Chateau	
"	5 "		On the afternoon arrangements were made for giving all the men a bath.	R.M.J.

WAR DIARY
INTELLIGENCE SUMMARY.
(Erase heading not required.)

Army Form C. 2118.

Place	Date	Hour	Summary of Events and Information	Remarks and references to Appendices
EMBRY	6 Sep	2 p.m.	Lovely weather. Details 1 Platoon daily on inlying Piquet. 12 men on the Sick list. Genl. HAKING - G.O.C. 11th Corps Commands saw the Officers of the 73 Bde at TORCY. Morning. Battn. route march, afternoon Adjt's parade.	
"	7 "		Lieut TANNER and 2/Lieut SOWREY with 4 N.C.Os of the Machine Gun Sect. proceeded to WISQUES for 5 days Course of instruction. Drew money from the Field Cashier to pay the Battn. Morning practise the attack, afternoon Adjutant's parade. 8 p.m. Alarm post parade, and afterwards Camp fire Concert - quite a success! — much talent [Concert not for parade]	3 men admitted to Hospital ETAPLES.
"	8 "		Majors COMPTON, Captain PHILLIPS and Captain WADDELL proceeded up to the trenches for the night. Morning Companies at disposal of Coy Commanders. 2:30 pm Adjt's parade. Weather still lovely. Snipers under 2/Lt ANDERSON, Bombers under 2/Lt BRYANT, and Scouts under Lt WALEY practising separately.	1 man admitted to Hospital ETAPLES and 1 man returned to Duty from there.
"	9 "		Lovely day. Morning, Battn. practised the attack. Afternoon, Adjt's parade. N°s 1, 2, & 4 Coys. N° 3 Coy did musketry, and nearly shot a Major SHERWOOD FORESTERS by accident. COMPTON, PHILLIPS & WADDELL returned from the trenches safe and sound.	Fourteen men on the sick list.
"	10 "		Morning, Coys at disposal of their Coy Commanders. Afternoon, ditto. N° 4 Coy musketry. In charging his magazine 1 man of latter Coy nearly shot the Quarter Master. The Colonel, the 2nd in Command & 4 other Officers went up to Div. Head Qrs at ROYON to be lectured about gas. They wore their gas helmets and walked through a trench filled with gas.	
"	11 "	2 pm	Breakfast at 6.30 am. 7.20 & 7.30 B.Cos. "Ready" roused by 8.30 am 72nd Bde feinted to have gone off to 160 much to the left as we had to set from half the morning until they changed direction. WE practised the evacuation of wounded & replenishing ammunition. — Back to EMBRY by 3.30 pm. 12 men for Sq.	72nd R. Fus. & 7th Norfolks attacked Pt. ST MICHEL with 13th Middlesex & 9th Sussex in support. The 73rd Bde feinted. 12 men on the sick list.

N.W.

Army Form C. 2118.

WAR DIARY
INTELLIGENCE SUMMARY.
(Erase heading not required.)

Instructions regarding War Diaries and Intelligence Summaries are contained in F. S. Regs., Part II. and the Staff Manual respectively. Title pages will be prepared in manuscript.

Place	Date	Hour	Summary of Events and Information	Remarks and references to Appendices
EMBRY	12	9.30 a.m.	Batt. paraded in a field N. of Oisthil from for Divine Service. Weather glorious — very hot. Drew another Lewis machine Gun, making 4 in all. This evidently proves that someone has realized that you cannot get a big outpost, even of death, without machinery. Also drew 60 bombs and 7 Practice bombs. A Grenadier Guard Corporal was sent down to instruct our bombers. 10 men on the Sick list. Headquarters detachment had their Sunday bath.	
EMBRY	13	9 a.m.	Batt. paraded for the Attack Practice — bombers, Scouts, Signallers, Snipers, & machine Gunners being trained separately under their respective Officers. No 1 Coy marched in afternoon, the three Coy Adjutants present. Weather fine. 2 men admitted to Hospital.	
EMBRY	14	8.15 a.m.	Batt. marched off to Practice Brigade Concentration. It rained. We formed up at the Rendezvous & got lost, and came back again. Lt E. NEYNOE and 2Lt J. EASTON & others on the Sick list came. influenza. 1 Lce Cpl. and 4 men attempted to Hospital, ETAPLES.	
EMBRY	15		2Lt A.J. TANNER went up to the trenches for a nights' instruction. Weather unsettled. Sgt WATTS & 1 man admitted to hospital. At midnight two young officers (one R.E. & the ARTIST RIFLES) lost their way in a motor car and wandered into Batt. H.Q. Chatroom asking for a map. The Guard detained them & we enquired and a reference to the Brigade HQ, were released. Number in Hospital this day 21. The N.A.S. reports sick this day 12.	

2353 Wt. W3544/1454 700,000 5/15 D. D. & L.   A.D.S.S./Forms/C. 2118.

Army Form C. 2118.

WAR DIARY
INTELLIGENCE SUMMARY.
(Erase heading not required.)

Instructions regarding War Diaries and Intelligence Summaries are contained in F. S. Regs., Part II. and the Staff Manual respectively. Title pages will be prepared in manuscript.

Place	Date	Hour	Summary of Events and Information	Remarks and references to Appendices
EMBRY	16		A quiet day. Normal parade. Fine weather. Capt WADDELL, 2/Lt SKEET, and 2/Lt EASTON were taken off the sick list. 1 man admitted to Hospital.	
EMBRY	17	9 a.m.	No 1, 3, & 4 Coys route marching — No 2 Coy musketry all the morning. Bombers, Signallers, & Machine Gun men parading separately under their respective officers. Fine weather.	
EMBRY	18	3 a.m.	No 1, 2, 3 & 4 Coy parade with all transport packed for Divisional Concentration near BOURBERS-les-Hesmon. Successes in finding ready. Rendezvous to time in the dark.	S. HUMBERT
	6 a.m.		9th Sussex & 13th Middlesex Regts occupies a ridge running E & W immediately S. HUMBERT. 12th R.F. supports Sussex. Reinforced. Got in the position for two hours. 71 Brigade came through & pursued the imaginary enemy. Had breakfasts. Came home to EMBRY. Back by 11 a.m.	
			2/Lt BRYANT with 8 NCos & men went to QUILEN to attend Brig.l Bombing School. 3 men admitted to Hospital. Weather fine.	
EMBRY	19	10.30 a.m.	Divine Service in field. 10 troops arrived and the Battalion practised entraining and detraining. Quickest time records for Entraining 25 fully equipped men 28 seconds, & for Detraining 19 seconds.	
	2.30 p.m.		2/Lt STEWART of the 9th Royal Sussex accidentally killed at the bombing School. Batt.n practises trench fighting. 2/Lt BUTTERWORTH, 1st Bedfords and 24 men went to QUILEN to the Bombing School. The two officers returned same night.	
EMBRY	20	9 a.m.	Batt.n practises night orders.	
	8 p.m.		The Batt.n practises night ready — Rendezvous and siting trenches in the dark in company bearing.	
EMBRY	21	7.30 a.m.	Receives Marching orders. 2/Lt BRYANT & men returned from QUILEN.	
	10 a.m.		2/Lt STEWART of the 9th Sussex was buried — 2/Lt STANTON & 3 Officers of this Battn attended.	
	10 a.m.		Three men of the Battn were tried by Field General Court Martial, namely Pte COCLOUGH for Insubordinate Language to a N.C.O., Privates MORRIS and LAND for refusing to obey an order. Thirty four men now in hospital. Weather fine but colder.	R.N.S.

8353. Wt. W2594/1454 700,000 5/15 D. D. & L. A.D.S.S./Forms/C. 2118.

Army Form C. 2118.

WAR DIARY
or
INTELLIGENCE SUMMARY.
(Erase heading not required.)

Instructions regarding War Diaries and Intelligence Summaries are contained in F. S. Regs., Part II. and the Staff Manual respectively. Title pages will be prepared in manuscript.

Place	Date	Hour	Summary of Events and Information	Remarks and references to Appendices
	21 September	5.55 p.m.	Battalion marches off from EMBRY. Order of march of Coys 4, 3, 2, 1. After passing PREHEDRE 1 Coy dropped a rear guard of 1 Platoon. At RIMBOVAL the Batt" followed the 9th ROYAL SUSSEX. The Transport waggons were unloaded and constantly checked the column. This was due to Battalions being ordered to draw and carry 250 rounds without any transport being allowed to carry them. 12th R.F. had a Civilian Cart privately — the only thing to do — but should never have been necessary. The route followed was through CREQUY, FRUGES, LUGY, & Billeting area BEAUMETZ–LEZ–AIRE. The Company got in at 1.30 a.m. on the 22nd, bringing along a number of stragglers from the other Battalions in the 73rd Brigade. About 69 men from 12th R.F. fell out during the march. All except 1 Sergt & 2 men reported present on morning of 22nd. The length of the march was about 16 miles. Beautiful moonlit night.	
BEAUMETZ	22nd Sept		Quiet day till 6.45 p.m. except that two of the 12th R.F. Transport men were badly kicked by some mules. Battalion Headquarters went in the School just behind the Church. The Battalion paraded and march(ed) off at the head of the 73rd Bn. Order of march (Companies 3, 2, 1, 4). The march was a long one through ST HILAIRE – LILLERS to Billeting area at BUSNES — 17 miles by road, and for the latter half of the march the roads were "pavé". This made the march heavier for the men. Halts were regular, 5 minutes in every hour, when the men took packs off.	
	6.45			

WAR DIARY
INTELLIGENCE SUMMARY.
(Erase heading not required).

Army Form C. 2118.

Instructions regarding War Diaries and Intelligence Summaries are contained in F.S. Regs., Part II. and the Staff Manual respectively. Title pages will be prepared in manuscript.

Place	Date	Hour	Summary of Events and Information	Remarks and references to Appendices
			moreover, heavy motor lorries were constantly passing the Column and smothering the men with dust. BUSNES was reached at 1:30 A.M. on the 23rd. The Quartermaster and Coy. Qm. Sergts. had preceded the Battalion earlier in the day, on bicycles, to the men were quickly put into their billets, but Mess were fed and very crowded. 150 men of the Battalion fell out during the march. The going of heavy guns was heard away in the distance all through the night. The Shrine at BUSNES to men were from hot tea which had been prepared on the way. It was a glorious moonlit night. All falling claims in the Company Orders. Left BEAUMETZ, but Mr. Lehane was a were settled before the Battalion temporary Industry, Carrying out the Majors' orders during the war. He was a Stupid agricultural Labourer too which there was a good deal of interpreting at the head of the Adjudant. Major GIBSON. 35 men in Hospital, 29 reported sick.	
BUSNES	23rd Sept		A quiet day. Battalion forms 1 platoon outlying picquet, 1 officer 9 30 men Bivouaced guard, and 1 N.C.O 1 bugler and 6 men for Brigade guard. In addition there were the regimental guard of 1 Sergt. 1 Cpl and 12 men. At midday there were still 20 men reports as not having rejoined the Batta after falling out on the march. Three aeroplanes were seen hovering high overhead. The Evening of Sunday still heavy all day. Brint H.Qrs and 73rd Bn H.Qrs both at BUSNES. Whether broke at 7pm & began to rain. Sandbags were drawn had a bathe in the river. The greater part of the men	

Army Form C. 2118.

WAR DIARY
or
INTELLIGENCE SUMMARY.
(Erase heading not required.)

Place	Date	Hour	Summary of Events and Information	Remarks and references to Appendices
BUSNES	23rd (continued)		In the morning at 11am. Pte S. Jennings was tried by F.G. Court Martial for (1) Drunkenness and (2) Refusing to go on Parade.	
BUSNES	24th		Colonel C.J. Slater attended a meeting at LILLERS where General Lakin Commanding II Corps explained the situation & the plan for closing up the troops around BETHUNE. The Battalion paraded at 9 pm & marched to BEUVRY where they arrived at about midnight.	
BEUVRY	25th		At 8.30 am Colonel Slater received an order to report himself at Dohenal (4th Division) Hdqrs Centre & to accompany it in advance. Handed over command of Battalion to Major Jim L.M. R.D. Barrow – In turn — The Battalion paraded at 11 am & marched over section to WINDEMILLES — at occupies some trenches. It was just dark	
			At 4 pm orders were received to march to LA FOSSE de BETHUNE. They were on their way when at about 11 pm the Battalion ordinarily closed on the night march of in close column of platoons following the 9th Royal Scots Regiment. The order of companies was 2, 1, 3, 4. after going 300 or 400 yards the lead platoon of No 1 Company lost touch with the leading platoon of No 2 Company. The leading platoon of No 1 Company proceeded on No 3 Company, and the leading platoon of No 3 Company under Lt Cd. Gambier-Parker	
WINDEMILLES				
VERMELLES				

WAR DIARY
or
INTELLIGENCE SUMMARY.
(Erase heading not required.)

Army Form C. 2118.

Place	Date	Hour	Summary of Events and Information	Remarks and references to Appendices
	25th Sept – 28 Sept		towards our R.O.B. at Bethune following the 9th Royal Sussex Regiment who were led by a guide. When about 400 yrds from the heap of clinkers (forming part of Fosse 8) they came under heavy shell and machine gun fire. They then found (for the first time) that they had become detached from the rest of the Battalion. On reaching the track & clinkers they were dispersed and were led by the Brigade Major 73rd I.B. through the town and placed in trenches which were then occupied by the Black Watch. At 10 am an attempt was made in conjunction with the Black Watch soldiers the trenches so occupied were almost continuously shelled from this time they suffered them until the time they arrived on the morning of the 28th Sept. The Germans attacked them heavier on the mornings of the 26th and 27th Sept but all their attacks were beaten off.	
In action			In the morning of the 28th Sept after a tremendous bombardment of our position the Germans attacked in force and gained a footing in the trenches occupied by the 7th Northants Regiment on the left flank (and in/light 7th Royal Sussex Regiment on the right flank). The Germans then proceeded to turn the soldiers out of these trenches from both flanks, so that they had to retire
VERMELLES				

WAR DIARY
INTELLIGENCE SUMMARY.
(Erase heading not required.)

Army Form C. 2118.

Place	Date	Hour	Summary of Events and Information	Remarks and references to Appendices
			and that they did under heavy shell & machine gun fire. It was during the retirement that most of their losses occurred. During this attack have they occupied the trenches they were without rations and water, and owing to the Confusion that put them was impossible the trouble went into action without any food to that day. He made to meet the attack of the Germans on the morning of the	
25th Sept – 28th Sept. (continued) In action N.E. of VERMELLES			27 Sept. All ranks behaved with great gallantry and coolness under my gravest trial. Experience of shell fire and both fast in 3 or 4 bayonet charges during the German counter attack occurred. Lt Naylor did admirable work in organising and leading a charge. Meanwhile Lt Col Gordon Williams had been severely wounded and all the time on duty all the officers of No 2 Company are among 2nd Lt Newcomb & No 1 Company are killed.	

WAR DIARY
INTELLIGENCE SUMMARY.
(Erase heading not required.)

Army Form C. 2118.

Place	Date	Hour	Summary of Events and Information	Remarks and references to Appendices
In action NE of VERMELLES	25th Sept - 28th Sept (continued)		Jo return to No 3 & 4 Coys and the 3 platoons of No 1 Coy who had been, as before mentioned, this part of the Battalion under Major H.N. Compton halted and tried to regain touch. As soon as they came out and they were located by the enemy and shelled in the open. They moved to the right and occupied some trenches which they had just passed on crossing in them until about dawn. They then moved into reserve trenches but almost at once were directed by a staff officer of the 2nd Brigade to a position in the old British firing line (immediately behind the wood). Captain Compton Germans firing long, having them left firing Isaac & de Bethune. The 1 & 9 Coys were placed in the firing line and No 3 Coy in the first support trench. These trenches were somewhat heavily shelled during the morning of the 26th Sept. Early in the afternoon 2 that day No 3 Coy was ordered by Major Compton to move into the firing line to fill vacant bays on the flanks of the position. This position was occupied by No 3 & 4 Coys and 3 platoons No 1 Coy until about 7 p.m. Tuesday 28th Sept. when they were relieved	

Army Form C. 2118.

WAR DIARY
INTELLIGENCE SUMMARY.
(Erase heading not required.)

Instructions regarding War Diaries and Intelligence
Summaries are contained in F. S. Regs., Part II.
and the Staff Manual respectively. Title pages
will be prepared in manuscript.

Place	Date	Hour	Summary of Events and Information	Remarks and references to Appendices
28 Sept – (continued) NE of VERMELLES	28 Sept.		On relief they retired to Noeux les Mines station and entrained for Brigade where they arrived early on the morning 29th 29 & Sept and marched 5 kilometers to FONTES where they went into billets.	
FONTES.	29.			
FONTES	30		The 29 & Sept were occupied in posting reinforcements and to collect stragglers	169

ATTACHED 24TH DIVISION
73RD INFY BDE

12TH BN ROY FUSILIERS
SEP 1915-OCT 1915.

2 T.

24th Division

12th Royal Fusiliers
Vol 2

Oct 15.

This batt. was transferred on Oct 18th to the 17th Bde but does not mention the fact in the Diary

Army Form C. 2118.

WAR DIARY
or
INTELLIGENCE SUMMARY.
(Erase heading not required.)

Place	Date	Hour	Summary of Events and Information	Remarks and references to Appendices
FONTES	1 Oct		This day was occupied in the work of reorganisation. Many packs, pithays (?) etc signed.	
do	2 Oct		The Battalion paraded at 7.45 a.m. and marched to TOERGUETTE STATION and entrained for GODENAERSVELDE STATION and marched from there to HERZEELE and went into billets which were very scattered.	
HAZEELE	3 Oct		Sunday. The Battn. was inspected by Major Lieut. Colonel Croft CMG but during 6 officers & 200 NCOs & men proceeded in motor lorries to BRIELEN for a course of instruction in trench warfare.	
do	4 Oct	9am	Weather wet — Companies engaged in cleaning up rifles, equipment & foot inspection & physical drill — Major R P Gibson reported previously wounded unfit, now reported wounded — The C.O. and Scanton left to take temporary command of the 22nd Brigade — Major Burgoyne assumed command during Major Gibson's absence — Lt Roger & 2nd Lt Bryant proceeded, reported, wounded unreported unwounded.	
	5 Oct		Major 5 Dec — 5 officers & 100 NCOs & men proceeded from HERZEELE to VLAMERTURGHE in Motor Lorries for 48 hours instruction in Trench Warfare — The Battalion paraded at 8:30am marched to PROVEN and took up scattered billets in farms about one mile west of the town.	
PROVEN	6 Oct		Fine 200 reservists & other returned from BRIELEN after course of instruction in Trench Warfare — Bat went on motoring to bombing range & during Pair. 6 officers & 80 other ranks left for a course of instruction in the Divisional School Remainder of day spent in ...	

Army Form C. 2118.

WAR DIARY
or
INTELLIGENCE SUMMARY.
(Erase heading not required.)

Instructions regarding War Diaries and Intelligence Summaries are contained in F. S. Regs., Part II. and the Staff Manual respectively. Title pages will be prepared in manuscript.

Place	Date 1915	Hour	Summary of Events and Information	Remarks and references to Appendices
PROVEN	8 Oct		Fine-overcast. 4 officers & 396 NCOs & men left in motor lorries for VLAMERTINGHE for a course of instruction in Trench warfare. A Draft of 4 officers & 446 NCOs when arrived. Party spent in instruction in bombing & drill for Transport Sechn & details — The party of 2 officers & 100 men who left on the 6th inst for a course of instruction in Trench Warfare returned this nmt.	
"	9 Oct		Fine-overcast. Roll & Bench — Boot inspection — Bombing instruction —	
"	10 Oct		Fine. Divine Service — Drill & cleaning up — Party 4 officers & 396 men returned from VLAMERTINGHE	
RENING HELST	11 Oct		Fine. Marched from PROVEN to RENINGHELST with Brigade & took up billets in this village. Wet nt & troops almost 1 mile S.W. of Town. An enemy aeroplane was turned about 6 p.m. night	
"	12 Oct		Fine. 5 officers visited the trenches to be occupied by the Battalion on the 14th instant. Battalion parade-drill — Physical training — Reorganization of Companies — out. Bathing parade. 2 parties of 60 men each.	
"	13 Oct		Wet morning. The CO. & Adjutant visited the trenches to be occupied by the Battalion. fine afternoon. on the 14th instant — 1 officer & 31 men Machine Gun Section left for the trenches — 4 officers, 2 NCOs & 4 men left for the trenches to be occupied by the Battalion on the 14th instant — Physical drill — Company drill — Inspection in relieving trenches & trench studies —	
"	14 Oct		Fine. Morning wearing hot rations, bathing parties — One man accidentally killed in billet by rifle bullet from another man practising loading — Battalion marched to trenches near YPRES-MENIN & took over a section from the 6 & KOYLI — Quiet night — only intermittent rifle fire — 2 men slightly wounded going up to the trenches.	

Army Form C. 2118.

WAR DIARY
or
INTELLIGENCE SUMMARY.
(Erase heading not required.)

Instructions regarding War Diaries and Intelligence Summaries are contained in F. S. Regs., Part II. and the Staff Manual respectively. Title pages will be prepared in manuscript.

Place	Date 1915	Hour	Summary of Events and Information	Remarks and references to Appendices
Near VOORMEZEELE.	15 Oct	morning Scotch mist afternoon fine	Trenches occupied found to require much work – Very little rifle fire & no enemy guns were noticed to fire – Working parties organized for night work – Front parapet, wire & drainage under R.E. – 2 Officers & 196 men left this section of trenches to relieve the 12th Sherwood Foresters at VOORMEZEELE. Bombers organized under Lt Blackpool –	
"	16 Oct	fine	Day quiet – only promiscuous enemy sniping – Our guns fired freq unfrly during afternoon – Rec'd no'd observed but no enemy guns were noted firing. 2 Working parties on Communication trench were under R.E. – Useful work done improving front line parapet & general sanitary on entrans – One man killed by sniper in front line – Several enemy snipers shot from our front line –	
"	17 Oct	fine, misty early	Reported 2 officers – 196 men at VOORMEZEELE moved to trenches in support NORTHANTS Reg. – Day quiet – Wiri & drainage improving parapet front trench, flow boards & sanitary conditions – Work under R.E. communication trench. Enemy trench mortar annoying no 4 Co silenced by T 108 fire – 40 fficers & Nort from Special Reserve Battalions & taken on strength – (2nd Lts Pindler, Hammond, Eames & Harvey) –	
"	18 Oct	fine	Party of officers 2nd Leinster Reg't came to see arrangements with a view to taking over 19th. – Day quiet – Our batteries shelled enemy during day – Work done improving trenches – One man killed in front line – going outside parapet	
"	19 Oct	fine	Day quiet – Work done improving trenches under R.E. – also incorporated wire improving inside of parapet – One man killed during night laying over parapet. Relieved (6.30 – 9 pm) by 2nd Batt Leinster Reg't – March into Rest Camp at St Hubertusenhop – HUIBERTUS HOEK.	

Army Form C. 2118.

WAR DIARY
or
INTELLIGENCE SUMMARY.
(Erase heading not required.)

Instructions regarding War Diaries and Intelligence Summaries are contained in F. S. Regs., Part II. and the Staff Manual respectively. Title pages will be prepared in manuscript.

Place	Date 1915	Hour	Summary of Events and Information	Remarks and references to Appendices
HUBERTUS HOEK	20 Oct		Some overcoat. cold. Cleaning up — kit inspection — Paying out — Physical training — Bombing instruction — Reorganisation of Companies (Redistribution of officers) MVC	
"	21 Oct		Route Physical training — Marching order parade — Boric clothing inspection. CO inspected trenches occupied by 1st Batt RF. — RE officer came to arrange building huts or dug-outs. — Party — 4 officers, 16 NCOs, 128 men/ machinery Instructors (a) 8 Signallers, Party Sgt Major, 1 NCO + 9 men MG section left for trenches (b) to be attached to 1st Batt for instruction in Trench Duties — 16 men sent to Hospital recommended as medical unfit —	MVC
"	22 Oct		Fine. cold. Route march — Training in bombs — Instruction in NCOs — Company schemes on Trench Discipline — Arranged with RE about building huts. Capt FREETH left for 1st Batt trenches —	MVC
"	23 Oct		Fine. cold. Early — Battalion parade in drill order — Bombing instruction — Instruction by NCOs. Party 5 officers, 16 NCOs + 128 men, 8 Signallers, 10 then Mac gun section left for the trenches for instruction under the 1/2 Batts. — 2 LL Caskell + 3 O.R. attended funeral service taken on the shores of the Battalion — Co + Company Commander attended a lecture at RE Nissing HELTIT + Trench Mortars — Party 4 + officers, 16 NCOs, 128 men, 8 Signallers, Bn LS Sgt Major, 1 NCO + 9 men MG section returned from the trenches — One man of outgoing trench party killed by stray bullet — MVC	
"	24 Oct		Fine cold & windy — Church parade Service — Rifle on inspection — Physical training — Representative of 1.C. Batt came re laying out camp — OC left for trenches — Enemy ... ... going up to trenches on the evening of the 23rd.	not MVC
"	25 Oct		Wet. Work under Company Commanders — OC inspected from trenches — Party 4 officers + 200 men left for the trenches — ... ... 4th ACPT officers, 16 NCOs, 128 men, 8 Signallers, 10 Mac gun — Party — ... returned — Section returned from the trenches —	not MVC

WAR DIARY
INTELLIGENCE SUMMARY

Army Form C. 2118.

Place	Date	Hour	Summary of Events and Information	Remarks and references to Appendices
ST HUBERTUS HOEK	26/10/15		Fine - cold - Marching order parade - Physical drill - Bombing instruction - Work commenced digging - dug outs - Enemy aeroplane flew over camp - chased away NW by one of our own - Enemy appeared to be shelling DICKEBUSCH a few shells were noticed to fall behind the village - Casualties - Man accidentally wounded from rifle	
"	27/10/15		Heavy showers - Digging trench for dug outs - Party 20 NCOs + men sent to RENINGHELST to parade before H.M. the King - Party to R.E. Dump to load material for dug outs - Physical training - Drill - Bombing instruction - Party 2 Officers + 200 NCOs + men attached to 1st Bn.R. for instruction - Casualties 3??? NC ? men left for trenches to be attached to 1st Bn for instruction	
"	28/10/15		Very wet. Digging trench for dugouts - O.C. visited trenches - Party 2 Officers 200 NCOs + men returned from trenches - following Officers joined - 2 Lts 12th RF F.G. SYMONS + C.R. BULL of RF MGC J.V.WILSON, MARTIN + 2 Lts Scots Fusiliers -	
"	29/10/15		Fine - Bathing parade - Work digging trench for dugouts - Physical training + drill - Party 4 Officers + 80 NCOs + men left for trenches for instruction - not	
"	30/10/15		Fine, Work digging for dugouts - drawing material - but inspection - Banking instruction - drill.	
"	31/10/15		Fine Morning cold. Church Parade - Work on Dug outs. Fatigue party drawing material for Main Gate dugouts - Capt R.HARE RE joined + was appointed acting See in Command - Heavy firing by our front at about 7pm -	

3 T.

17/24

12th Roy: Fus:
Vol: 3

121/7656

24th Nuncun

Nov. 15.

WAR DIARY or INTELLIGENCE SUMMARY

Army Form C. 2118.

Place	Date 1915	Hour	Summary of Events and Information	Remarks and references to Appendices
RENING-HELST	1st Nov		Very wet. Moved from Camp A at HUBERTUSHOEK to Camp D. RENINGHELST exchanging with 8th BUFFS — C.O. & Capt HARE went up to trenches to arrange relief with 1st Batt — 2nd Lt J.M. CAMPBELL & G.H.V. JEFFERIES joined — (previously served in the ranks London Rifle Brigade) — 2nd Lt COBBETT sent away — sick.	M.O.
"	2nd		Very wet. G.O.C. 24th Division inspected drafts received since joining 2nd Army. Capt F. FREETH left 1st trenches as Intelligence Officer (he recently handed over the duties of A.C.A.S. & in Command to Capt HARE on the 31st October)	two
VOORMEZEELE SECTOR	3rd		Wet. Relieved 1st Bn R.F. in trenches night of Canal Bank 2 miles E. of VOORMEZEELE.	one
"	4 "		Fine. trenches in very bad state, very wet, dug outs collapsed — Began work to make good defects — About midday an enemy aeroplane came over, was attacked by a French aeroplane & brought down in our lines — both occupants killed & machine burnt. Enemy shelled bluff on our side of canal during afternoon with heavy fire — (One man slightly wounded) Our first trench 27 also shelled but no damage done + one man killed — abt 2.E BETTESWORTH reported wounded in the 27/10/15	two
"	5 "		Slight rain early afternoon & [illegible] — Work continued on improving & repairing trenches — dug outs — 2nd Lt Warmwood wounded out of head — Ypernum, enemy shelled bluff & H.Q. 2 men accidentally wounded —	
"	6 "		Fine. Mostly. Work improving trenches — great day. 2nd LtBETTESWORTH previously reported pm wounded, was reported dead — One man wounded.	
"	7 "		Fine. mostly. Work improving & repairing trenches continued — Scouring & search party at H.2. — Relieved by 8th Queens & took over men near trenches 33, 34 & about 1 mile to left of the trenches from St Amerns	

Army Form C. 2118.

WAR DIARY
or
INTELLIGENCE SUMMARY.
(Erase heading not required.)

Instructions regarding War Diaries and Intelligence Summaries are contained in F. S. Regs., Part II. and the Staff Manual respectively. Title pages will be prepared in manuscript.

Place	Date	Hour	Summary of Events and Information	Remarks and references to Appendices
VERBRANDEN MOLEN	8/11/15		Heavy showers - The line of trenches taken over were found in bad repair but well drained being on top of rising ground with a wood behind - The Reserve Company & H.Q. being in the wood 200 to 300 yds behind first line - Much work done repairing & improving trenches - Trenches & wood shelled during day otherwise was quiet -	
	9/11/15		Quiet until evening. Enemy shelled wood & country round, communication trench shewn up by shell work making dugouts in wood (consisting dugouts with overhead (?) cover) sandbagging in trenches & general improvement - Lieut CAPPS R.W. Devon's Spent some time in trenches with CO Examining Enemy's line - 2 dead Germans were seen by enemy's wire, supposed to have been killed by our bombers the night before - C.S.M.T. TUCKWELL No 2 Co killed by bullet while in sitting in his dugout, bullet penetrated through space between sand bags - Very wet night & little protection from it owing to bad shell of dugouts - 4 men killed & wounded - (7th & 8th & 9th)	
	10/11/15		Lieut R.O.C. Hingate (?) & Lieut CORRELL went round trenches with Co - 24th D. v Artillery & Belgians registering on German trenches some men unknown from first line, but one of our men killed by a short shell - Enemy retaliated & shelled wood killing one man - Relieved by 4th Batt & marched to Camp D at PENNINGHELST. 2/Lt SOWER(?)(R?) & 2 Lt Bath wounded to Camp D (?Camphuis) - 2 men killed & 1 wounded Reported sent to Base (Camphines) - 2 men killed & 1 wounded	
PENNING-HELST	11/11/15		Quiet windy - Rest & cleaning up as Camp Carpenters did not arrive until about 4 am - Army Chaplain Rev. B. BROWN joined men being attached to Camp D - 2 Lt F.G. WILSON appointed Act. Transport Officer from - 2nd Lt COBBETT reported himself from LONDON as arrived there. S/gt. READER 1 NCO accidentally wounded at Bomb School.	

2353 Wt. W3544/1454 700,000 5/15 D. D. & L. A.D.S.S./Forms/C. 2118.

WAR DIARY
or
INTELLIGENCE SUMMARY.
(Erase heading not required.)

Army Form C. 2118.

Instructions regarding War Diaries and Intelligence Summaries are contained in F.S. Regs., Part II. and the Staff Manual respectively. Title pages will be prepared in manuscript.

Place	Date	Hour	Summary of Events and Information	Remarks and references to Appendices
RENINGHE-HEIST	12/11/15		Very wet & high wind. Very little could be done but kit inspection & foot inspection – An Engineering fatigue party proceeded to a point indicated but could find no one to give instruction as to work to be done – The CO had an interview with Divisional General re appointment of 2nd in Command. MOC	
"	13/11/15		Wet & high wind. Work on huts practically at a standstill owing to the bad weather conditions – Efforts were however made to improve the state of the camp in the way of drainage as the ground was very very wet.	
"	14/11/15		Fine & cold wind. 300 men attended Devine Service at YMCA Tent, & two platoons met Col had baths – CO & D men & returned to Camp A to arrange 5 about moving. Here in the afternoon – Moved from D to A Camp in the afternoon – 20 officers & 150 NCO & men. No 1 C left in trenches to relieve 16 Somersets number of 8.5/Buffs – Lt BLACKFORD left for Grenade School to act as Instructor for one month – 2nd Lts MATTEYBACH & JEFFREYS returned from a short course at Grenade School – Capt DICKCLELAND & Lt & the latter being posted HQC duties of Adjutant from 2nd LT VENTRESS to 2nd Lt C
ST HUBERTUS HOEK	15/11/15		Fine cold. Working parties under RE & also building dugouts in Camp. Still under Company arrangements cleaning clothing, bombing instruction, also training extra machine gunners – Our Artillery shelled the enemy's "dumps" & communications –

WAR DIARY or INTELLIGENCE SUMMARY

Army Form C. 2118.

Place	Date	Hour	Summary of Events and Information	Remarks and references to Appendices
ST HUBERTUS / HOEK (Conj A)	16/11/15		Fine morning, cold showers afternoon – Working parties under R.E. – All men had a bath at RENNINGHELST – C.O. went to 17th Brigade H.Q. to lunch – Capt HARE left to be attached to the 1st Batt N Staffords & Capt FREETH & Capt BARRINGTON – left to be attached to the 1st Batt Royal Fusiliers – Capt BARRINGTON – FOOTE appointed 2nd in Command vice Capt HARE – Casualties – one man killed – one man wounded no 1 Co –	
	17/11/15		Heavy showers morning – Working parties under R.E. – Orders received to relieve 1st Batt in trenches on the 18th. C.O. informed that the Brigade would be relieved by a Brigade of the 3rd Division on the night of 21/22 – Later – Orders received 1st Batt cancelled trench fatigue by our force of morning. Things at 3pm – Battalion parade drill order. Bombing instructed by NCOs. – Work	
	18/11/15		Many showers & and afternoon very wet – Battalion parade drill order. Bombing instructed & Machine Gun instruction – R.E. – Instruction dwelt to Jr NCOs – Work parties in Camp – 7 Officers & headed lectures at RENNINGHELST – photograph of dug out in Camp – S.A. German aeroplanes came over in the morning & dropped bombs on of trenches – Jerry night	
	19/11/15		Cold pent. – Working parties under R.E. – & rift – Instruction in Bombing & Machine Gun – Work on dug outs. Drag off & lightning & signing from hospital here	
	20/11/15		Cold fine. Fatigue & working parties under R.E. – Marching order inspection – Work on dug outs & drainage – Drill – Physical training & cleaning up – 2nd Lt WILSON rejoined from hospital – Rev MORGAN attached –	

WAR DIARY or INTELLIGENCE SUMMARY

Army Form C. 2118.

(Erase heading not required.)

Instructions regarding War Diaries and Intelligence Summaries are contained in F. S. Regs., Part II. and the Staff Manual respectively. Title pages will be prepared in manuscript.

Place	Date	Hour	Summary of Events and Information	Remarks and references to Appendices.
ST. JBERT's HOEK Camp A	21/1/15		Fine, very cold – Divine Service 10am – Foot inspection with Medical Officer & greasing feet – loading transport for mule – Lt BLACKFORD rejoined from Grenade School – Lt Watts & 2 Lt Bull & 100 men rejoined from trenches. 2 Lt MARTIN & party 25 men rejoined from fatigue work with 1st Batt. Rev BROWNE attended during morn – marched from Camp A to PIPERINGHE at 4.05pm, arrived 6.30pm. Took up billets in town. Very wet, fuel, fingers hard on the march – left Pioneer Sgt & fine pioneers behind at Camp A to fix crosses on graves of men killed in trenches –	MAC
POPERINGHE	22/1/15		Cold, foggy – Day spent in billets – rifle inspection & – marched out at 4.45pm in ELCKE – started in dense fog – cleared later – very good road – arrived MAC 9pm –	
ELCKE	23/1/15		Cold, damp – CO visited Dutch – very contented & crowded in town. Brigade's made no arrangements. Rifle inspection & –	MAC
ARNEKE	24/1/15		Mild, showery – left at 9am in Brigade for ARNEKE – marched in rear of Brigade – through CASSEL long hill – about 6 mile – billets beyond thro' about 2 mile in town – very crowded – much straggling fair constantly took of packet hit about 3 men fell out mostly Labour Draft.	
WATTEN	25/1/15		Fine, cold. Left ARNEKE at 9.45 am with Brigade – 12th Batt. leading – marched to WATTEN about 12 miles arriving 2pm – went into billets – hard – fair march improvement noticed in march discipline & only 4 men fell out.	MAC

Army Form C. 2118.

WAR DIARY
or
INTELLIGENCE SUMMARY.
(Erase heading not required.)

Instructions regarding War Diaries and Intelligence Summaries are contained in F. S. Regs., Part II. and the Staff Manual respectively. Title pages will be prepared in manuscript.

Place	Date	Hour	Summary of Events and Information	Remarks and references to Appendices
EST MONT	26/11/15		Left Strenens, Ambre – moved into billets via EST MONT, OUEST MONT + WEST MONT. Very difficult to find accommodation, regt scattered + small being many out weather bad – Officers GRINDLEY, WILKINSON + CORNISH joined 1st Battⁿ. Right very cold + hard frost.	Mar
EST MONT	27/11/15		Issue cold. Battn billeting scheme made. Company arrangements. Cleaning up + changing sewer men into better billets – General – GOC/3rd Brigade + later GOC/3 Brigade called. Divine service 11.30 a.m.	Mar
"	28/11/15		Inspected very hard frost during night. Divine service 11.30 a.m. frosty. Pack-horse Mule to Brigade H.Q. Engineers.	Mar
"	29/11/15		Warm + not raining. Coat very slippery – Battalion parade. Drill under Company arrangements. Billets, Fur jackets – GOC 3rd Division came + gave some of the billets a look – arrangements to be made for men to use community as most weather permits – 2 Lt. Regiments from 13th Batt.	Mar
"	30/11/15		Inclid frost. Commenced programme of training – Drill physical training, machine guns, bombing instruction – also instruction of Officers N.C.O.s – 26 Part 15 overhid duties of Transport Officer.	Mar

4 T.

12/24

12/Nov. Iwars. transfer
Vozice 1915

7/31

7978

Army Form C. 2118.

WAR DIARY
or
INTELLIGENCE SUMMARY.
(Erase heading not required.)

Instructions regarding War Diaries and Intelligence Summaries are contained in F.S. Regs, Part II. and the Staff Manual respectively. Title pages will be prepared in manuscript.

Place	Date	Hour	Summary of Events and Information	Remarks and references to Appendices
ESTMONT	1.12.15.		Some rain. Drill, physical training, bombing instruction under Company arrangements. Football in afternoon. The C.O. Lt-Col H.W.COMPTON left for England on leave in evening. CAPT BARRINGTON-FOOTE in command of the Battalion. 6 P.M. Lecture by COL. COMPTON to Platoon Sergeants.	
"	2.12.15.		Battalion Route March. Kit and foot inspection. Fine. The Adjutant, LT TANNER, and 2 LT BULL attended Court Martial at Brigade H.Q.	
"	3.12.15.		Fine. Drill and Physical training under Company arrangements. No 3 Company had baths at Creurey. No 4 Co H.Q. 6 P.M. Lecture to N.C.O's by 2 LT VENTRESS. CAPT CAHIR R.A.M.C. lectured on home leave. Only indoor training possible. Football match with Brigade H.Q. postponed. LT and "Q.M. RICE and 2 LT ANDERSON left on home leave. 5 P.M. Lecture by MAJ. GEN. CAPPER to officers and N.C.O's. LT. E. CHESTER-MASTER and LT. G.M. GORDON joined the Battalion from the 5th Battalion and were posted to 3 and 1 Cos respectively.	
"	5.12.15.		Rain in evening. Divine Service in morning. Football Match v Brigade H.Q. in afternoon. Result. 12 "R.F.B." goals. H.Q. nil. 2-T.J.B. WILSON returned from a grenade course.	
"	6.12.15.		Heavy Rain. Drill etc under Company arrangements. 6 P.M. Lecture on bombing to platoon Sergeants by 2 LT GIRDLER. Inter-Company football match in afternoon. No 4 beat No 2. No 3 and No 1 drew.	
"	7.12.15.		Fine. Battalion Route march and Brigade parade. No 3 Company again drew with No 1 Coy Football. 8 P.M. Lecture by 2 LT. GIRDLER to officers on bombing. LT NEYNOE and 2 LT. F.G. WILSON returned from leave.	

WAR DIARY
or
INTELLIGENCE SUMMARY.

(Erase heading not required.)

Army Form C. 2118.

Instructions regarding War Diaries and Intelligence Summaries are contained in F.S. Regs., Part II. and the Staff Manual respectively. Title pages will be prepared in manuscript.

Place	Date	Hour	Summary of Events and Information	Remarks and references to Appendices
ESTMONT	8.12.15		Fine. Drill and bombing instruction under Company arrangement. 2 Lt EAMES went with a party of 20 officers from the Division to visit a Supply Railhead, an Ammunition Railhead and the Headquarters of the Second Army at CASSEL. Football Match v 3rd Rifle Brigade. Victory for 3rd Rifle Brigade by 5 goals to nil. Lectures to N.C.O's in evening under Company arrangements on gas.	AE
"	9.12.15		Wet. Battalion parade abandoned owing to bad weather. 4 officers and 200 men digging practice German trenches near ST OMER-CALAIS road. Lectures on trench routine under Company arrangements. Preliminary inter-Company ties in shooting won by No 4 Company, Nos 1 and 3 Companies tied with boots. Lecture by 2 Lt EAMES to Officers on his visit to Army H.Q. Col COMPTON returned from leave.	AE
"	10.12.15		Wet. Brigade Route March postponed accordingly. 2 Companies tied with boots. No 2 Company taken over obstacle course in afternoon. Capt FREETH rejoined the Battalion from LEIST. 5.30 P.M. Lecture to officers by Col. COMPTON.	AE
"	11.12.15		Wet. Brigade Route March and inspection by Army Commander, GEN...	AE
"	12.12.15		Divine Service. Parades for Roman Catholics and Nonconformists. 2 Lt CORNISH left on Bombing Course.	AE
"	13.12.15		Battalion parade. Lecture on wire Entanglements. Lt RICE and 2Lt ANDERSON returned from leave. 5.30 P.M. Lecture to officers by Col COMPTON	AE
"	14.12.15		Fine. 500 men and 2 officers per Company attended gas demonstration and passed through a trench filled with gas. Lecture to officers by Col COMPTON. 2 Lt WATENBACH and 2 Lt JEFFERIES returned from Course at Technical School. Capt DICK-CLELAND left on home leave, 2 Lt EAMES acting as Adjutant in his absence.	AE

Army Form C. 2118.

WAR DIARY
or
INTELLIGENCE SUMMARY.
(Erase heading not required.)

Instructions regarding War Diaries and Intelligence Summaries are contained in F. S. Regs., Part II. and the Staff Manual respectively. Title pages will be prepared in manuscript.

Place	Date	Hour	Summary of Events and Information	Remarks and references to Appendices
ESTMONT	15.12.15.		Fine. Col. Battalion parade. Col COMPTON and three other officers attended a lecture at NORDAUSQUES on Machine gun Tactics. 6 p.m. Lecture to Platoon Sergeants by Col COMPTON.	182
"	16.12.15.		Fine. 2 Lt BENJAMIN a member of a Court-Martial at H.Q. 1st R.F. Holiday. Sports — Boxing, Tug of War, Grooms' Race, Flat races, Obstacle race etc. 2 Lt CAMPBELL left for Technical School.	182
"	17.12.15.		Battalion Route March — Football Match Officers v Sergeant, won by former.	18E
"	18.12.15.		Dull but no rain. Nos 2 and 4 Companies constructing trenches and entanglements for attack practice. Nos 1 and 3 Companies marching order parades. Football match 6 a side ten minutes each way between Nos 3 and 4. Victory for latter. CAPT CAHIR R.A.M.C. returned from leave.	18E
"	19.12.15.		Fine. Church parades for Cof E, R.C. and Nonconformist. C.O. and Company Commanders inspected practice German Trenches at MONNECOVE.	18E
"	20.12.15.		Attack practice in Battalion area. C.O. and Ag Adjutant attended lecture at 1st Northeants H.Q. on the Campaign in German WEST AFRICA. LT NEYNOE lectured to N.C.O.s	182
"	21.12.15.		Brigade Route March fixed for today abandoned owing to continuous rain. Col COMPTON discussed schemes of attack with Company Commanders Evening LT NEYNOE lectured N.C.O.s (subject discussed lectures)	18L
"	22.12.15.		Training under Company arrangements. Lecture to Officers by Col COMPTON in Evening. CAPT BARRINGTON-FOOTE left on home leave. CAPT DICK-CLELAND returned from leave. LT NEYNOE returned to Battalion and one officer and one officer from each Company left for the new Divisional area. 5 officers and 5 Sergeants	

2353 Wt. W3441/1454 700,000 5/15 D. D. & L. A.D.S.S./Forms/C. 2118.

Army Form C. 2118.

WAR DIARY
or
INTELLIGENCE SUMMARY.
(Erase heading not required.)

Instructions regarding War Diaries and Intelligence Summaries are contained in F. S. Regs., Part II. and the Staff Manual respectively. Title pages will be prepared in manuscript.

Place	Date	Hour	Summary of Events and Information	Remarks and references to Appendices
ESTMONT	23.12.15		VISITED TILQUES to see model trenches etc.	
	23.12.15		Very wet. Training carried on under Company arrangements. 4 officers attended lecture at NORDAUSQUES on the new Divisional area, illustrated by aeroplane photographs of trenches.	
"	24.12.15		Very wet. Route March fixed for today postponed owing to rain. The Officers had their Christmas dinner at No 4 Co H.Q. — a great success. The trench party returned. 2 Lt BLACKFORD rejoined.	
"	25.12.15		The men had their Christmas dinner from 12:30 p.m. in the barns at their billets. No 4 Co managed to arrange for all the Company to dine together. The remainder were in a large groups as the accommodation allowed. The Sergeants dined at 2 p.m and finished the same day.	
"	26.12.15		Fine. The Battalion did a practice attack at the model German trenches at MONNECOVE. In the afternoon the Officers of Nos 1 and 2 Coys played the Officers of Nos 3 and 4 Coys at football. The game resulted in a victory for the latter. The play was more vigorous than scientific. 2 Lt TUERSLEY joined the Battalion from 1st Royal Fusiliers.	
"	27.12.15		Hitler under Company arrangements. The Commander in Chief passed through the district. Lecture to Officers by Col COMPTON at 5:30 p.m. 2nd Lt TUERSLEY posted to No 2 Coy. Lt Bonnett to No 1.	
"	28.12.15		Battalion Route March. Foot inspection in afternoon. Lecture to officers on "Vigour of Operations" by Col COMPTON at 5:30 p.m. CAPT CHESTER-MASTER assumed command of No 1 Company. LT YEATS was appointed Ag Assistant Adjutant. 2 Lt COX was transferred from No 4 to No 3 Coy.	

Army Form C. 2118.

WAR DIARY
or
INTELLIGENCE SUMMARY.
(Erase heading not required.)

Instructions regarding War Diaries and Intelligence Summaries are contained in F.S. Regs., Part II. and the Staff Manual respectively. Title pages will be prepared in manuscript.

Place	Date	Hour	Summary of Events and Information	Remarks and references to Appendices
ESTRÉHEM	29.12.15		Drill, bombing instruction etc. under company arrangements. The C.O. inspected Company with view during the morning in view of G.O.C.'s inspection. Drill and Football were indulged in during the afternoon. In the evening 2nd Lt. Armstrong lectured to Sergeants. The day was mild and dry.	/M.
"	30.12.15		The G.O.C. 24th Division [Major Gen. J.E. Capper] inspected the 17th Bn. on the Brigade Parade ground near La COMMUNAL this morning. He usually saw first a company at drill. He inspected Brigade and workshop of the G.O.C. on the CALAIS – ST OMER road. The afternoon was given to sport, football etc. In evening at 5.30 p.m. LT. BLACKFORD lectured the Battalion on bombing.	/M.
"	31.12.15		The morning was occupied with bombing instruction, physical drill etc under Company arrangements. No 3 Coy musketry musketry on the Mt Gr Range on the CALAIS – STONER road during the morning. Rain in the afternoon prevented No 1 Coy attending of the range. Companies to use helped production. The bad weather also interfered with the night work which was arranged for Companies. 2nd Lt. F.G. Symons was admitted to hospital.	/M.

CAPT. P.W. BARRINGTON FOOTE returned from home leave.

Lt Compton
DI Cox
Colonel 17/Royal Fusiliers

17th Brigade.
24th Division.

12th BATTALION

ROYAL FUSILIERS.

January 1 9 1 6.

Feb '18

17/24

12th Reg: Foot
Vol: 5

245

WAR DIARY
or
INTELLIGENCE SUMMARY.
(Erase heading not required.)

Army Form C. 2118.

Place	Date	Hour	Summary of Events and Information	Remarks and references to Appendices
ESTMONT	1.7.16		The battalion marched to an open field north west to LA CALOTTERIE in accordance with arrangement. Officers & N.C.O.s and selected men did work. The day was spent in company training. Capt. A.H. Tanner proceeded to home Hospital sick. Capt. G. Hickson proceeded to WISQUES bathing & headq. the troops. 2nd Lieut. PS. Wilson returned to regimental transport. 2nd Lieut. J.T. Cox took over.	
"	2.7.16		Sunday. Whole Church Parade at 11.30 am. Lieut Col Compton, Capt. Neynos, Capt. Chester-Master 2nd Lieut Anderson and 2nd Lieut Harvey proceeded to take over the new trenches. Lieut Gen Kyford Kay proceeded on leave.	
"	3.7.16		Brigade route march. Weather fine and warm. Shaftesbury returned from hospital. Capt. Chester-Cleeve and Capt Dick-Cleland allowed at NEROH GROVE hot. Some officers inspected Capt. Foote's and Capt Dick-Cleland allowed at NEROH GROVE.	
"	4.7.16		O.C. left to take over South Kensington Dumps to specially prepare the new position for the enemy companies arrived. The move 12 bodying description. Day spent in preparation for move. Lieut Varley proceed in home on leave.	
POPERINGHE	5.7.16		Battalion moved to EST MONT — STOMER. Car & entrained for POPERINGHE arriving there about 7.30 p.m.	
Outendom	5.7.16		Occupied Camp F. Battalion prepared to go into trenches. Advance party sent to H trenches to take over.	
H.Trenches	6.7.16	9 p.m.	Relieved Sherwood Foresters. Quiet night. Casualties nil.	
"	7.7.16		Very quiet day. Equipment inspected. Roughplan for drainage drawn up. Sniping posts arranged. Night quiet. Machine guns traversed front line. Casualties. 2 or 3 killed 1 wounded.	

R.B. Ch. Ch.w Cpt.

Army Form C. 2118.

WAR DIARY
or
INTELLIGENCE SUMMARY.
(Erase heading not required.)

Instructions regarding War Diaries and Intelligence
Summaries are contained in F. S. Regs., Part II.
and the Staff Manual respectively. Title pages
will be prepared in manuscript.

Place	Date	Hour	Summary of Events and Information	Remarks and references to Appendices
H. trenches	8.1.16		Fairly quiet day. Moon. Believe a Boll Bte Bomer heavily shelled. Into our Coy rob off carried out during night. Enemy sniper killed by us at 7 pm. exposed H20. Enemy machine guns silenced by rifle grenades. Casualties. o.r. 1 wounded	
"	9.1.16		Artillery active today. During night heavy bombardment heard in direction of St ELOI. from 3.30 AM to 4.30 AM. Caught enemy working party. Visible over m. gun. also dropped enemy working party by rifle grenades. Otherwise night quiet. Casualties. o.r. 3 killed.	
"	10.1.16		Quiet day. Good deal of enemy shelling in vicinity. Night passed uneventfully. During evening enemy machine fired intermittently on H.11 & rifle fire and then ceased to outpost posn. Casualties nil.	
"	11.1.16		Enemy put 25 HE shells into our front trenches, and in front of S16. but did no material damage. Night quiet. Casualties nil.	
"	12.1.16		Enemy again shelled in front of S.16. and close to outpost from at 8 am and 10 am. They also shelled front line and Huddy Lane at 4.30 pm. No damage. We returned our artillery retaliation in 5 minute. Night quiet. Casualties nil.	
"	13.1.16		Very quiet day. Few shells in front of S.16. Casualties o.r. one wounded. Relieved by 1st Roy Irish at 10 pm. Marched to Camp H13Dq 1. All in by 3 AM.	
Camp H13D q 1	14.1.16		Rested and cleaned up.	
"	15.1.16		10 inspection. rifle &c. foot ditto. Baths arranged. Issue of clothing.	
"	16.1.16		Training programme commenced. First parade 7 AM. Batt. inspection 9.30. drill and instruction. Commanded to clean Camp. Fatigues supplied to R.E.	

C.B.V.L.C.[signature] Capt.

Army Form C. 2118.

WAR DIARY
or
INTELLIGENCE SUMMARY.
(Erase heading not required.)

Instructions regarding War Diaries and Intelligence Summaries are contained in F. S. Regs., Part II. and the Staff Manual respectively. Title Pages will be prepared in manuscript.

Place	Date	Hour	Summary of Events and Information	Remarks and references to Appendices
Camp H13 D91 (Outersham)	17.1.16		Usual camp routine. Inspection. drill. instruction in grenade work. Sniping and scouting parties organised. R.E. fatigues supplied. Baths. Bayonet exercise.	
"	18.1.16		Kit and rifle inspection. Issue of clothing. Route march by Companies. Battalion inspection by C.O. Fatigue parties supplied. Gas helmets inspected.	
"	19.1.16		Special work done to complete drawing of camp. Foot inspection. Fatigue parties for Sherwood Foresters. Grenade instruction. Practice surmounting obstacles.	
"	20.1.16		Camp fatigues. Rifle inspection. Grenade instruction. Gas helmet instruction.	
"	21.1.16		Battalion inspection by C.O. Company drill by O.C's. Bayonet exercise. Musketry.	
"	22.1.16		Sniping practice. Grenade instruction. Camp fatigues. Working parties for R.E. & Sherwood Foresters. Two hrs Drill in ranks.	
"	23.1.16		Work as per programme. Kit inspection. Rifle & foot inspection. Issue of clothing. Baths.	
"	24.1.16		Battalion parade. Inspection by C.O. Company drill. Gas helmets inspected. Fatigues for R.E. Scouting parties at night.	
"	25.1.16		Company parades and inspections. Lectures by O.C's on Gas. Grenade instruction. Camp fatigue. Scouting parties at night. Fatigue for R.E.	
"	26.1.16		Preparations begun for taking over trenches. Clothing, boots and ammunition inspected and made up. Grenade instruction. Bayonet exercise. Practice surmounting obstacles. Gas helmets practised.	
"	27.1.16		Advance parties prepared for trenches. Foot inspection. Grease issued and used. Issue of socks. Fatigues supplied for R.E. Grenade instruction. Sniping and Scouting practised.	

[signature] Lt Col

2353 Wt. W3544/1434 700,000 5/15 D. D. & L. A.D.S.S./Forms/C. 2118.

Army Form C. 2118.

WAR DIARY
or
INTELLIGENCE SUMMARY.
(Erase heading not required.)

Instructions regarding War Diaries and Intelligence Summaries are contained in F. S. Regs., Part II. and the Staff Manual respectively. Title pages will be prepared in manuscript.

Place	Date	Hour	Summary of Events and Information	Remarks and references to Appendices
Camp H13 Dq1 (huder dam).	28.1.16		Battalion parade and inspection by C.O. At 3.45 p.m. Prematire explosion of grenade (No 5 Mills) thrown during grenade instruction caused serious wounding of Lt Benjamin, Sgt Mjr Allen, Scout Wilde, Ptes Morley, Campbell, Humphrey & Hilton. Court of inquiry returned opinion that occurrence was accidental.	
"	29.1.16		C.O. and Company Cdrs. started out for trenches and took over from 9th R. Sussex. C.O. spent day inspecting trenches and returned to Camp at night. Batt. made ready to move off	
A.3 & C.3	30.1.16		Relief of R. Sussex completed at 9 p.m. Night quiet. Enemy shelled Appendix but did no material damage. Casualties nil.	
"	31.1.16		Enemy artillery not very active. At 10 a.m. he shelled Appendix. Two kills in trench. no one hurt & no material damage. Enemy seen in daylight working right of Keep. One hit by our sniper. Wire inspected front of C3 and found to require repairs. Casualties nil. One wounded. Drainage of trenches started. New dugouts begun.	

2353 Wt. W3544/1454 700,000 5/15 D. D. & L. A.D.S.S./Forms/C. 2118.

17th Brigade.
24th Division.

12th BATTALION

ROYAL FUSILIERS.

February 1916.

17/24

12th R. Fus

Vol 6

24

WAR DIARY or INTELLIGENCE SUMMARY

Army Form C. 2118.

Place	Date	Hour	Summary of Events and Information	Remarks and references to Appendices
Bq to C 3.	1.2.16		Quiet night. Single Red & Green lights seen opposite C.2. & C.1. Enemy aeroplanes over our lines dropped two smoke balls on Zouave Wood and spot was shelled afterwards. Working party dispersed by our machine gun in Appendix at 3 a.m. Wire in front of C.1. repaired. Drainage of trenches proceeded with. Two new shelters made in R.7. Casualties. O.R. 2. wounded.	
"	2.2.16		Day & night fairly quiet. Patrol across C.2 and front of R of C.3. Listening post of enemy located in front of C.3. Three direct hits on our machine gun and grenade posts. S/che. Barrington re-established the posts quickly and showed great coolness but presence of mind under very trying circumstances. Front line cleared during morning to allow our artillery to shell keep. Casualties. O.R. 3. killed. 3. wounded.	
"	3.2.16		Inter-Company grenade post reliefs carried out. Drainage and sand bagging done in front line R.S. 6 and R.S. 7 repaired and chained A.L. 8. trans ferred to R.7. C.2. patrolled. Enemy working party fired at by our machine gun and two hits noted? Casualties O.R. 2. wounded. Command of Grenade Post in C 3 taken over by 3rd R.B. me to Suppl' men. Keys to Suppl trenches. 2nd Sq sent to front line at night. 2nd Lt. Cox and 2nd Lt. Empson, 3rd R.B. me to Suppl. H.W.S.Gp Community B Royal Fusiliers	

WAR DIARY
or
INTELLIGENCE SUMMARY.

(Erase heading not required.)

Army Form C. 2118.

Instructions regarding War Diaries and Intelligence Summaries are contained in F.S. Regs., Part II. and the Staff Manual respectively. Title pages will be prepared in manuscript.

Place	Date	Hour	Summary of Events and Information	Remarks and references to Appendices
B.7.W.C.3	4.2.16		Line inspected by Brigadier. Several direct hits in German Royal/enemy Post shelled badly from 10 to 12 noon. About 100 shells dropped in area. Appendix and R1 shelled whilst by war there of fire which obtained opposite Craker as white light was sent up when direct hit. Snipers reported to have punctured C2 and two Officers made search but could not move. Very noticeable that number of shells used by enemy has decreased. Casualties. O.R. 1 wounded. Drainage and scaffolding done.	
	5.2.16		Quiet day & night. Patrols in. Patrolling. 8th Canadians sent Str. Canadians our tonight. Inspection hunted and side by Officer at 1st R.F. Brigade Grenades at Yeomanry Post places Rest and Sentry guide in shade. Rifle Grenades teams over Keep at 2 am this morning. Reported that fuses of shells fired into Yeomanry Post yesterday are dated 19/16. Handful out corrected and releasing in B.W.7. Royal Sussex. Expected by 11 pm and Bath. Men relief by parties to 2 Lille Beke Dugouts. Casualties. O.R. 2 killed. 4 wounded.	
2nd Corps Dugouts	6.2.16		Short day rest and cleaning up. Two other Artist rifle left. Lighters Si.Os shewn cleaned and Dugouts repaired. Five parties at wiring for R.E. Capt. D.V. Bannister & Foote prevented to supervise work.	
	7.2.16		Quiet day. Rifle inspection. Fatigues for R.E. at night at House. One party shelled in another street. Casualties. 1 O.R. wounded.	
	8.2.16		Artillery active on both sides. Sunday closing party. Fatigue parties at night for R.E. Capt. A.G. J.A. Clarke. H.W. Coupland Capt, 2 Royal Sussex Commanding.	

Army Form C. 2118.

WAR DIARY
or
INTELLIGENCE SUMMARY.
(Erase heading not required.)

Instructions regarding War Diaries and Intelligence Summaries are contained in F.S. Regs., Part II. and the Staff Manual respectively. Title pages will be prepared in manuscript.

Place	Date	Hour	Summary of Events and Information	Remarks and references to Appendices
Zillebeke Dugouts			Appointed 2 i/c Command from this date vice Capt P.W. Beresford Peirse who has vacated this appt through ill health. Capt Gorton Arthington transferred from this date to 2nd Tunnelling Coy. Proceeded to England on leave.	
"	9.2.16	11.30 am	Twelve heavy shells dropped in and around Forvin Trk Cemetery. OR 2 Killed 5 wounded. Enemy artillery active	
"	10.2.16		Quiet day. Some gas shells dropped close this morning but no damage done. 152 went up to relieve E 3 Trench tonight. Capt L Carvill OR wounded. Relief completed at 11 pm. Lieut Mjr. Z. Ensor. E3 Counsellor OR 2 wounded.	
C.e. Py.	11.2.16		2 St Mathurin 2 St Martin proceeded to start on leave.	
"	12.2.16		Heavy bombardment of E.3 all day. 1 OR Killed & his women in 2 St Martin.	
"	13.2.16		Heavy shell fire lasted till midnight. Cylinder explosion from gh reg. res. seen by us. Bombardment started again this morning & lasted 7 pm. Sniping all day. Casualties 8 OR wounded.	
"	14.2.16		Bombed through to Canal ed all day. quiet night. Free. but our enhance. Casualties 6 OR wounded.	
"	15.2.16		Bombardment recommenced early this morning. We were heavily shelled for & minutes. Two explosions of landmines to rear of boy's dump & 2 St Mk/s G Bruce severely wounded. 3 OR killed 8 OR wounded by E Greens and marched to Camp D (Q15 a5) 2 St	
Camp D.	16.2.16		Quiet day. Relieved by E3 Greens and marched to Camp D (Q15 a5) 2 St Came died of wounds.	
"	17.2.16		Complete rest. Badly draft of 30 OR posted to Coy Ballarfred eff'd recd the 9.S.C. 17 Conjtr has expressed his great satisfaction at the manner in which the battalion carried out its duties	

H.W. Anjath Lt Colonel
Commanding 12 Royal Fusiliers

Army Form C. 2118.

WAR DIARY
or
INTELLIGENCE SUMMARY.
(Erase heading not required.)

Instructions regarding War Diaries and Intelligence Summaries are contained in F. S. Regs., Part II. and the Staff Manual respectively. Title pages will be prepared in manuscript.

Place	Date	Hour	Summary of Events and Information	Remarks and references to Appendices
Camp D.	18.2.16		Arrived. We took over in the hutches. Programme of duty commenced. Saturday Camp Routine. 5 P.M. Cot treated as Appointment at T.O.	
"	19.2.16		Early morning Physical training. S/Sgt. Coates down with Carpenters inspection Repairs and Sanitary Inspection. A.P. Received kits and clothing of Commanding Officer. Effects of Capt. Adams to the list. We attended to Equipment. Cricket for men in evening. Capt. Normal Routine on Saturday.	
"	20.2.16		Digree Church in Cafine.	
"	21.2.16		Practice Attack. Instruction by Bayonet. The Battalion returning To 5½ Coy. Reserve.	
"	22.2.16		Normal Routine. Marching Parties on road and at Dickebusch. Capt. T. W. Somerton A/1727 2nd Lt. St Leger/No. V.A./5076? Should Self the struggle Authority 2nd Army A/1727. 2 Capt. No. V.A./5076 Practice Attack Normal Routine as per programme of work. Scheme b attacks by Coll. Campbell.	
"	23.2.16		Normal Routine. Spline hoisting Scheme instruction in trifling as for Rev. G. G. Bre Sue leclerce to see officers & N.C.Os. 2 Sgt. S not less G. Se. Confl. of Iniated Gas in Camp.	
"	25.2.16		New Programme of lst work commenced. Reconnoissance sent by Night to the Bluff. Heavy Snow Jell & Effect out about three days? 2 Sgt. Wilkinson Struck off the Strength V.A./5509 Many Candles Requested. Stamped by Order received Ball ready to move	
"	26.2.16		Instruction Nothing further. By 2nd Lt. Greenwood. 1st R.E. Barks. Lt Col Compton returned from leave.	
"	27.2.16		Practise Attack. Grenade and Sniping Instructors. A. V. Humphry & George Sinclair Committee is Bijoy & Sinclair	

Army Form C. 2118.

WAR DIARY
or
INTELLIGENCE SUMMARY.
(Erase heading not required.)

Instructions regarding War Diaries and Intelligence Summaries are contained in F.S. Regs., Part II. and the Staff Manual respectively. Title pages will be prepared in manuscript.

Place	Date	Hour	Summary of Events and Information	Remarks and references to Appendices
Camp D	28.2.16		Routine duty. Inspection of General Culper. Lecture to Officers by Col. Compton. Draft of 30 OR posted to this battalion.	
	29.2.16		Divine Camp Routine. Baker Capt. E.L. Wymore returned from leave.	

H.W.Compton Lt. Colonel
Commanding 12 Royal Fusiliers

17th Brigade.
24th Division.

12th BATTALION

ROYAL FUSILIERS.

March 1916.

24th Div

12 R Fus

Vol 7

Army Form C. 2118.

WAR DIARY
or
INTELLIGENCE SUMMARY.
(Erase heading not required.)

Place	Date	Hour	Summary of Events and Information	Remarks and references to Appendices
Camp D Outer Vimereux	1.3.16		Work as per programme of training. Lecture to Officers by Col. Jno Compton	
"	2.3.16		Work as per programme of training.	
"	3.3.16		Attack practice – Athletic parade.	
"	4.3.16		Work as per programme of training.	
"	5.3.16		Work as per Church parade 9.45 training. Lecture to young officers by Lt.Col. J.W. Compton.	
"	6.3.16		Work as per programme of training.	
"	7.3.16		Capt. A.B. Dick-Cleland, Capt. C.L. Neyroz & Capt. N.G. Tanner proceeded to the gas schools conducted by 4th Army Corps, 2nd Wallentack attached I.O.	
Somehwere? West? France? Trenches? D.13 to D.14	8.3.16		Relieved of East Yorks. Our sheets to leave continued by O.C. & Batt. to right about 7.30. Some of ours wounded during the night by snipers.	
	9.3.16		Fairly quiet. An Officer patrol examined ground in front of B.3. Casualties O.R. 7 wounded.	
	10.3.16		Snow fell in the early hours of the morning. Enemy Artillery active about 2 pm. over 200 shells been fired in sections Regt. Casualties. O.R. 2 wounded.	
"	11.3.16		More snow fell during the night. Enemy Artillery rather active especially round B.2. Casualties. O.R. 2 killed. 5 wounded. 7 shell shock.	
"	12.3.16		Enemy Artillery & trench Spanderls especially our Zouave Wood & its vicinity. Casualties. O.R. 1 killed. 11 wounded. 1 shell shock.	

J.W. Compton
Lt. Colonel
Commanding 12. Royal Fusiliers

#353 Wt. W2544/1454 700,000 5/15 D. D. & L. A.D.S.S./Form/C. 2118.

WAR DIARY or INTELLIGENCE SUMMARY

Army Form C. 2118.

(Erase heading not required.)

Place	Date	Hour	Summary of Events and Information	Remarks and references to Appendices
"	13.3.16		A fairly quiet day. We worried the enemy with land grenades especially in the evening. 11.0 pm WM Kafir over Bt. Casualties OR 1 killed, 1 wounded, 1 shell shock	
"	14.3.16		Enemy exceedingly active, his attention to Somme Rd Clearing Cross & Somme Walk & Bt. H.Q. being very marked. Casualties O.R. 2 killed, 11 wounded, 1 shell shock	
"	15.3.16		Enemy again very active especially round Bat.H.Q. Somme Walk, Bat. HQ decided to move to Winchester Avenue. Casualties OR 5 killed, 1 wounded, 6 shell shock	
"	16.3.16		Enemy Artillery active all day. New Bat. H.Q. Winchester Avenue struck his rifle grenade. 2 Lt Campbell wounded & since died from the effects of his wound. Casualties OR 1 killed, 17 wounded & shell shock	
"	17.3.16		Enemy shell active. Concrete Dugouts shelled. 2 Lts Tom Sheffield & D.W. Umpstead wounded. Casualties O.R. & tracers wounded 11 shell shock	
"	18.3.16		A quiet day. Relieved by 1st R.F. — marched to Camp C	
Camp C.	19.3.16		Bn. had started cleaning up. Capt A.B. Dick Cunyng & Capt A.S. Tanner proceeded to England on short leave. Capt A.B. Dick supervising work and the duties of Commandant during Capt. F. Transport absence	
"	20.3.16		arrived at Camp F.	
Camp F.	21.3.16		Work in the Company arrangements	
Endham	22.3.16		Work in the Company arrangements. 1 Officer & 23 men marched on leave. Baths carried out. Capt A.B. Dick elected in the rank of Major on 5.10.15	

H. Cunyngham Lt Colonel
Commanding 12th Royal Fusiliers

Army Form C. 2118.

WAR DIARY
or
INTELLIGENCE SUMMARY.
(Erase heading not required.)

Instructions regarding War Diaries and Intelligence Summaries are contained in F.S. Regs., Part II. and the Staff Manual respectively. Title pages will be prepared in manuscript.

Place	Date	Hour	Summary of Events and Information	Remarks and references to Appendices
	23.3.16		Temp: St. 6. L. Jeynes to be Temp. Capt. 28.9.15. Temp. Lieut: D.L. Blackford to be Temp. Capt. 5.10.15. Temp. 2nd Lieut D.C. Anderson (Vincent) in Brigade. Capt. D.C. Anderson proceeded to England on leave.	
Gomiecourt	24.3.16		Billets in trenches. 2 St. H.J. Dinkney joined	
"	25.3.16		Work in the Company encampment. Heavy fall of snow	
"	26.3.16		Church Parade clergy on account of weather. 2 Lt. E.E. Yeatan joined from 29th R.F.	
"	27.3.16		Work in the Company encampment. Application. The following letter dated 24.3.16 has been received from the S.O.C. 24th Division by the B.S.C. 17th Infantry Brigade. "Please report from General [illegible] that the 17th Brigade on the march yesterday [illegible] their turn out march discipline and general soldierly appearance did them great credit after the hardships they have had in the trenches."	
"	28.3.16		Work in the Company encampment. 2nd Lt. D.S. Gibson joined Temp. 2nd Lt. C. Anderson to be Temp. Capt. 26.1.16.	
"	29.3.16		Battalion moved by march route to billets at Gouy-en-Artois. Clear and warm. Billets are new ones far the Canadians.	

A.W. Murphy St. Colonel
Commanding 12 Royal Fusiliers

Army Form C. 2118.

WAR DIARY
or
INTELLIGENCE SUMMARY.

(Erase heading not required.)

Instructions regarding War Diaries and Intelligence Summaries are contained in F.S. Regs., Part II. and the Staff Manual respectively. Title pages will be prepared in manuscript.

Place	Date	Hour	Summary of Events and Information	Remarks and references to Appendices
"	30.3.16		Relieved 7th Battalion Canadian Regt in Trenches 132 to 135 + Field O.P.	
"	31.3.16		Very quiet day. St. Jeans proceeded to England on leave.	

W. Gosp.m
Lt. Colonel
Commanding 12th Royal Fusiliers

17th Brigade.
24th Division.

12th BATTALION

ROYAL FUSILIERS

April 1916.

WAR DIARY or INTELLIGENCE SUMMARY

Place	Date	Hour	Summary of Events and Information	Remarks and references to Appendices
PLOEGSTEERT (VIEUX Bq) Trenches 132-138 Hill 63.	1.4.16		A quiet day. Very little shelling. Casualties 2 O.R. wounded. Draft of 51 O.R. arrived. Major Dirk Cleland and Capt Tanner returned from leave. 2nd Lt. Rice proceeded on leave.	
"	2.4.16		Another very quiet day. Casualties 1 O.R. wounded.	
"	3.4.16		Enemy more active today. Shelled Irish Farm & Lonely Casualties 1 O.R. wounded. Capt Cahir proceeded to Ireland on leave.	
"	4.4.16		A quiet day. Capt. D.E. Anderson returned from leave. A draft of 59 O.R. joined.	
"	5.4.16		Casualties. Quiet day. A few shells on front line, Irish Farm & vicinity. Relieved by 1st R.I.F. and proceeded to Bulford Camp. Casualties nil.	
Bulford Camp	6.4.16		Men had baths. 400 O.R. & 4 Officers worked in front line during the night. 2nd Lt Yeatmay & 2nd Lt Snider proceeded on leave. St John reported in his rank as A/Lt from 5.2.16.	

H.W. Cunynghame Lt.Col.
Comm 12/ Royal Irish Rifles

Army Form C. 2118.

WAR DIARY
or
INTELLIGENCE SUMMARY.
(Erase heading not required.)

Instructions regarding War Diaries and Intelligence Summaries are contained in F. S. Regs., Part II. and the Staff Manual respectively. Title pages will be prepared in manuscript.

ORDERLY ROOM
15 MAY 1916
No.
12TH (SERVICE) BATTN. ROYAL FUSILIERS

Place	Date	Hour	Summary of Events and Information	Remarks and references to Appendices
Bulford Camp	7.4.16		The C.O. inspected the new draft. Coys carried on with programme of work. 200 O.R. + 4 Officers worked in Front Line during the night. The Q.O.C. inspected the Transport.	
"	8.4.16		Divine Service Parade. Capt. Clark Maxted + 2nd Lt. Gordon proceeded on leave. 200 O.R. + 4 Officers worked in Front Line during the night.	
"	9.4.16		Coys carried on with programme of work. 200 O.R. + 4 Officers worked in Front Line during the night. St. Yeats returned from leave.	
"	10.4.16		Played 1st Leinsters at Football + won 2–1. 200 men + 4 Officers worked in Front Line during night. Casualties 2nd Lt. N. Downey wounded.	
"	11.4.16		Relieved 1st R.F. in the evening in Trenches 132 to 135 inclusive and behind Ilse 63. St Rib returned from leave.	
Trenches 132 to 135 Ilse 63	12.4.16		Quiet day, raining most of the time. A few shells over Front Line. All leave cancelled & everyone on leave recalled.	

H. Winghim Lt Col
Commd 12/Royal Fusiliers

Army Form C. 2118.

WAR DIARY
or
INTELLIGENCE SUMMARY.
(Erase heading not required.)

Instructions regarding War Diaries and Intelligence Summaries are contained in F. S. Regs., Part II. and the Staff Manual respectively. Title pages will be prepared in manuscript.

Place	Date	Hour	Summary of Events and Information	Remarks and references to Appendices
Trenches 132 to 135 & Hill 63	13.4.16		The Hun was rather more active than usual. Trench Farm & Trench 132 & our wire trench all damaged. Casualties O.R. 2 wounded.	
"	14.4.16		Enemy Artillery active again Trench 132 & wire trench slightly damaged. Casualties. O.R. 2 wounded.	
"	15.4.16		Enemy very active. Trench 132 - Wire trench damaged - Maedelstede Farm Completely destroyed. Two of our snipers wounded by Shrapnel. Casualties O.R. 7 wounded.	
"	16.4.16		A quiet day. An enemy aerial torpedo fell into Trench 134. Casualties. 1 O.R. killed.	
"	17.4.16		Relieved by 1st R.F. Went into Brigade Reserve at GRAND MUNQUE Farm & adjoining wood. 2 St Yvettes & 2 St. Quidée returned from leave.	
GRAND MUNQUE FARM	18.4.16		Found working parties at 310 O.R. & 4 Officers for work in front line & forts. 2 St Quidée proceeded to Base as in charge of new drafts.	

H. W. Compton Ch. Col.
Commandg 12 Royal Fusiliers

Army Form C. 2118.

WAR DIARY
or
INTELLIGENCE SUMMARY.
(Erase heading not required.)

Instructions regarding War Diaries and Intelligence Summaries are contained in F.S. Regs. Part II. and the Staff Manual respectively. Title pages will be prepared in manuscript.

Place	Date	Hour	Summary of Events and Information	Remarks and references to Appendices
GRAND MUNQUE	19.4.16		Congrès Marchand inspected by B.E.C. Men had baths. Found working parties of 310 O.R. & 4 Officers for work in Front line & forts. 2/Lt Gordon returned from leave.	
—	20.4.16		Found working parties of 310 O.R. & 4 Officers for work in Front line & forts. 2/Lt Symons returned from hospital.	
—	21.4.16		Good Friday. Voluntary Services for all denominations in Y.M.C.A. Hut & Field dressing Station. Found working parties of 310 O.R. & 4 Officers for work in Front line & forts.	
—	22.4.16		Found working parties of 310 O.R. & 4 Officers for work in Front line. 2-Lts R.E. Cullen & E. Walker joined.	
—	23.4.16		Easter Sunday. Services held in Same locality. Found working party of 50 O.R. & 1 Officer for work behind Hill 63. Relieved 1st R.F. in trenches. Casualties O.R. 1 wounded	
Trenches 32&135 Hill 63	24.4.16		A quiet day. Enemy trigmachine except that his machine guns were heavily employed firing on our ropads immediately behind the trenches between the hours of 7 pm - 9 pm. Casualties O.R. 1 wounded	

H.W. Compton Lt. Col
Command 13 Royal Fusiliers

WAR DIARY or INTELLIGENCE SUMMARY

Army Form C. 2118.

Place	Date	Hour	Summary of Events and Information	Remarks and references to Appendices
Trenches 132 b 55 Sheet 63.	25.4.16		Another quiet day. A few rifle aerial torpedoes were fired onto trench 134. 2nd Lt. Venables went to Indirect Divisional School as instructor. 2nd Lt. Hughes went on a Trench Divisional Course. Casualties. O.R. 1 killed. 3 wounded.	
"	26.4.16		Another quiet day. Every again active in the evening with his machine guns. 2nd Lt. Cooper went on Transport Course. Casualties. O.R. 1 wounded.	
"	27.4.16		The enemy were inclined to be more offensive than usual. With trench mortars in for a good deal of shelling. In the evening a false gas alarm was given to everyone stood to ready to fire on gas helmets. Our guns opened fairly heavy fire. 2nd Lt. Stowe & 2nd Lt. Moakley proceeded to England on leave. Casualties. 2nd Lt. Shepherd. T.M. wounded. O.R. 5 wounded.	
"	28.4.16		An intense shrapnel fire enemy threw a few shells over our trenches & on to the edge of Niel. G3. Casualties. 1. O.R. wounded.	

H.W. Compston Lt Col
Commanding 2/ Royal Dublin

WAR DIARY or INTELLIGENCE SUMMARY.

(Erase heading not required.)

Army Form C. 2118.

Place	Date	Hour	Summary of Events and Information	Remarks and references to Appendices
	29.4.16		A very quiet day. Relieved by 1st R.F. & proceeded to Bedford Camp where the Battalion took over from 8th Buffs. 2 Strong patrols proceeded to England on leave.	
Bedford Camp	30.4.16		In the early hours of the morning the enemy discharged Gas from the direction of Kemmel Knowles. With the wind over the camp. All Officers & men were warned & turned out with Gas Helmets on time to avoid any Casualties. A good deal of discomfort was experienced as it was very short that no instruction to this form of fighting. The Battalion received orders to move to a certain Queery [Quarry] point but immediately after this order was cancelled & the Battalion remained in Camp in a state of readiness to move at a moments notice until 12.30 p.m. A draft of 40 O.R. joined. Transferred from 19th R.F.	

H. W. Compton Maj RF "
Comnd 1st Royal Fusiliers

17th Brigade.
24th Division.

12th BATTALION

ROYAL FUSILIERS

May 1916.

Army Form C. 2118.

WAR DIARY
or
INTELLIGENCE SUMMARY.
(Erase heading not required.)

Place	Date	Hour	Summary of Events and Information	Remarks and references to Appendices
Rupford Enfute	1-5-1916		Clear spring weather. Parades all day.	
Do.	2-5-1916		2nd Lt J.W. Wilson appted O.C. 1 Coy from 10-4-16 during absence of Capt. E. Chester Masler on leave in England. Gas alarm given & battalion stood to for a short time. Working parties of about 200 OR & 3 officers supplied for front line. Casualties 10 R wounded. Weather warm with occasional showers. Capt E Chester Master, Sick in England, struck off strength accordingly from 17-4-1916. Authy 2nd Army 2/1873/3 of 29.4.16. The officers played NCO at hockey & won 5-2. 2nd Lt Whitworth proceeded to England on leave.	
Do.	3-5-1916		Weather very hot. Confirmatory of Lieut G.M. Gordon in his appointment as Adjutant published for 6-11-16 & was cancelled pending official recognition his appointment as acting adjutant confirmed. Officers played NCO at Football and won 5-3.	
Do.	4-5-1916		Delightful weather. 2nd Lt Richardson returned from Hospital. The B.G.C. inspected transport and expressed his satisfaction at the superior turn out.	
Meurches 132-135. H.e. 63	5-5-1916		Weather hot with showers. Draft of 20 OR joined battalion. Casualties wounded 2 OR. Relieved C/1st R.F. in trenches. Gas alarm sounded & everyone stood to, but like the last it was too far away on the right to reach us.	

OBOI Ch/ng
(K R Fowles)

Army Form C. 2118.

WAR DIARY
or
INTELLIGENCE SUMMARY.

(Erase heading not required.)

Instructions regarding War Diaries and Intelligence Summaries are contained in F. S. Regs., Part II. and the Staff Manual respectively. Title pages will be prepared in manuscript.

Place	Date	Hour	Summary of Events and Information	Remarks and references to Appendices
Trenches 132-135 Hill 63	6-5-1916		Weather close & somewhat dull. The enemy fired ten 5.9 shells at Such Farm, one of which dropped short into Winter Trench (about) hit 2nd Lt D.W. Knirkard. This officer was buried about 10 p.m. in Canadian Cemetery on Hill 63.	
Do	7-5-1916		Weather dull & showery. Lieut J.J. Mann joined from Hangoak Instruction School Pont Royal. A quiet day, little shelling, casualties 1 O.R. wounded.	
Do	8-5-1916		Weather dull & inclement. 2nd Lt N.E. Walker proceeded to 2nd Army Grenade School for course of instruction. The enemy shelled top of Hill 63 at various times throughout the day.	
Do	9-5-1916		Weather fine west. A quiet day on our front, but the enemy were very busy on our left. Capt Beckford proceeded to England on leave.	
Do	10-5-1916		Very warm. Another uneventful day. Casualties O.R. 2 wounded. Lt Journalier expiration of Field Gratitude. 2nd Lt Wilson proceeded on leave. 14 O.R. to England.	
Do	11-5-1916		Dull. Relieved by 1st R.F. proceeded to Grand Munque Farm. Working parties 120 O.R. + 1 Officer.	
Grand Munque Farm.	12-5-1916		Very hot. Found various working parties totalling 385 O.R. 2nd Lt. Richardson + Mealor proceeded to Div. Tech School. Draft of 25 O.R. joined from 2nd Entrenching Battalion.	

R B C ...
12 Royal Fusiliers

Army Form C. 2118.

WAR DIARY
or
INTELLIGENCE SUMMARY.

(Erase heading not required.)

Place	Date	Hour	Summary of Events and Information	Remarks and references to Appendices
Grand Mongue Mun.	13-5-16		Lost day. Lieut Cox & Bridge proceeded on leave to England. 2nd Lt Barker returned from Trench Mortar School. Found working parties of 315 NCOs & men	
Do	14-5-16		Guee 9 Clock. working parties of 290 NCO's men were found by us.	
Do	15-5-16		Hot & rather close. Football match was played. Officers v. NCOs & men. Latter won 3-2. Found working parties of 260 NCO's men	
Do	16-5-16		Very Hot. Football match was played against 2 Royne Scots & was won by 3-2. Found working parties of 285 NCO's men.	
Do	17-5-16		Fine & warm. Relieved 1 R.F. in trenches. Gas alarm sounded & my right, but was too far away to reach us. Passed off in a few moments.	
Trenches B3-B5 Hill 63	18-5-16		Weather hot. Enemy very quiet. Casualties 1 OR. wounded. Capt Blackford returned from leave.	
Do	19-5-16		Lovely day very hot. plenty of sunshine. Enemy fairy active especially with Machine Guns. 1 OR killed, 5 OR wounded	
Do	20-5-16		Another hot day. plenty of sunshine. Just & Wilson tell from leave. enemy artillery not very active. W/2a Thompson truce Canadian Cemetery 9.30 p.m. about 45 casual Trench mortars fired over ten at 11.34. A draft of 35 OR joined Batt.	

Army Form C. 2118.

WAR DIARY
or
INTELLIGENCE SUMMARY.

(Erase heading not required.)

Instructions regarding War Diaries and Intelligence Summaries are contained in F. S. Regs., Part II. and the Staff Manual respectively. Title pages will be prepared in manuscript.

Place	Date	Hour	Summary of Events and Information	Remarks and references to Appendices
Trenches 132 to 135 N.E.63.	21.5.16		Anther glorious day. Sunshine all day long. Enemy Artillery fairly active on trench 135 which hangs. 2 O.R. killed. B.B. buried at Cameron Cemetery at 1-30 a.m. 22.5.16. 5.O.R. Wounded.	
"	22.5.16		Fine morning. Rained in the afternoon from 4 p.m. until about 8 p.m. S.F.S. Sgnrs. fired. About 50 aerial torpedoes fired over 134 & 135 trenches. Sent S.R.Mule cpr. joined from 5th Royal Fusiliers. 2nd Lieuts. R.G.F. Ordego & N. Somerhough, 2nd Lt. Thomson left joined as from 16th Royal Fusiliers.	
"	23.5.16		Settled fine, plenty of sunshine. Enemy fairly quiet. 2nd Lt. F.S.Symns. limed up 10 m in Birklehie Cemetery. Sent W.B. Donaghie 2 Bt. Mullan joined from 14th Royal Fusiliers. 2 O.R. Commisk proceeded to England on leave. Wounded 1.O.R.	
"	24.5.16		Fine morning. Occasional showers in the afternoon. No casualties	
"	25.5.16		Fine morning. Relieved 11 p.m. by 1st R.F. 1 O.R. wounded, 2 O.R. A. Myles returned to Snipers Course. 2 Bt. Robertson returned from Div. Red Shoot. Front working party. Strength 130 officers & men.	

OBJ.W. Chal. Mojo.
12th Royal Fusiliers

WAR DIARY
or
INTELLIGENCE SUMMARY.
(Erase heading not required.)

Army Form C. 2118.

Place	Date	Hour	Summary of Events and Information	Remarks and references to Appendices
Vallant Camp	26.5.16.		Very fine day. 2/Lt A.H. Lee & C.T. Roberts joined the battalion from 16th R.I. in 1st Echelon returned from Div Tech School. Found working parties Adduly 160 NCO+ men. Wounded 3 O.R.	
"	27.5.16.		Very hot day. Sergt. G.M. Gordon appointed Adjutant dated 8 February 1916 vice 2 Lt. L. Verchere (to Rejoin the duty). Found working parties totalling 180 NCOs + men	
	28.5.16.		Sunday. Very hot day. Battalion church parade at 10 am. Conduct aided in the afternoon Officers versus Sergts. Officers won by 40 runs. Found working parties totalling 130 NCO + men	
	29.5.16.		Very warm day. No 1 + 2 Coys inspected by C.O. Cricket match in afternoon Signallers versus machine gunners. Signallers won by 19 runs. Medal ribbons presented in the morning by 1st Army Commander to 17 Sergt Int. Bles working parties found totalling 198 NCOs + men. Colonel H.V. Compton & Capt El gegen proceeded to England on leave. Maj-Sr. A.M. Dick Cleland took over command of the Battalion during absence of Col. H.V. Compton.	

R.B.O. Col. Mgr
1st Royal Fusiliers

Army Form C. 2118.

WAR DIARY
or
INTELLIGENCE SUMMARY.
(Erase heading not required.)

Instructions regarding War Diaries and Intelligence Summaries are contained in F. S. Regs., Part II. and the Staff Manual respectively. Title pages will be prepared in manuscript.

Place	Date	Hour	Summary of Events and Information	Remarks and references to Appendices
Outtesteem Camp	30.5.16		Wet morning. Turned out very quite in the afternoon. The Company emitted match M1 & E9 versus W9.0, 2 E9, W9.0 & E9 won by 10 runs. Working parties 195 men 5 men wounded 1 O.R.	
"	31.5.16		Very hot day. I. W. Company cricket match M9.3 E9 versus W9.1 E9 W9.1 E9 won by 1 run. Bath's allotted for 275 men & men. Found working parties. W9 W9.2. 190 O.R. W9.o.3 & E9's inspected by B.O. School from South Gazett d/27.5.16. the whom ordered to be sent for Lewis. 2-Lt. C.L. Traveller Oct. 5. 1915. 3-Lt. AR Snider Oct. 14. 1915	

OB (?) Oakman Major
12th Royal Fusiliers

17th Brigade.
24th Division.

12th BATTALION

ROYAL FUSILIERS

June 1916.

12. R. Fus.

Army Form C. 2118.

Vol 10

10.T

WAR DIARY
or
INTELLIGENCE SUMMARY.
(Erase heading not required.)

Place	Date	Hour	Summary of Events and Information	Remarks and references to Appendices
Bulford Camp	1.5.16		Another very warm day. Final Inter-Coy Cricket match played. 90 & batg CO-1 Coy by 20 runs after a very exciting game	
"	2.6.16.		Rather cool, with slight showers. Relieved 1st R.F. in Trenches, 132 – 135 + trench 63 a quiet relief. Casualties. 1.O.R. wounded	
Trenches 132,135 Ditch 63	3.6.16.		Very warm day. Enemy machine guns very active in early hours of the evening. Our Snipers kept down Sie Petite Douve – Ash Road Douries at midnight by enough to prepare our raid by 72nd Brigade on our left.	
"	4.6.16		Dull. – In the early hours the enemy detonated a mine 132 – 135 + Water trench for our bombardment of Petite Douve – 2nd Lieut E. Maclin wounded. 6.O.R. killed. 15.O.R. wounded. 1.O.R. shell shock.	
"	5.6.16		Showery morning, with some sunshine. Our Left Company in action with rifle grenades. The enemy retaliating with Trench Mortars. Casualties. 1.O.R killed. 8.O.R. wounded.	
"	6.6.16.		Showery & dull. Enemy again very troublesome with his Trench mortars especially trees trench 135 + 2nd Lieut Oyé caught snipers in trenches on Machine Gun case. Casualties. 1.O.R. killed. 9.O.R wounded	
"	7.6.16.		4 D.C.C. bag with occasional glimpses of sun. Casualty. 1.O.R wounded.	
"	8.6.16.		Weather still dull. C.O. returned from leave	

H.W. Compy. Major
Comme 8o Royal Fusiliers

Army Form C. 2118.

WAR DIARY
or
INTELLIGENCE SUMMARY.
(Erase heading not required.)

Instructions regarding War Diaries and Intelligence Summaries are contained in F. S. Regs., Part II. and the Staff Manual respectively. Title pages will be prepared in manuscript.

Place	Date	Hour	Summary of Events and Information	Remarks and references to Appendices
Jette	9.6.16		Drill occurred, trench. Sunshine. Casualty 1 O.R. wounded. Brig. Maj. Rice proceeded on leave.	
"	10.6.16		Weather unchanged. Relieved by 1st R.I.F. Battalion marched in to GRAND MUNQUE FARM & adjacent huts. Casualties. 3 O.R. wounded.	
GRAND MUNQUE	11.6.16		Sunday. Cold & dull. 2 Lt. Tiffany joined Battalion. 2 Lt. R.E. Cutler & Lt. White left afternoon 1.6.16 and Regt. Serjt. Major Gohm sick to R.E. Cave. Major A/Lt Col. Aitken & Capt. Travis proceed on leave.	
"	12.6.16		Cold & dull. Draft of 50 O.R. arrived.	
"	13.6.16		Wet morning. Slight memorial service owing to death of Lord Kitchener held at Farm. Casualty 1 O.R. wounded.	
"	14.6.16		Dull, cold & wet. Time advanced at 11 pm by 60 minutes.	
"	15.6.16		Dull — inclined to rain again.	
"	16.6.16		Dull & warmer. Draft of 15 O.R. arrived. 2 Lt. G.R. Buel struck off the strength.	
"	17.6.16		Bright & fairly sunshine. General ... The following were mentioned in Sir Douglas Haig's dispatches dated April 30.13.16 of gallant & distinguished conduct in the field: 11380 S. Flynn S.P. 4727 Pte Hart W. Casualties Capt. D.E. Anigson wounded 5 O.R. wounded.	

F.W. Comyn Major
Commanding 2/Royal Fusiliers

WAR DIARY
or
INTELLIGENCE SUMMARY.

Army Form C. 2118.

(Erase heading not required.)

Place	Date	Hour	Summary of Events and Information	Remarks and references to Appendices
Grand Tomague	16.6.16		Weather fine. Relief of Sunshine. Relieved 1st Royal Fusiliers in trenches 132 & 135. & Died 63.	
Trenches 132-135 & Died 63.	19.6.16		Weather rather dull. Gas alert cancelled. Trench 132 communication trench heavily shelled in the afternoon. Own aeroplane reported by German aviez about midnight. R.G. & S. Snps proceeded to Aleuch by rail. Casualty. 1 O.R. slightly wounded.	
"	20.6.16		Weather dull - no chance to air trench scenery sent by trenches 132-135. 2 St. O.C. injured sent from Div. Field School. Major AB Dick Cecil & Capt. A.J. Turner returned from leave.	
	21.6.16		Weather. A little sunshine. Draft of 1 Officer & 23 O.R., all old 12" R. Fus., arrived. 3rd Lt. Gjordt returned from Base. Australian representatives visited the line. Casualties 2 O.R. wounded	
"	22.6.16		Weather rather bright. Enemy artillery busy on roads. St. Jacks & St. Jevery proceeded to England on transfe to M.G. Corps. Gas Alarm sounded on my right about 12 midnight. To far. Came over our front. Enemy Artillery open on own trenches. Casualties. O.R. 7 wounded	
	23.6.16		Weather fine in the afternoon about 5pm a shower. Hunder storm. Relieved by 5 Batt. Attaching grenadiers very active during relief. Casualties 4 O.R. wounded. Battalion march to the night.	
Rgt. Rgi Kule Sn.	24.6.16		Weather rain early morning. Batt. marched to Meteren. Draft of 1 Officer & 20 O.R. arrived 2 Lt. O'T Butler.	

Commanded 1st Royal Fusiliers

Army Form C. 2118.

WAR DIARY
or
INTELLIGENCE SUMMARY.
(Erase heading not required.)

Instructions regarding War Diaries and Intelligence Summaries are contained in F. S. Regs., Part II. and the Staff Manual respectively. Title pages will be prepared in manuscript.

Place	Date	Hour	Summary of Events and Information	Remarks and references to Appendices
X.u.c.4.4.95.	6.16		Weather - very hot. Capt. D.I. Blackford proceeded to 2nd Army Rifle School for Course of Instruction.	
"	26.6.16		Weather - Showers & rain. Woodcutting party of 10 men rejoined battalion. 2 Lt Yeoham transferred from 90th L.T.M.B. to No. 3 Coy. 2 Lt C.L. Twersley sick to England 12.6.16 & struck off the strength accordingly. G.O.C. congratulates all ranks on their steadiness & fortitude during gas attack & bombardment of 16/17 = 4 2 stormen from 2nd Army School. 2 Stretchers return from Div. Tren. school. 2 Lt Lee return from Grenade school.	
"	27.6.16		Showery. Marched to LOCRE = to BAJATOS HUTMENTS occupied by 4 Coys.	
BAJATOS HUTS	28.6.16		Weather Dull & rain, parties from each Company rearranged KEMMEL DEFENCES	
"	29.6.16		Weather Dull. Parties from each Coy reconstructing KEMMEL DEFENCES. Ration party of 150.O.R. going for cable burying.	
"	30.6.16		Morning dull & inclined to rain. 90's 1 & 2 Coy parties as ordered by Command'g Officer. Ration party of 150 O.R. going for cable burying.	

H.W. Compton
Colonel
Comm'd'g Royal Fusiliers

17th Inf.Bde.
24th Div.

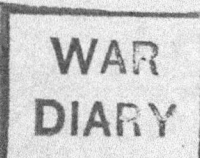

12th BATTN. THE ROYAL FUSILIERS.

J U L Y

1 9 1 6

Army Form C. 2118

24 July
12 R Fus
Vol II

WAR DIARY
or
INTELLIGENCE SUMMARY
(Erase heading not required.)

Place	Date	Hour	Summary of Events and Information	Remarks and references to Appendices
Dranoutre (Billets)	1-7-1916		Weather very warm and sunny. Moved to Dranoutre & took over Billets & adjacent Camp from 8th Queens. Draft of 15 men joined from 15th R.F. A few rifles & long range gun dropped in Dranoutre, slight damage done. Great British/French advance commenced in front of Albert.	
Do	2-7-1916		Weather fine and warm. A 6 days course of instruction of NCOs in Physical Training & Bayonet fighting by Sergt Major of Army Gymnastic Staff commences. Sixteen Officers pitched 10am from whole under 2nd Lt Venters.	
Do	3-7-1916		Another fine day Cricket Match played between No 1 & 3 Coys v No 2 & Hd Coys won by 110 runs to 48. Physical Training & Bayonet fighting continued. Capt D.G. and men wounded in action, 17.6.16 rest to duty today.	
Do	4-7-1916		Morning fine & warm. Thunder shower in the afternoon. 3 wounded other ranks rejoined & 2nd Lt Venters. Physical Training & Bayonet fighting continued. No 2 Coy field a concert. wounded in action 1 O.R.	
Do	5-7-1916		Early morning wet. Fine sunny afternoon. Cricket match, Officers 12 R.F. v Officers 13th Sherwood Foresters. 12th won by 148 to 29. Fatigue party found for work under R.E. Physical drill my weekly training carried on.	
Do	6-7-1916		Fine morning. Fatigue party of 330 men NCOs 13th R.F. & 172nd Sherwood Foresters (NCOs) The latter for work under R.E. 12th NCO wounded in action 1 O.R. Accidentally wounded by Grenade S.O.R.	
Do	7-7-1916		Fine & close, inclines to rain. Working party of 310 NCOs & men found for work under R.E.	
Do	8-7-1916		Relieving 58th Australian Inf Bde in trenches Cnt 6 D4, near Wulverghem. 2nd Lt Lee attending course at Sniper School.	

H.W. Campbell
Comdg 12 Royal Fusiliers

Army Form C. 2118.

Instructions regarding War Diaries and Intelligence Summaries are contained in F. S. Regs., Part II. and the Staff Manual respectively. Title Pages will be prepared in manuscript.

WAR DIARY
or
INTELLIGENCE SUMMARY

(Erase heading not required.)

Place	Date	Hour	Summary of Events and Information	Remarks and references to Appendices
Trenches Cit 6 D.4.	9-7-1916.		Weather fine & warm. The enemy fired a good many large Trench Mortar shells at our trenches, most of which fell just over the parados. Sergt Jones relieved to the rank of Corporal for drunkenness (by F.G.C.M. held on 7th inst.). 1 Sect 2 O.R. wounded 6 O.R. accidentally wounded (Grenade) 5 O.R.	
Do	10-7-1916.		Weather warm & sunny. 2nd Lt. Frank Hammond attended Bombing course. Capt J.L. Blackford returned from Sig. Course. Capt H.T. 2nd Lt. Rawbone D.M. joined from 16th R.F. During the night the 3rd Rifle Brigade on our left carried out a minor offensive in retaliation by the enemy we had the following casualties:- 1 Other 5 O.R. wounded 6 O.R. wounded 2 O.R. (2 wounded at duty) Slightly wounded Sheve 6 O.R.	
Do	11-7-1916.		Weather warm. Relieved by 9th Royal Sussex Regt and proceeded to Wakefield Huts near Loos.	
Wakefield Huts.	12-7-1916.		Rather windy all day with rain during the evening. Baths alloted to all Coys.	
	13-7-1916.		Windy & inclined to rain. Baths alloted to Coys. Military Medals awarded to No 5210 Pte J. Pattenden for bringing to No 13967 Pte W. Wyatt for bringing in & to No 5362 Pte H. Tomlins 2 wounded men under heavy Trench Mortar fire, when attacked by a patrol of the enemy & the enemy trench for defending two listening posts. He himself was wounded. Congratulations of 8th Bde. General were conveyed to recipients. Received 1 Pte R.F. in trenches.	
Trenches E1 – F5.	14-7-1916.		Fine & warm. A very quiet day. A number party of 3 Officers 176 O.R. Commenced training for a minor operation.	

H.W. Crispin Lt. Col.
Comd 8/th Royal Sussex

Army Form C. 2118.

WAR DIARY
or
INTELLIGENCE SUMMARY

(Erase heading not required.)

Place	Date	Hour	Summary of Events and Information	Remarks and references to Appendices
Trenches E.5 - F.5	15-7-1916		Bright & warm. 2nd Lt Lee returned from Snipers School. Training for minor operation continued. The B.G.C. visited the men & watched the training. Aerial activity. Wounded 1 O.R.	
Do	16-7-1916.		Warm, plenty of sunshine. The enemy a little more active. Our guns busy all day wire cutting. Kieels 1 O.R. wounded 2 O.R. slightly wounded 2 O.R. (remained on duty).	
Do	17-7-1916.		Misty morning with little wind. We carried out our minor Operation about 11 P.M. The raid was very successful, 16 Germans being returned for and many wounded. The raid was made very difficult owing to the Moon being so bright but the party slowly forced attention until our barrage commenced. They being too close to the enemy wire. 2nd Lt G.H. McNaught wounded & missing. 2nd Lt AE. Hughes wounded. Killed 1 OR. Wounded 8 O.R., slightly wounded 1 O.R.	
Do	18-7-1916.		A fairly quiet day. 2nd Lt. H. Frankamith returned from Grenade School & proceeded to join 17th T.M. Batty. The Divisional General visited & congratulated the raiding party on their work last night. Killed 1 O.R. Wounded 2 O.R. Accidentally wounded 1 O.R.	
Do	19-7-1916.		Sunny all day. Relieved by 9th Durham Lyle Infantry. T. proceeded to Halcipine huts. 2nd Lt H.E. Rice + 2nd Lt GE Davie joined from 5th R.F. Wounded 1 OR.	

H.W. Company Lt E
Commdg 8/21 Royal Fusiliers

Army Form C. 2118.

WAR DIARY
or
INTELLIGENCE SUMMARY
(Erase heading not required.)

Place	Date	Hour	Summary of Events and Information	Remarks and references to Appendices
WAKEFIELD HUTS.	20-7-1916		Very warm all day. The Battalion received all day. Orders to about to move at a moment's notice were received.	
Billets near Meteren	21-7-1916		A lovely day. Battalion moved to Billets in vicinity of Meteren. Military Medal awarded to No. 17827 Sergt J. Lamont for bringing in a badly wounded man from No Man's Land under heavy machine gun fire. Congratulations of Army Corps, Division & Bde Commander conveyed to recipient.	
Do	22-7-1916		Free Close, inclined to rain. Physical drill — Bayonet fighting carried out.	
Do	23-7-1916		A very fine day. No. 1 Coy held sports and No 2 & 4 Coys held a concert, both of great success. 2nd Lt was attached returned from 2nd Army Technical School. The following is an extract from 5th Army Corps. memo Q591. dated 23.7.1916 re the 17th I.B. "Reference raid carried out by 12th Royal Fusiliers. The Army Commander considers that the operations carried out by the 12 Royal Fusiliers reflects much credit on all concerned & were well planned and carried out. The Divisional Commander has great pleasure in forwarding the above remarks of the Army Commander to & heartily endorses the same. The fact that no identifications could be obtained in no way detracts from the good work so ably carried out by all ranks." The Bde Commander also added his congratulations to those of the Divisional &c	J.H.J. Coope [Maj] H.C. Comm'd'g 12/Royal Fusiliers

2449 Wt. W14957/M90 750,000 1/16 J.B.C.&A. Forms/C.2118/12.

Army Form C. 2118.

WAR DIARY
or
INTELLIGENCE SUMMARY

(Erase heading not required.)

Instructions regarding War Diaries and Intelligence Summaries are contained in F. S. Regs., Part II. and the Staff Manual respectively. Title Pages will be prepared in manuscript.

Place	Date	Hour	Summary of Events and Information	Remarks and references to Appendices
Billets near Meteren	23-7-16		The Minor operation was carried out under the supervision of the 2nd in Command, Major A.B. Dick Cleland, it was entirely owing to the carefully thought out plan arrangements made by him that the success was so full	
do	24-7-16		Damp & close, slight rain. Battalion entrained at Bailleul at 1.30 pm & detrained at Longueau near Amiens at 10 pm. At 10.30 pm the Battn marched off to Pibrax at St Remy a Gry, a distance of approximately 14 miles, which was accomplished with only 2 men falling out a very satisfactory result, taking into consideration that the men had not practiced Route marching having been in trenches so many months.	
Billets St Pierre a Gouy	25-7-16		Very Hot. Battalion arrived in new area at 8 am & rested for the rest of the day.	
do.	26-7-16.		Dull & close. Battalion carried out Musketry, Physical Training & Bayonet fighting.	
do	27-7-16		Very warm & sunny. Musketry, Physical training & Bayonet fighting.	

H.W. Murphy Lt Col
Commandg 12/Royal Dublins

WAR DIARY
or
INTELLIGENCE SUMMARY

Army Form C. 2118.

Place	Date	Hour	Summary of Events and Information	Remarks and references to Appendices
do.	28.7.16		Dull & warm. Lecture on Consolidation of Captured positions by Major King, R.E. to all Officers & N.C.O's.	
do.	29.7.16		Fine & Sunny. Attack possibly carried out.	
do.	30.7.16		Very fine day. Battalion route marched a distance of 15 miles in marching order. Cols. one man falling out. Orders to move into forward area received.	
do.	31.7.16		Scorching hot. Battalion entrained at PICQUIGNY for MERRICOURT. Arrived about 2 pm, & marched to billets in BOIS des TAILLES.	

H. W. Compton? Lt Col
Commdg Royal Fusiliers

17th Brigade.
24th Division

12th BATTALION

ROYAL FUSILIERS

August 1916.

Headquarters,
24th Division

Confidential

A19/1

Herewith War Diary of 12th Royal Fusiliers for the month of August

9.9.16

A P Sparks Capt for
B.G.C. 17th Infy Bde

Army Form C. 2118.

Vol 12

WAR DIARY
or
INTELLIGENCE SUMMARY

(Erase heading not required.)

12 Royal Fusiliers

Place	Date	Hour	Summary of Events and Information	Remarks and references to Appendices
BOIS des TAILLES	1.8.16		A scorching hot day. Battalion rested and cleaned up. At 5.30 pm paraded and marched to SAND PITS near MEAULTE just south of ALBERT and bivouaced for the night.	
SAND PITS	2.8.16		Very hot all day. Physical Drill, Bayonet fighting for & drill by an aeroplane signalling for an attacking force. Draft 1.O.R.	
"	3.8.16		Very hot. Physical Drill & a Bath parade carried out. Bathing in the afternoon. 2nd Lt A.D. Lee wounded nightly 2nd Lts. Gazette 9/5/7/16. 2nd Lt J.Y. Nelson to be temp. Capt. whilst commanding a Company.	
"	4.8.16		Fine day. Cool breeze. Bayonet fighting Drill & lecture	
"	5.8.16		Very warm all day. Attack practice and Bayonet fighting. Officers from Grenade Supplement of 3.8.16. Capt. & Adjutant to be temp. Major from June 8. 1916.	
"	6.8.16		Fine day. Brigade Church Parade.	

H.W. Empey 2Lt a/c
Commanded 12 Royal Fusiliers

WAR DIARY
INTELLIGENCE SUMMARY

12th Royal Fusiliers

Place	Date	Hour	Summary of Events and Information	Remarks and references to Appendices
"	7.8.16		Very hot. Supplied working party for work in Old German trench. One headed 100 Officers men.	
THE CRATERS CARNOY.	8.8.16		Again very hot. The Battalion supplied to the Craters of CARNOY. Found working party of 200 for ammunition dump. Rest of other numbers to 17th I.Bde. Casualties 1 O.R. wounded.	
"	9.8.16		Blazing hot day. Relieved 2nd South Staffords in BERNAFAY WOOD. Enemy artillery very active on road outside H.Q. 2 Lt. E. WALKER wounded, also Regt. S.M. SABEY. Casualties wounded 1 Officer, 10 O.R.	
BERNAFAY WOOD.	10.8.16		Dull & misty. A lot of gunning all day. One shell falling just outside H.Q. causing casualties. Draft 20 O.R. Casualties killed 3 O.R. wounded 6 O.R.	
"	11.8.16		Very hot all day. Enemy Artillery busy all afternoon. Relieved by 2nd R.B. and returned to CRATER TRENCHES. Sgt. Taylor proceeded to Cadet school Cambridge. 2 Lt. S.W. Bridge transferred to Gen. Sect. for duty as Adjt-Gen in Salvation Guards Division 26.6.16. Auth. W.O. List 93. N/1. 8.16. Casualties killed 1 O.R. Wounded 7 O.R. Lt. W. Campbell wounded (Blue Shock) 2 O.R. Crossed to Royal Fusiliers.	

Army Form C. 2118.

WAR DIARY
or
INTELLIGENCE SUMMARY

12th Royal Fusiliers

(Erase heading not required.)

Place	Date	Hour	Summary of Events and Information	Remarks and references to Appendices
CRATER TRENCHES CARNOY	12.8.16		Very hot. Suffered carrying parts of 400 ofs front line. Casualties 3. O.R. wounded.	
"	13.8.16		Very warm. Relieved 10th & 8th Batt'n in Trenches between DELVILLE WOOD & GUILLEMONT. Enemy Artillery very active. Battalion in trenches in front of 70.1. e.g. & 70.2. e.g. Casualties 4. O.R. wounded.	
TRENCHES between DELVILLE WOOD & GUILLEMONT	14.8.16		A fine day. Continued digging assembly trenches. Artillery on both sides very active. 2nd Lt MARTIN wounded. Casualties. Wounded 1 Officer, 13 O.R. " (Shellshock) 3 O.R.	
"	15.8.16		A showery day. Artillery very active. Casualties Killed 10. O.R. Wounded 18. O.R. " (Shellshock) 5 O.R.	
"	16.8.16		A cold day. Artillery very active. We let off smoke bombs along from of our front to cover an attack made by 73rd Bde. 2nd Lt. D.W. Tiffany slightly wounded but remained at duty. 2nd Lt C.R. Langer wounded. Casualties. Wounded 2 Officers 45 O.R. Killed 3 O.R. H.W. Campbell Lt. Col. Comd'g 12/Royal Fusiliers	

Army Form C.2118.

WAR DIARY
or
INTELLIGENCE SUMMARY

(Erase heading not required.)

12th Royal Fusiliers

Place	Date	Hour	Summary of Events and Information	Remarks and references to Appendices
TRENCHES between DELVILLE WOOD & GUILLEMONT	17.8.16		Weather fine. Relieving by 8" Buffs. & proceeded to CRATERS at CARNOY. One Officer & 6 O.R. who were slightly wounded return to duty.	
CRATERS CARNOY.	18.8.16		A warm day. Sent 16 Officers & 50 men to join R.E. for construction work during attack about to be made on GUILLEMONT. Found camp & party of 4 Officers & 220 O.R. for carrying bombs & S.A.A. to front line on road to BERNAFAY WOOD at 11.30 a.m. Attack on GUILLEMONT by the 17th & 73rd Bdes with Div on left & 3rd Div might in conjunction with the French took place at 2.30 pm. The attack on MACHINE GUN HOUSE & RAILWAY STATION & hence to immediate vicinity was carried out by 8th BUFFS & 3rd R.B. with 1st Royal Fusiliers in close support & ourselves in reserve. The objectives were all taken by our Brigade & consolidated but the attack in general was held up by a strong point in front, at the 73rd Bde, the Division last about 35 Officers & 1200 O.R. in casualties. The following message was received after the attack was over: "The Corps Commander has asked me to convey to troops his extreme appreciation of gallant conduct of troops and satisfaction at success gained. We have broken into GUILLEMONT and must grip like bull dogs the recedeges when we have." H.W. Camp hn. Lt. Col. Command 12/Royal Fusiliers.	

WAR DIARY or INTELLIGENCE SUMMARY

Army Form C.2118.

12th Royal Fusiliers

Place	Date	Hour	Summary of Events and Information	Remarks and references to Appendices
"	"		The following wire received from 17th F.B. "The B.G.C. wishes to congratulate all on their brilliant success of yesterday and wishes all ranks to know how pleased he is." 9th W. Coy. had Capt. Ahearn "proceeded to post his other dug out" C.T. from an old line to position taken. Casualties wounded. 9 O.R.	
BERNAFAY WOOD.	19.8.16.		Slightly misty. One 2nd Company Parties for fuel " (Shrapnel) 4 O.R. Killed. 1 O.R. line of trenches. 1200 men to carry water and rations. Artillery on both sides active Casualties 1 O.R. wounded	
			2 O.R. previously wounded returned to duty.	
	20.8.16.		A very warm day. Enemy artillery active. Casualties. Killed. 1 O.R. Wounded. (Shell Shock) 1 O.R.	
			1 O.R. previously wounded returned to duty.	
	21.8.16.		Fine & warm. Enemy artillery fire very active. Ammunition dump in rear of trenches of D.H.Q. set on fire causing many explosions & splinters of their ammunition & casualties to our men who were trying to put the fire out. No 3 Coy. P. son. Lobby having lost 2 S.gts. 1 L/Cpl. & 7 men. Never felt quite safe in recovery quickly when shown who first any exposure. At 4.30 p.m. the attack on GUILLEMONT was renewed by the 12th (Bde.) when the front of the 73rd Bde. the attack is places Command by 73rd Royal Fusiliers	

WAR DIARY
or
INTELLIGENCE SUMMARY
(Erase heading not required.)

Army Form C. 2118.

12th Royal Fusiliers

Place	Date	Hour	Summary of Events and Information	Remarks and references to Appendices
"	"		Very successful tour, nothing taken was been complained. The 1st Royal Fusiliers after B Coy's reinforcing the attacking Party of 6" Battn 7 R.B., The Division lost about 35 Officers & 1100 men. In the evening we relieved the 3rd R.B. & 1st R.F. in nearly won line. Casualties Killed 2 O.R. Wounded B. O.R. " (Shellshock) 1 O.R.	
Maricourt 22.8.16. to Gullimont			2 O.R. previously wounded returned to duty. Fine day. Enemy shelling very erratic. Ammunition dump again set a fire. The Battalion relieved about 12 midnight by the 7 J. D.L.I. and proceeded to HAPPY VALLEY near BRAY sur SOMME. Casualties Killed 2 O.R. Wounded 11 O.R. 1 O.R. previously wounded returned to duty. 6.8.16. A.M. + 2 Master 2nd Lt W.A. Rice to England Sick 8.8.16. 2nd Lt Roberts Gt " " 6.8.16.	
HAPPY VALLEY	23.8.16.		Rather cool. The Battalion rested. Bathed & refitted. 2 Lt Gibson & 2 O.R. proceeded on M.G. Course at LE TOUQUET.	

H. W. Compton Lt Col
Commanding 12/Royal Fusiliers

Army Form C. 2118.

WAR DIARY
or
INTELLIGENCE SUMMARY
(Erase heading not required.)

12th Royal Fusiliers

Place	Date	Hour	Summary of Events and Information	Remarks and references to Appendices
"	24.8.16		Weather warmer.	
"	25.8.16		Very fine & warm. Battalion moved to vicinity of DERNANCOURT in France. A number of horses seen here & outskirts of new camp. Casualties wounded 1 O.R. R.S.M. Palliser appointed A/R.S.M. vice A/R.S.M. Salez.	
DERNANCOURT (near Ap)	26.8.16		Fine & Sunny with showers. Battalion carried out drill, P.T. rifle & gas helmet inspections.	
"	27.8.16		Showery. Some sunshine. Draft of 51 O.R. joined battalion. Many T. Rynne died & others.	
"	28.8.16		Showery & close. Rynne died. Draft of 50 Sergt fifty committed officer inspected the new draft. The G.O.C. addressed the Brigade. Congratulated them on their fine work. 2/Lt A.L. GIRDLER struck off the strength with effect from 27.8.16 (Auth D.A.G.'s list of officers evacuated sick & wounded no. 496.)	
"	29.8.16		No change in weather. Casualties wounded 1 O.R. through bomb exploding in incinerator. Rynne died. Battalion parade. sgd M12/R[?]	

2449 Wt. W14957/M90 750,000 1/16 J.B.C. & A. Forms/C.2118/12.

Army Form C. 2118.

WAR DIARY
or
INTELLIGENCE SUMMARY

(Erase heading not required.)

12 Royal Fusiliers

Instructions regarding War Diaries and Intelligence Summaries are contained in F. S. Regs., Part II. and the Staff Manual respectively. Title Pages will be prepared in manuscript.

Place	Date	Hour	Summary of Events and Information	Remarks and references to Appendices
"	"		Sgt Turner appointed A/C Sm 109. " Taylor " " 309. Officers in Camp. Reserve ready to move at four hours notice.	
"	30.8.16		Wet, my high cold wind. Battalion moved to Camp in vicinity of FRICOURT. R.O.'s. Sect orders transfer temporary Commission as Lieut + Q.M. posted to 16 (B) Bn. The Welsh Regt. Auth. AG. A/16357. of 22.8.16.	
FRICOURT 31.8.16 vicinity.			Fine morning. Bn. spent day cleaning up. H.W. Cooper, Major Comnd'g 12/Royal Fusiliers

17th Brigade.
24th Division

12th BATTALION

ROYAL FUSILIERS

September 1916.

Army Form C. 2118.

WAR DIARY
or
INTELLIGENCE SUMMARY
(Erase heading not required.)

12th Royal Fusiliers

Place	Date	Hour	Summary of Events and Information	Remarks and references to Appendices
CARLTON Trench between HIGH WOOD & DELVILLE WOOD	1.9.16		Battn. fell in and suddenly to move up to Trenches. Arrived in Trenches at 3.30 A.M. after being delayed in CATAPILLAR VALLEY for some way to a very heavy gas shell barrage + our guides going astray. An exceedingly unpleasant experience. Many men very sick from the effect. No 3 Coy sent up to reinforce the 3rd R.B's who had little trouble reaching it. An attack on Orchard Trench which they captured + and holding. Casualties 6 OR wounded	
ORCHARD TRENCH OPPOSITE WATER LANE	2.9.16		Weather misty and dull. 1 Platoon + 10 bombers & 1 team Stoker Mot. Coy sent off to reinforce 3rd R.B's in bombing fort in WoodGate Trench. The enemy made a determined bombing attack on this post and turned the guns captured on Paris + overran it. 2nd Lt Burton was reported very active all day. He remained in the Buttering Canary in the evening took over the trouble held by 3rd R.B's opposite from J. Ted Tunnel + captured by the Remain of 13th Middlesex Casualties. 1 Officer wounded. 5 OR killed 20 OR wounded. 1 Missing	
Do.	3.9.16		Trenches Same. Our Div. represented by 8th Buffs in conjunction with 12th Div. on our left and 7th Div. on our right made an attack at 12 midday. The attack by 8th Buffs was on H.W. Copse in High Wood Lane. Commanded by Royal Sussex.	

13/T

WAR DIARY or INTELLIGENCE SUMMARY

Army Form C. 2118.

12th Royal Fusiliers

Place	Date	Hour	Summary of Events and Information	Remarks and references to Appendices
Camp N. FRICOURT	4.9.16		and a starting point ab junction of this trench and a strong point Capt Anderson accompanied by working up No 2 LONE trench with details by 8th Buff trench through the rising point. The Bde formed holders preparation firing joined our ring to east of ORCHARD trench. Our two Coys from ORCHARD trench did considerable damage to the enemy causing him at least 100 casualties. Enemy Artillery very active. Casualties 10 OR killed, 48 OR wounded, 1 OR missing. 3 OR shell shock.	
Camp N. FRICOURT	5.9.16		Very wet. Enemy artillery again heavy throughout the day. Relieved by 6th R. W. Kent. Regiment and proceeded to Camp in vicinity of FRICOURT. 10 slightly wounded men returned to duty. Casualties. 1/10 OR killed. 8 OR wounded. 1 OR missing. Yr. Battalion arrived about 7am & moved off again to Camp near DERMANCOURT. Buff arrived 15 O.R.	
Camp nr DERMANCOURT	6.9.16		7.0 E. marquees not erected during the afternoon. Battalion marched to EDGEHILL SIDING & entrained for LONGPRE, arriving there at 7.30 pm. Marched to billets in village of BUSSUS.	
Billets in BUSSUS	7.9.16 8.9.16		Very fine and warm. Day spent cleaning up and resting. It Bn Complete were brigade day. Companys carried on work under there own arrangements. Musketry Dulls.	

2449 Wt. W14957/M90 750,000 1/16 J.B.C. & A. Forms/C.2118/12.

WAR DIARY / INTELLIGENCE SUMMARY

Army Form C. 2118.

12th Royal Fusiliers

Place	Date	Hour	Summary of Events and Information	Remarks and references to Appendices
Billets in BUSSES	9.9.16		Very fine day. Company arrived out and B Board held. Troops arrived. Physical drill, Drill, Musketry, Bath Parade. **Observation** "The passing message from Commander in Chief 6th Army begins. The total success gained by the 4th Army during the operations last 3 days are very satisfactory & reflects great credit on the preparatory made & on the troops who have carried out the attacks. The rapid advance on LEUZE WOOD preceding on the capture of GUILLEMONT & FALFEMONT FARM showed vermont judgment determination and has been considered invisible to the French army on our right. I warmly congratulate you, R.C. Commander Staffs & Troops under you on the result already achieved & feel the energy and determination with which they are being pursued will	
D	10.9.16		Fine day. Battalion Church Parade. Lt. Col. Cohen attended H.Q. Army Baptist Services.	
D	11.9.16		Fine day. Physical Drill. Battalions arms out drive. Training & Lewis Gun & Bombing. Capt DC Anderson to hospital sent. L. Rifle Gun Inspection. NorEr.	
D	12.9.16		Very hot. Physical Drill. Training & Lewis Gun & Bombing Musketry.	
D	13.9.16		Fine day. Physical training. Bn Musketry. Battn parade Instruction r/arms drawn. Fatigues M.Ps. 2nd Lt. Sergt. Officers sent to Corps pistol shooting 26. Other personnel att 253rd Coy RE stages & strength. Supp. n OR absent Lt Col Mullens adopted artillery Draft arrived. Capt Stevenson out to England	

Army Form C. 2118.

WAR DIARY
or
INTELLIGENCE SUMMARY
(Erase heading not required.)

Instructions regarding War Diaries and Intelligence Summaries are contained in F.S. Regs., Part II. and the Staff Manual respectively. Title Pages will be prepared in manuscript.

Place	Date	Hour	Summary of Events and Information	Remarks and references to Appendices
Billets in Busnes	14.9.16		Capt. Ansell 15 O.R. joined. 1 O.R. previously wounded return to duty. Officers congratulate Transport section on Prize Competition yesterday that respects. Can't Transport for Prize Competition being above, all great credit all concerned noted in order that the general appearance of men not always state, that amongst whole sections no one failing left side up to the mark. It is hoped that these will be a further opportunity shortly of taking part in this Competition.	
	15.9.16		Fine & sunny. Parties of 16 officers & 450 men under Major Neynoe, proceeding to billets for full tactical r. nat. Fees 10 spraying cases arose returning Monday. Mount Sgt. 25 R.D.C. Kinton ordered Command 'F' & 'G' Coy during absence of Capt. Rawbone. Myxom fine. Hygiene Training Musketry. Orders received to be prepared to entrain at short notice. Further orders received during day to stand fast.	
	16.9.16		Signs attached Box Respirators Exhibition given during day to Officers. The Divisional Entertainers gave a Gramophone Entertainment.	
	17.9.16		Draft 3 Offrs, 1 Sgt, 1 Corp. joined from 49 I.B.D. Army Orders just dated Mar. 29/16.	

H.W. Brockell?
Annals 12/Royal Scots

Army Form C. 2118.

WAR DIARY
or
INTELLIGENCE SUMMARY
(Erase heading not required.)

12th Royal Fusiliers

Instructions regarding War Diaries and Intelligence Summaries are contained in F.S. Regs., Part II. and the Staff Manual respectively. Title Pages will be prepared in manuscript.

Place	Date	Hour	Summary of Events and Information	Remarks and references to Appendices
BILLS in BUSSUS	18.9.16		Showery. Ordinary morning in entrenching. Physical Drill, Bayonet Fighting, Inspection of Gas Helmets. Musketry	
	19.9.16		Wet day. Battalion marched to Pont Remy and July for AULT & entrained for THIENNES detrained at THIENNES at 8pm. arrived at CAUCHY A LA TOUR about 9.30am & marched to billets at CAUCHY A LA TOUR.	
CAUCHY A LA TOUR	20.9.16		Wet morning, rest & fine afternoon. Day spent cleaning up & resettling in Billets.	
D⁰	21.9.16		Fine Morning. Physical Drill, Bayonet Fighting, Drill. Major St Heynier proceeded on leave. Coy. refit clothing.	
D⁰	22.9.16		Fine Morning. Physical Drill, Saluting Drill, Bayonet Fighting, Squad Drill & new drafts. Orders received to move tomorrow to BRUAY.	
D⁰	23.9.16		Fine day. Battalion marched to BRUAY. Much thunder for the night. Under authority granted by SS 144 the King "i" the Corps Commander has awarded the following Medals to the following NCOs men:— 4796 Cpl R.F. MOORE & 5097 Pte H. WALKER, London Gazette extract. Lt. G.M. GORDON (Special Reserve) Adjutant to be Temp. CAPTAIN. June 8th 1916	

H.W. Crispin (Lt Col)
Commanding 12th Royal Fusiliers

WAR DIARY or INTELLIGENCE SUMMARY

Army Form C. 2118.

12th Royal Fusiliers

Place	Date	Hour	Summary of Events and Information	Remarks and references to Appendices
BRUAY	24.9.16		Fine day. Major A.B. Firth Ireland proceeded on leave. Capt A.S. Tanner appd Acting 2nd in Command. Battalion marched to ESTREE CAUCHIE & billeted. Gen staff message received about 10 pm. 1 Officer and 40 OR att. 182 T Coy R.E. Strength 21 OR joined	
ESTREE CAUCHIE	25.9.16		Still fine & sunny. Battalion relieved 15 Royal Scots in Trenches. Relief complete 8 pm. Gas alert message received 14.9.16 for H.H. Men. Sent to England 14.9.16, Strength 25.9.16. Authy. Lieut. 525 Other Ranks 21.9.16	
Trenches	26.9.16		Very warm day. Work of repairing & relieving trenches commenced 1 Officer & 50 OR No. 1 Coy attached to 182 T Coy in addition	
ALHAMBRA & COLISEUM Dugouts	27.9.16		Fine day, very quiet. Day spent in maintaining & repairing trenches, trench dugouts etc	
CABARET ROUGE	28.9.16		Very fine day. Working in trenches, dugouts fatigue parties found for R.E. – T.M. Battery	
"	29.9.16		Dark misty morning. Fatigue parties found for R.E. etc	

H.W. Cooper Lt Col
Commanding 12/Royal Fusiliers

Army Form C. 2118.

WAR DIARY
or
INTELLIGENCE SUMMARY

(Erase heading not required.)

12th Royal Fusiliers

Place	Date	Hour	Summary of Events and Information	Remarks and references to Appendices
Trenches ALHAMBRA COLISEUM trenches to CABARET ROUGE	30.9.16		Very fine & sunny. Fatigue parties from men in the Battalion attended Trench Warfare Sch: PERNES. under authority granted by HM. the King. The Base Army authority to authorize detentions to be nominated. Appts Capt D.T. Anderson 2nd Lt Ian Tiffany Military Govr.

A.W. Crutherston
Comdt 12 Royal Fusiliers | |

To D.A.G.

    3rd Echelon.

Please attach the following sheets to War Diary.

Sheet 1. after Sept. 30th-1915.

Sheet 2. after Nov. 30th-1915.

CASUALTIES. Sept. 25t 28th-1915.

	KILLED.	WOUNDED.	WOUNDED and MISSING.	MISSING.	REMARKS.
OFFICERS.	Lt. Col. R.D. Garnons Williams. Capt. J.D. Waddell. Capt. S. Phillips. 2nd Lt. C. Newcombe.	Major. R.R. Gibson. Capt. J.K. Ireland. Lieut. E.E. Ridger. Lieut. A.J. Waley. 2nd Lt. C.J. Riley. 2nd Lt. W.E.G. Bryant.		✱ 2nd Lt. C.H.L. Skeets. ✱ 2nd Lt. J. Easton.	✱ Officially reported Prisoners of War.
OTHER RANKS.	20.	27.	64.	142.	

R.B.A.L. Clay Major
1st Royal Fusiliers

17th Brigade.
24th Division

12th BATTALION

ROYAL FUSILIERS

October 1916

Army Form C. 2118.

WAR DIARY
or
INTELLIGENCE SUMMARY
(Erase heading not required.)

Vol 14
12 Royal Fusiliers

Place	Date	Hour	Summary of Events and Information	Remarks and references to Appendices
Franvillers Albamera Polisrum Carnoy Rouge a.	1.10.16		Major Sunny Villiers came into forces at 1 am. was struck but luck us here des 4632 S/Sgt Stubbs. 19773 S/te G.E. Riley, wounded, 19164 Mcpl. 2813 G.m.R Banton — R.m. Dannigan joined.	
"	2.10.16		Very wet day. Battalion relieved about midday by 1st York Staffords & proceeded to billets. Nos 1 & C & Coy to CAMBLAIN L'ABBE. Nos 2 & Y to Coys to VILLIERS au BOIS. 25 O.R. was M.L.A to 104 Field Coy R.E.	
CAMBLAIN L'ABBE & VILLIERS AU BOIS	3.10.16		Weather very wet during & morning. Inspected by etc. Platoon by Coy Comdts. & ... & infected many clothes to all ranks. Commenced 2 hours daily. Coy G.M. Gordon Javaline in Camp. 2/Lt R.C. Cully attached into Battalion. Gazette 25.4.16 L. Yorkers from the Kings Battalion & will attend to 23.9.15 M.S.I 10/2 dtd/4970 24/19.16 Capt. D.L. Beaufort of this unit of Quartermaster from 23.9.16 - 2 St. H. Martin joined.	
"	4.10.16		Weather very unsettled. Physical drums & squad lasts, platoon drill etc. Continued. & rifles cleaned one company daily. Inoculation of all...

M.O.Loffoty Lt Col fusiliers

Army Form C. 2118.

WAR DIARY
or
INTELLIGENCE SUMMARY
(Erase heading not required.)

12th Royal Fusiliers

Instructions regarding War Diaries and Intelligence Summaries are contained in F. S. Regs., Part II. and the Staff Manual respectively. Title Pages will be prepared in manuscript.

Place	Date	Hour	Summary of Events and Information	Remarks and references to Appendices
	5.10.16		Route march. Tyfent emenced. 2/Lt. XW. Tiffany & 2/Lt. D.J. Cox joined to Retrieve Scheme (Brisonel)	
"	6.10.16		Weather still unsettled. Physical drill, platoon drill, bayonet fighting, musketry, etc.	
"	7.10.16		Drill & showery. Bde. Physical drill & rifle exercise squad marches etc. Sgt. J. Stewart joined from 12" Commins. 2 N.C.Os & 29 ORs from Ans. Div. Reim returned from leave.	
"	8.10.16		No change in weather. Bde. Physical drill, Guards Mounting, Battalion drill ord rifle ex. 2/Lt. A Martin proceeded on 8 days Course. Capt. J.D. Calier RAMC. M.O. left the battalion & proceeded to join 34" Field Ambulance Sgt. E.A. Vaughan RAMC. M.O. from 109" Bde. RFA joined. Casualties. 1 O.R. wounded.	
"	9.10.16		Sunday. Not much battle. 2/Lt. W.F. Crofts proceeded on L.S. Lef. 2/Lt. R.W. Jennings proceeded for instruction to 183" Tunnelling Co RE. Divine service held in Divisional Cinema.	
"	9.10.16		Weather fine. Bde. Physical training, platoon drill, musketry etc. All N.C.Os handed letter C.O. of Middlesex Rgt. at 11 am — 2d	

F.W. Coughin Lt Colonel
Commanding 12 Royal Fusiliers

Army Form C. 2118.

WAR DIARY
or
INTELLIGENCE SUMMARY

(Erase heading not required.)

12th Royal Fusiliers

Place	Date	Hour	Summary of Events and Information	Remarks and references to Appendices
CARENCY Sub-sector	10.10.16		CAMBLAIN L'ABBE at 12 noon. 2nd Bn. R. Fus. relieved from 4th Army 24 Bd and Battalion relieved 4th Royal Scots in left sub-sector trenches in front of SOUCHEZ. Casualties: Wounded 2 O.R.	
"	11.10.16		Day misty morning. Snipers were more active. 2 S.M.G. Rifles mounted in Brighton Corner. 2.St (?)m. Rations relieved from the mid-way shew. Casualties. 1.O.R. killed. 1.O.R. wounded.	
"	12.10.16		Dull day. Fine; fresh breeze. The R.E.'s sprung two small mines in front of our line at 9-20 am, destroying two dug-outs and led by 2nd Lieut M.D.B. Ely, who had surveyed it with orders.	
"	13.10.16		Damp + misty. Capt. J.W. Wilson proceeded on leave. The enemy sent over his usual supply of trench mortar shells.	
"	14.10.16		Dull morning, fresh wind. Very quiet day.	
"	15.10.16		Damp + close. 2nd Lieut. 25.O.R. proceeded to 17 Corps Lewis Gun Railway, Maroeuil. 2nd Lt. W.W. Cooper proceeded on leave. Casualties. 1 O.R. killed. H.W. Caughey. 1 O.R. Bois Vincent. Somerby 12 Royal Fusiliers.	

WAR DIARY or INTELLIGENCE SUMMARY

Army Form C. 2118.

12" Royal Fusiliers

Place	Date	Hour	Summary of Events and Information	Remarks and references to Appendices
	16.10.16		Fresh wind, drier. The enemy a little more active than usual.	
	17.10.16		Fine with little sunshine. 2/Lt. Nathan returned from Division. We attempted a small raid on a Sap running out from the DUDDING FARM site. The raid being mostly 2/Lt FONTEYN D'ARTHY. The Sap was entered & found to be empty of the enemy & full of tangled wire. As the party had been out over 1½ hrs + it was pouring with rain & very dark, they returned to our trenches. Casualties 1. O.R. wounded.	
	18.10.16		Dull inclined to rain. Battalion was relieved by 1st Royal Fusiliers & proceeded to billets three companies at VILLERS AU BOIS AT one company in CARENCY in Bde Support.	
VILLERS AU BOIS	19.10.16		Wet + some fog. Battalion had baths + spent remainder of day cleaning up. 2/Lt Sir Gen Cupton + Lieut L Yerbeck proceeded on leave. Major A.B. Iith Recruit attached Commanding Officer during absence of C.O. + major E.L. Raynor attached 2nd in command v.ce major A.B. Dick Cecred. 2/Lt. A.H. Lee returned from 3rd R. Bde.	

H.W. Cupton
St Peland
Commanding 12" Royal Fusiliers

WAR DIARY
or
INTELLIGENCE SUMMARY

Army Form C. 2118.

12th Royal Fusiliers

Place	Date	Hour	Summary of Events and Information	Remarks and references to Appendices
"	20.10.16		Very cold but fine. Battalion bathed & filed clothing. Training was Coy manoeuvres. 289 & Other attached to 104th Field Coy R.E. 2/Sec. Dig Schools & Divl. Tiffany schemes from Divl. Scheme	
"	21.10.16		Cold but very fine. Physical Drill Squad drill & bayonet fighting, foot inspection.	
"	22.10.16		Fine & sunny but cold. Battalion Officers mess & fired ch[?] full mess & dinner at Battn. H.Q. were given to all 2/Lt. Bryant proceeded to T.M. Course. Church parade & march 6 2nd H[?] returned from Sniping Course.	
"	23.10.16		Bitter frost & cold. Officers played football match v M.G. Staffords & won. Some nine min for Drill Platoon & Capt Jenner proceeded to lecture on the new sector of trenches which the Battalion were about to go to.	
"	24.10.16		Damp & wet. Physical drill, Gas helmet inspection. 289 AB Rice returned to entry Camps.	
"	25.10.16		Clear & inclined to rain. Battalion was relieved by 2 Canadian Bn & proceeded to billets at ESTRÉE CAUCHIE. Lewis gun teams Joseph Tringham Commanding 12th Royal Fusiliers

Army Form C. 2118.

WAR DIARY
or
INTELLIGENCE SUMMARY

(Erase heading not required.)

12th Royal Fusiliers

Place	Date	Hour	Summary of Events and Information	Remarks and references to Appendices
ESTREE CAUCHIE	26.10.16		Proceeded to MAZINGARBE to take over the trenches. 2nd Lt. Collison & Jennings returned from 162 Tunnelling Coy. R.E. 1 O.R. 39. O.R. Capt. J.V. Wilson returned from leave.	
MAZINGARBE			Weather unsettled. Battalion marched to MAZINGARBE. Relief of the right S.O.R. proceeded to England & later completed.	
	27.10.16		Dull, cold & very windy. Battalion relieved 13th Yorks in trenches. Left Sub-section. Loos area. Cas: 45 Tunnelling proceeded on leave.	
14 B.S Sector	28.10.16		Fine - mild. 25 O.R. returned from work on Fges Railway.	
"	29.10.16		Wet & mild. 2/Lieut. M.R. Markes proceeded on course of instruction at 1st Army School. 2nd Lt. De Coysten & Lieut. L. Venters returned from leave. Casualties. 1 O.R. killed. 1 O.R. wounded.	
"	30.10.16		Dull. 2/Lt. M.R. Dean returned from L.G. Course. At Officers patrol went out to examine a Sap & M. 9a/Ham went out to examine a Suffwork Sap in the enemy front line. Found Sap to be sixty yds distant up drainage purposes.	H.W. Murphy Major Commanding 12th Royal Fusiliers

2449 Wt. W14957/M90 750,000 1/16 J.B.C. & A. Forms/C.2118/12.

Army Form C. 2118.

WAR DIARY
or
INTELLIGENCE SUMMARY

(Erase heading not required.)

12 Royal Fusiliers

Instructions regarding War Diaries and Intelligence Summaries are contained in F. S. Regs., Part II. and the Staff Manual respectively. Title Pages will be prepared in manuscript.

Place	Date	Hour	Summary of Events and Information	Remarks and references to Appendices
"	31.10.16		Mild but unsettled weather. 3. O.R. transferred to M.G.Corps. 1. O.R. wounded. Self field.	

H.W. Hughes Lt Colonel
Commanding 12 Royal Fusiliers

2449 Wt. W14957/M90 750,000 1/16 J.B.C. & A. Forms/C.2118/12.

17th Brigade.
24th Division

12th BATTALION

ROYAL FUSILIERS

November 1916.

Army Form C. 2118.

WAR DIARY
or
INTELLIGENCE SUMMARY

(Erase heading not required.)

12th Royal Fusiliers

Vol 15

Place	Date	Hour	Summary of Events and Information	Remarks and references to Appendices
Trenches new BOIS SUD SECTION 14 Bns.	1.11.16		Weather fair. Lieut. J.D. Stewart & 2nd R.J. Benjamin struck off establishment with effect from Sept. 1. 1916. 2nd Lieut. Artly b457/3 (M.S.K.) 2nd Lt. Cromwell struck off establishment with effect from Sept. 1. 1916. Artly 1756/3 (M.S.K.) A quiet day.	
"	2.11.16		Damp morning. 2Lt. D.G. Gibson proceeded on leave. We Battn. were relieved by 1st Royal Fusiliers and proceeded to Brigade Support VILLAGE LINE.	
VILLAGE LINE	3.11.16		Very fine day. The usual working parties were found for front line.	
"	4.11.16		Fine. Working parties as usual.	
"	5.11.16		Fine day. Lewis Gun Books at MAZINGARBE transferred to M.G. Coy. L.O.R. Corps. for 9 Os. 2 + 3	

H.W. Grigoby Lt. Colonel
Commanding 12th Royal Fusiliers

Army Form C. 2118.

WAR DIARY
or
INTELLIGENCE SUMMARY

(Erase heading not required.) 12" Royal Fusiliers

Place	Date	Hour	Summary of Events and Information	Remarks and references to Appendices
"	6.11.16		Wet morning. Fine later. Working parties found.	
"	7.11.16		Very wet & boisterous. Usual working parties found.	
"	8.11.16		Dull. Inclined to be showery. Working parties found.	
"	9.11.16		Fine morning. 2/Lt. D.J. Stewart returned from L.G. Course. Working parties found.	
"	10.11.16		Fine day. Battalion relieved 1st Royal Fusiliers in trenches. Left sub-section 14 B.S.	
Trenches 14 B.S.	11.11.16		Fine but dull. Lieut. E.A. Whittingham (M.O.) proceeded on leave.	
"	12.11.16		Dull. 2nd Lieuts. Cutter, Emerson & Collison proceeded to 24th Divisional School on a course of instruction. 3 O.R. joined the Battalion. A quiet day.	
"	13.11.16		Fine. Some sunshine. Our heavy & trench mortar active. 3 O.R. transferred to 33rd Labour Battn. R.E.	

H.W. Anyon St. Colonel
Commanding 12th Royal Fusiliers

Army Form C. 2118.

WAR DIARY
or
INTELLIGENCE SUMMARY

(Erase heading not required.)

12th Royal Fusiliers

Place	Date	Hour	Summary of Events and Information	Remarks and references to Appendices
"	14.11.16		Since the enemy retaliation on LOOS for our wire cutting of the last two days.	
"	15.11.16		Early morning. We carried out a raid on the enemy trenches. The wire being blown up by a Bangalore Torpedo. Two parties started, but only one were under 2/Lt. H.W. Tiffany & 2/Lt. R.G. Fortey succeeded in getting through the wire. The party failed to get in owing to our trench mortars firing on them by mistake. Casualties. Missing believed killed. 2/Lt. H.W. TIFFANY. Killed 2. O.R. Wounded. 7. O.R.	2/Lt. H.W. Tiffany
"	16.11.16		Very quiet morning. Battalion relieved by 1st Royal Fusiliers & proceeded to huts in MAZINGARBE. Capt. D.L. Blackford proceeded on leave. 1. O.R. transferred to 174 M.G. Corps.	

H.W. Compton Lt. Colonel
Commanding 12th Royal Fusiliers

WAR DIARY or INTELLIGENCE SUMMARY

Army Form C. 2118.

12th Royal Fusiliers

Place	Date	Hour	Summary of Events and Information	Remarks and references to Appendices
MAINGARBE NORTHERN TRS.	17.11.16		Very cold - frost. Day spent cleaning up + Billy man Bn. Regimental. The experience of N.C.O.s + men he "on Fatigue" duties to Brigade in the Field. following were mentioned 2542 Sergt. J.C. Aldworth. 681 Sgt. F.A.H. Dix. 2926. Pte. Mylee. F. Robert to London Gazette. 5193 Pte. J.J. Brown. 4227 Corpl. W. Hart. 3656 S/Sgt. A.N.C. Davies I.O.R. Joined. The following letter has been received from the B.G.C. "The Divisional Commander expects to hear that 2nd Lieut Tiffany, 12th Royal Fusiliers is missing as the result of the raid on the night of 15/16" inst. The Major-General wishes to express his sincere regret and at the same time is much gratified at the gallantry shown by the parties of 2nd Battalion who went out, and though they failed to recover 2/Lt. Tiffany, succeeded in bringing safely back several other casualties.	
"	18.11.16		Exceedingly cold. Turned to sleep later. M.O. Coy led Lewis Signal + Company drill carried out. Lecture ref. Book requirement likely. Lewis Gun instruction 2/Lt. Frankyside talked to 17 T.M. Battery - Strength of the Battalion 2 St. Lts.+ 615 others.	

H.W. Compton St. Colonel
Commanding 12th Royal Fusiliers.

WAR DIARY
or
INTELLIGENCE SUMMARY

(Erase heading not required.) 12th Royal Fusiliers

Army Form C. 2118.

Instructions regarding War Diaries and Intelligence Summaries are contained in F. S. Regs., Part II. and the Staff Manual respectively. Title Pages will be prepared in manuscript.

Place	Date	Hour	Summary of Events and Information	Remarks and references to Appendices
"	19.11.16		Damp morning. Ceremonial Parade took place at 2nd Divisional H.Q. BRAQUEMONT where the First Army Commander presented Medal ribbons to the undermentioned Officers, N.C.O.s & men. 2 Lt. A.H. LEE. 5150 Sgt. D. SNOOKIE. 3125 Pte. F. STEWARD. 5077 Pte. J. WALKER. 17873 Sergt. G.F. BISHOP. 2542 Sergt. J.C. ALDWORTH 2926 Pte. F. MYALL. 3656 L/cpl. H.N.C. DAVIES. No. 3 Coy had baths. 6 O.R. joined. 2/Lt. F.J. Jenkin proceeded on T.M. course.	
"	20.11.16		Very fine day. No.1 Coy had baths. Dull later. New Respirators Rifle exercises. A Seven a Side Football Competition this was won by No.4. Coy. The Friedrich Leonfg. Nos. 4 & 3 Coys were in M.O.H.Y. Respirator drill, Company drill. Rifle exercises.	
"	21.11.16		Bright & sunny.	
"	22.11.16		Cold & fine. Battalion relieved the 1st Royal Fusiliers in Trenches the Bus sub-section, front line.	
Trenches 14 Bis.	23.11.16		Fine. 2/Lt. H.J. Cox proceeded on leave. Enemy very quiet.	

H.W. Crispin Lt. Colonel
Commanding 12th Royal Fusiliers

2449 Wt. W14957/M90 750,000 1/16 J.B.C. & A. Forms/C.2118/12.

Army Form C. 2118.

WAR DIARY
or
INTELLIGENCE SUMMARY

12th Royal Fusiliers

(Erase heading not required.)

Place	Date	Hour	Summary of Events and Information	Remarks and references to Appendices
"	24.11.16		Cold. Somewhat damp. Some Trench mortar activity on our side.	
"	25.11.16		Drizzly rain. 2nd Lieut W.B. Hone-Goss joined. 2nd Lt. Dm. Rawlins proceeded on L.G. Course. A quiet day.	
"	26.11.16		Mild & dull. Another quiet day.	
"	27.11.16		Very fine & frosty. 2nd Lieut Colt. 2nd Lt. A.B. Ritz attached to 14th T.M. Battery. 2nd Lt. E.V. Watherhead proceeded on leave. A little more shelling than usual. Casualties:- Killed. 1 O.R. Wounded 3 O.R.	
"	28.11.16		Very fine. Battalion was relieved by 1st Royal Fusiliers & proceeded to VILLAGE LINE in Brigade Support.	
VILLAGE LINE	29.11.16		Dull & foggy. 2 Companies had baths at LES BRÉBIS. Working parties found.	
"	30.11.16		Cold & dull. 2 Companies had baths at LES BRÉBIS. Working parties found.	

H.W. Grijoh. St. Colonel
Commanding 12th Royal Fusiliers

Sheet 2.

Corrections in Casualties from Sept.29th/1915 to Nov..28th-1915.

Additional Casualties O.R. Wounded

Date.	No.
17-10-15.	3.
23-10-15.	1.
25-10-15.	1.
5-11-15.	4.
6-11-15.	1.
7-11-15.	1.
8-11-15.	1.
17-11-15.	1.
18-11-15.	1.

R.B.O.E. Clow of Major
1/2 th Bn Royal Fusiliers

17th Brigade.
24th Division

12th BATTALION

ROYAL FUSILEERS

December 1 9 1 6.

Army Form C. 2118.

Vol 76

12th Royal Fusiliers

WAR DIARY
or
INTELLIGENCE SUMMARY

12th Royal Fusiliers

(Erase heading not required.)

Place	Date	Hour	Summary of Events and Information	Remarks and references to Appendices
VILLAGE EN NE	1.12.16		Fine + mild. Usual working parties found for front line.	
"	2.12.16		Rather colder. Usual working parties found.	
"	3.12.16		Dull – mild. 2nd St. R.G. Fortescue proceeded on leave. 2nd St R.G. Fortescue awarded the Military Cross by the G.O.C. in chief. Relieved 1st R.F. in front line trenches.	
Trenches	4.12.16		Fine day. London Gazette extract. "The undermentioned temp. Captn. from Reg. Batt. to be temp. Capts. (attd.) 1st Sept. 1916. R.C. Rutter." Casualties. 1.O.R. Wounded	
14 Bde				
"	5.12.16		Dull + wet. Very quiet day.	
"	6.12.16		Mild. Lt. H. Reynolds proceeded on leave. 2nd Lt. J.D. Stewart proceeded to Grist Army School. Casualties. Killed. 1.O.R. Wounded 1.O.R. (slightly at duty).	
"	7.12.16		Dull. Casualties Wounded 2.O.R.	

H.W. Cooper Lt. Colonel
Commanding 12th Royal Fusiliers

16 T.

WAR DIARY or INTELLIGENCE SUMMARY

Army Form C. 2118.

12th Royal Fusiliers

Place	Date	Hour	Summary of Events and Information	Remarks and references to Appendices
"	8.12.16		Damp & misty. Capt. A.G. Tanner proceeded on Specie Bodys leave.	
"	9.12.16		Mild. Casualties. Wounded 1.O.R.	
"	10.12.16		Dull. Battalion relieved at midday by 1st R.F. & moved to Huts in MAZINGARBE. 2Lt. A.G. Hughes rejoins at the Battalion.	
NORTHERN DIOPS MAZINGARBE	11.12.16		Very fine & sunny. Day spent cleaning up. 2Lt. H. Deakin proceeded on leave. Details in billets.	
"	12.12.16		Snow & sleet, very cold.	
"	13.12.16		Very cold. Reprinter divise, musketry & rifle exercises. Baths. London Gazette Extract. Royal Fusiliers. Temp 2nd. (acting Capt) whilst commanding a company) J.V. Wilson to be temp Capt to complete establishment (Jan 27). Temp Lt. L. Vachere to be temp Capt (June 8)	
"	14.12.16		Cold & dull. Reprinter divise. Platoon drill. Wiring party provided for work near MAZINGARBE KEEP.	

C.H.W. Grigor Lt Colonel
Commanding 12th Royal Fusiliers

WAR DIARY
or
INTELLIGENCE SUMMARY

(Erase heading not required.)

Army Form C. 2118.

12th Royal Fusiliers

Place	Date	Hour	Summary of Events and Information	Remarks and references to Appendices
	15.12.16		Cold + dull. Pewter & Gas helmet drill. Some wiring parties found. Baths for No. 1. Coy.	
TRENCHES 14 Bis.	16.12.16		Cold + fine. Battalion relieved 1st R.F. in trenches 14 Bis. near Loos. 2nd Lt. Penrie returned from Div. School. Capt. L. Vachon & 2nd Lt. M. Collison proceeded to training camp as instructors.	
"	17.12.16		Dull. A very quiet day.	
"	18.12.16		Dull. The supports lightly shelled. No wind.	
"	19.12.16		Cold + dull. 'Military Medal' awarded by the Corps Commander to 5105 Sgt. Schermier. C. 3 Coy. Casualties. Wounded 2. O.R. Missing 2. O.R.	
"	20.12.16		Very fine day. Draft of 75 O.R. arrived from training camp.	
"	21.12.16		Mild inclined to rain. Casualties. Wounded 1. O.R.	

H.W. Compton Lt Colonel
Commanding 12th Royal Fusiliers

Army Form C. 2118.

WAR DIARY
or
INTELLIGENCE SUMMARY

(Erase heading not required.)

12th Royal Fusiliers

Instructions regarding War Diaries and Intelligence Summaries are contained in F. S. Regs., Part II. and the Staff Manual respectively. Title Pages will be prepared in manuscript.

Place	Date	Hour	Summary of Events and Information	Remarks and references to Appendices
"	22.12.16		Very wet. Battalion relieved by 1st R.F. & proceeded to Ontario Reserve. Village Line	
Village Line	23.12.16		Wet - without incident.	
"	24.12.16		Wet. Enemy fired a number of Gas shells	
"	25.12.16		Very windy but fine. Cemeteries. Killed. 1 O.R.	
"	26.12.16		Fine. Enemy shelled with Gas shells.	
"	27.12.16		Fine. Major A.D.S. Dirk Cleeve & 2 Lt. W.F. Cooper proceeded on leave. Battn. at LES BREBIS. 2 Lt. E. Gill joined. One of our aeroplanes was shot down & dropped behind our lines. Enemy shelled the vicinity of this machine.	
"	28.12.16		Fine. Relieved the 1st R.F. in trenches. Wet afternoon.	
Trenches	29.12.16		Showery. Enemy quiet. 2 Lt. W.S.Q. Adam returned from Div. H.Q.	
H.B. 15.				

H. W. Crispin Lt Col
Commandt 12th Royal Fusiliers

Army Form C. 2118.

WAR DIARY
or
INTELLIGENCE SUMMARY

(Erase heading not required.)

12th Royal Fusiliers

Instructions regarding War Diaries and Intelligence Summaries are contained in F. S. Regs., Part II. and the Staff Manual respectively. Title Pages will be prepared in manuscript.

Place	Date	Hour	Summary of Events and Information	Remarks and references to Appendices
	30.12.16		Showery. Enemy sent a few "crumps" over on our front line. 2/Lts. A.F. Watson & R.F. Bielow joined the battalion.	
	31.12.16		Showery. 2 Bangalore torpedoes were blown up in enemy wire. Enemy active with "crumps". X. Parties near B.Tn. O[M] [trenches] & 2 St. Souleyn M.C.	

H. W. Compton
Lt. Colonel
Commdg 12th Royal Fusiliers

Army Form C. 2118.

Vol 17
12th Royal Fusiliers

WAR DIARY or INTELLIGENCE SUMMARY

(Erase heading not required.)

Place	Date	Hour	Summary of Events and Information	Remarks and references to Appendices
TRENCHES 4 B 15	1-1-17		Showers. Enemy active with minnies. The following letter was received today from O.C. No. 2. Squadron R.F.C. "Would you convey the thanks of myself and the 6 officers of No 2 Squadron R.F.C. to the men of the 12th Royal Fusiliers and all those who gave such very able and generous assistance to the pilot and observer who were shot down on Dec 29th/16. We are very grateful to them for their help and would be much obliged if you would let them know how much their assistance was appreciated. (Sd) Reginald Cooper, Major, O.C. No. 2 Squadron R.F.C. The 17th Bde Commander also wishes to add his thanks to you and your Battalion for your gallant assistance rendered to the injured airmen." Capt. R.C. Cutter proceeded on short leave to England. Corporation 2. O.R. wounded.	
"	2-1-17		2/Lt G.M.R. Emmerson transferred to England sick. 2/Lt W.R. Dean returned from leave.	
"	3-1-17		Windy and damp. Battalion relieved by 1st Royal Fusiliers and proceeded to Northern Hts. MAZINGARBE. The General Officer Commanding in Chief has awarded the Military Medal to No. 4800 Sgt. L. Bright. Lieut J.D. Stewart proceeded on short leave to England.	

H.W. Cowptwhite? Colonel
Commanding 12th Royal Fusiliers

Army Form C. 2118.

WAR DIARY
or
INTELLIGENCE SUMMARY

(Erase heading not required.)

12th Royal Fusiliers

Place	Date	Hour	Summary of Events and Information	Remarks and references to Appendices
Northern Hutts Marzingarbe	4-1-17		Fine. Battalion Xmas dinner for the N.C.O.s and men together with cinema show and concert troupe, was held at the local Brasserie and was greatly enjoyed by all ranks.	
"	5-1-17		Fine and Sunny. Musketry and Lewis gun training carried out. Sergeants Xmas dinner was held at a local restaurant from 3 P.M. to 9 P.M. Bath allotment from 26 O.R. per Coy. Lewis gun training and Rifle Range.	
"	6-1-17		Dull. Musketry and drill under Coy arrangements carried out. 2 Lieut. W.J. Cooper returned from leave.	
"	7-1-17		Very Sunny but Cold. No. 1 Coy played No. 4 Coy in the final inter Company Competition. Result No. 1 Coy 9 goals No. 4 Coy 1 goal. 2 Lieut H.S. Davidson performed the duties of O.C. No. 3 Coy for period 8-12-16 to 7-1-17. Major A.B. Dick Cleland returned from leave.	
Trenches 14 Bde	8-1-17		Cold. The Battalion relieved the 1st Royal Fusiliers in front line trenches 14 Bde. 4 I.O.R. wounded on short leave to England. Capt A. Janmay returned from 30 days leave.	
"	9-1-17		Cold and Dull. 2 Lt W.J. Cooper appointed Acting Adjutant during absence of Capt C.M. Green on leave. Casualties Killed 1 O.R. Wounded 3 O.R. Died of wounds 1 O.R.	

H. W. Campbell Lt Colonel
Commanding 12 Royal Fusiliers

Army Form C. 2118

WAR DIARY
or
INTELLIGENCE SUMMARY

(Erase heading not required.)

12th Royal Fusiliers

Place	Date	Hour	Summary of Events and Information	Remarks and references to Appendices
Trenches 14 B sec	10-1-19		Cold – Capt G.M. Gordon proceeded on short leave to England. Work under Coy arrangements.	
"	11-1-19		Cold – unchanged to anew. Capt L Ventress returned from 24th Division Training Camp. Capt R C Cutter returned from leave. Milder. Casualties Wounded 3. O.R.	
"	12-1-19			
"	13-1-19		Cold. Sleet. 2 Lt A.E. Hughes returned from Infantry Course. Major E L Huyson proceeded on 30 days special leave. 2 Lt G.E. Dauer proceeded on leave.	
"	14-1-19		Very Cold and some snow. Lieut J.S. Stewart returned from leave. Lieut H.B. Horne-Gall proceeded on medium French Mortar Course. Casualties Wounded 1. O.R.	
"	15-1-19.		Cold but fine. Capt R Hare returned to the Battalion. Casualties Wounded. 1. O.R.	
"	16-1-19		Cold and Dull. 4 6 O.R. joined. 2 Lieut J.R. Barlow proceeded to 24th Division School. Casualties Wounded 1. O.R.	
Village Linea.	17-1-19.		Battalion relieved by 1st R.F. and proceeded to Village Lines in Brigade Reserve.	

H.W. Crighton Lt Colonel
Commanding 12th Royal Fusiliers

Army Form C. 2118.

WAR DIARY
or
INTELLIGENCE SUMMARY

(Erase heading not required.)

Instructions regarding War Diaries and Intelligence Summaries are contained in F. S. Regs., Part II. and the Staff Manual respectively. Title Pages will be prepared in manuscript.

Place	Date	Hour	Summary of Events and Information	Remarks and references to Appendices
Village Lines	17-1-19		Very cold, several inches of snow fell during the night and continued throughout the day. Naval working parties found for front line. 2 Lt D.M. Rawbone returned from leave.	
"	18-1-19		Very cold. Baths for Companies. 85 O.R. joined Battalion. 2 Lt D.M. Rawbone admitted to Field Ambulance.	
"	19-1-19		Cold and Sleeting. Baths for Companies. Working parties found. 2 Lt A.E. Rice proceeded on short leave to England.	
"	20-1-19		Very cold. Baths for Companies 38 O.R. joined Battalion. Capt S.Y. Wilson & 2 Lt E.A.H. Fordham proceeded on short leave to England.	
"	21-1-19		Cold. 2 Lt E.A.H. Fordham proceeded on course at First Army School. Extract from London Gazette dated Jan 4/1919. Temp Major E.L. Heynes and G/13648 Pte Richardson P.E. mentioned in despatches for distinguished and gallant services and devotion to duty.	
"	22-1-19		Very Cold. Casualties. Wounded 1. O.R.	
"	23-1-19		Very fine day but cold. East Wind. Battalion relieved the 1st Roy. Inn. front line trenches 14 Bn. returned from leave. Casualties Killed 1. O.R. 2 Lt A.E. Davis Wounded 2. O.R.	
Trenches 14 Bde.	24-1-19		Fine day. 2. O.R. joined Battalion. Casualties Killed 1. O.R.	

H.W. Croydon Lt Colonel
Commanding 12th Royal Fusiliers

Army Form C. 2118.

WAR DIARY
or
INTELLIGENCE SUMMARY
(Erase heading not required.)

12th Royal Fusiliers

Place	Date	Hour	Summary of Events and Information	Remarks and references to Appendices
Trenches 14 Bis	25-1-17		Fine. A/RSM. Parker returned to C.S.M. & Sgt. Barham A.1/RSM. as attached to this Battalion & appointed A/RSM.	
	26-1-17		Very bros. Fine. Attempt at daylight raid was carried out in conjunction with the 8th Buffs, other party, numbers 100 O.Rs. & Officer (2nd Lt. Mounters, 2nd Lt. Attenborough, 2nd Lt. Rotton, 2nd Lt. Rotenburg) and under the direction of Capt. Watkins. Our objective was the German front line & close support. The 8th Buffs objective was the German front line only. All objectives were reached. Many Germans were killed, dugouts bombed T.M. Gun emplacements destroyed, 16 prisoners were taken. Our casualties were fairly heavy. The enemy barrage was very accurately placed on No Man's Land & our front line & communication along trenches. All officers were wounded. 2nd Lt. JR Mounters & 2nd Lt. Attenborough very severely wounded. 2nd Lt. Rees S.O.R. Meaney believes killed S.O.R. Casualties Killed 3 O.R. Wounded 11 O.R. Wounded 4 Officers Missing Wounded 3 O.R. Wounded 25 O.R.	
	27-1-17		The Corps Commander, the Army Commander, the G.O.C. B.G.C. &c. sent Congratulations to Commanding Officer & all ranks who took part in the successful raid, carried out on the 26th inst.	
	28-1-17		Very fine dull eve.	
	29-1-17		Very fine.	

H. W. Cugly, Lt. Colonel
Commanding 12th Royal Fusiliers

Army Form C. 2118.

WAR DIARY
or
INTELLIGENCE SUMMARY

(Erase heading not required.)

Instructions regarding War Diaries and Intelligence Summaries are contained in F. S. Regs., Part II. and the Staff Manual respectively. Title Pages will be prepared in manuscript.

Place	Date	Hour	Summary of Events and Information	Remarks and references to Appendices
TRENCHES 14. B.13.	30-1-17		Fine, cold wind. Batalion was relieved by the 1st Royal Fusiliers & proceeded to Northern Huts, Mazingarbe. 1 OR died in Hospital (Sick)	
Northern Huts. Mazingarbe.	31-1-17		Very cold. Snow fell. Bn was afforts cleaning up & taking [?]	

H.W. Augustin Lt Colonel
Commanding 12 1st Royal Fusiliers

Army Form C. 2118.

WAR DIARY
or
INTELLIGENCE SUMMARY

12th Royal Fusiliers

(Erase heading not required.)

Instructions regarding War Diaries and Intelligence Summaries are contained in F. S. Regs., Part II. and the Staff Manual respectively. Title Pages will be prepared in manuscript.

Place	Date	Hour	Summary of Events and Information	Remarks and references to Appendices
NORTHERN HUTS MAZINGARBE	1-2-1917		Very Cold. Fine. Box Respirators treated with Glycerine. Captain A.S. Jameson admitted to Hospital.	
"	2-2-1917		Very Cold. Fine. The Raiding Party under Captain L. Ventrees inspected by the Corps Commander. No 1 & 3 Coys used the rifle range. No 1 & 4 Coys had Baths.	
"	3-2-1917		Exceedingly Cold. Coys exercised in Box Respirator drill and musketry. Baths allotted to No 3 Coy. Transport inspected by the Colonel. 2 Lt E.E. Sewin, 2 Lt H. Penrose, 2 Lt C. Gill attended lectures at Theatre BRUAY subject "Offensive use of Gas". Lt W.B. Hume fell returned from Trench mortar Course. The following was the British Communique of the 1st & 2nd at 1917 published in the daily papers of 3rd Feb 1917. "British Official, Thursday, 9·15 P.M. We again improved our position slightly north of BEAUMONT HAMEL. Enemy attempted to rush our posts in neighbourhood of GRANDCOURT was driven off.	

H.W. Smyth Lt Col
Commanding 12th Royal Fusiliers

Army Form C. 2118.

WAR DIARY
or
INTELLIGENCE SUMMARY

(Erase heading not required.)

12th Royal Fusiliers

Instructions regarding War Diaries and Intelligence Summaries are contained in F. S. Regs., Part II. and the Staff Manual respectively. Title Pages will be prepared in manuscript.

Place	Date	Hour	Summary of Events and Information	Remarks and references to Appendices
NORTHERN HUTS MAZINGARBE	3-	2-17	We carried out a successful raid S E of NEUVILLE ST VAAST. We had no casualties. Hostile attempts to approach our lines SE of ARMENTIERES and E of YPRES repulsed with loss. Two other attacks near WYTSCHAETE made by strong parties of enemy dressed in white beaten back before they could reach our trenches. Enemy suffered heavy casualties. We took a few prisoners. The total number of Germans captured by the British forces in FRANCE during the month of January is 1228, including 27 officers. Following regiments specially distinguished themselves:— 2nd Royal Scots, 8th East Kent Regiment, 12th Royal Fusiliers, 1st Kings own Scottish Borderers, 1st Royal Inniskillen Fusiliers, 1st Border Regiment, 2nd Border Regiment, 1st South Staffordshire Regiment, 10th Loyal North Lancashire Regiment, 21st and 22nd Manchester Regiment, 8th and 10th Gordon Highlanders, 2nd Leinster Regiment, 2nd Monmouthshire Regiment, 20, 21, and 49th Canadian Regiment, Newfoundland Battalion, 2nd Battalion, 3rd New Zealand Rifle Brigade. Captain L Ventures proceeded on leave. H. W. Cowper Lt Col Commanding 12th Royal Fusiliers	

WAR DIARY or INTELLIGENCE SUMMARY

Army Form C. 2118.

12th Royal Fusiliers

Place	Date	Hour	Summary of Events and Information	Remarks and references to Appendices
NORTHERN HUTS MAZINGARBE	4-2-19		Exceedingly Cold. 2nd Lieut. R.G. FONTEYN and 5105 L/SGT. SCHEURMIER presented with Medal Ribbons by LT. GENERAL Sir C.A. ANDERSON K.C.B. 26 Officers and 43 O.R. paraded as Guard of Honour. No. 2 & 4 Coys. found working parties.	
"	5-2-19		Cold. 2nd Lieut. No. 1 & 3 Coys. found large working parties. No. 2 & 4 Coys. ward Rifle Range. No. 2 & 4 Coys. had Bath. Captain T.V. WILSON, 2nd LT. H. DOWDNEY, 2nd LT. W.S. NATHAN, attended Lecture given by LT.COL W.L. TWISS. M.C. subject "The German Army" 2nd LT. R.G. FONTEYN proceeded on Bombing Course. 3702 A/CSM YOUNG J. 14145 SGT. COOPER W. 9346 SGT NAISH F. 8128 Pte ARCHER, awarded the Military medal	
TRENCHES 14 BIS	6-2-19		Cold. 2nd Lieut. The Battalion relieved the 1st ROYAL FUSILIERS in the trenches. Killed 1 O.R. Wounded 2 O.R. Enemy active with minnies and Pineapples	
"	7-2-19		Cold. 2nd Lieut. Enemy fairly quiet. LIEUT H.R. MURLESS awarded the Military Cross.	

H.W. Amphlett
Commanding 12/Royal Fusiliers

Army Form C. 2118.

WAR DIARY
or
INTELLIGENCE SUMMARY

12th Royal Fusiliers

(Erase heading not required.)

Place	Date	Hour	Summary of Events and Information	Remarks and references to Appendices
TRENCHES 14 BIS	8-2-17		Cold. Fine. Enemy artillery active. LT H.R. MURLESS died in Hospital at BETHUNE of wounds received in action. 2LT H. PENROSE admitted to Hospital. Killed 2 O.R. Wounded 2 O.R.	
	9-2-17		Very Cold. Enemy quiet. Funeral of LT H.R. MURLESS took place at BETHUNE. MAJOR A.B. DICK-CLELAND, CAPTAIN D.L. BLACKFORD and 20 O.R. attended the funeral. 2LT H. MARTIN admitted to Hospital.	
	10-2-17		Very Cold. Enemy very active with minnies and pineapples all day. Heavy hostile shelling by enemy in the early hours of the morning. Enemy made a raid on the Right Coy of the Right Battalion HULLUCH SECTOR (1st North Staffords). The raid was unsuccessful, the enemy were met when they got to the wire and severe casualties were inflicted upon them by Lewis gun. Prisoners taken 16 Officer and 3 O.R. 2LT [J.D] EAKIN, LT W.B HOMEGALL and 38 O.R. Battalion from the R.E's. 2LT E. COHEN and 24 O.R rejoined the Battalion from the 104th Field Coy R.E. 2LT E.L. MOODY joined this Battalion and was posted to No 2 Coy. Killed 3 O.R.	

H.W. Augher Lt Col
Commanding 12th Royal Fusiliers

Army Form C. 2118.

WAR DIARY
or
INTELLIGENCE SUMMARY

12th Royal Fusiliers

(Erase heading not required.)

Place	Date	Hour	Summary of Events and Information	Remarks and references to Appendices
TRENCHES 14 BIS	11-2-19		Milder. Enemy active with Minnies and Pineapples during	
"	12-2-19		Mild. Enemy very quiet the day. Killed 1 O.R. Wounded 2 O.R.	
"	13-2-19		Mild. The Battalion was relieved by the 10th York & Lancs and proceeded to Billets MAZINGARBE. Wounded 2 O.B.	
BILLETS MAZINGARBE	14-2-19		Fine. The Battalion marched to Huts at NOEUX LES MINES. Coys had Baths. 2LT A E HUGHES awarded the Military Cross	
HUTS NOEUX LES MINES	15-2-19		Cold & fine. Coys had Baths. Coys spent the day in haveing Rifle kit. So Helmet and Iron Rations inspections also refitting Clothers and changing up. 2LT. R G Latter rejoined the Battalion from the 24th Divisional School	
"	16-2-19		Fine. Coys at the disposal of Company Commanders for training. MAJOR E L NEYNOE returned from 30 days special leave.	
"	17-2-19		Mild. Coys inspected by Company Commanders in full marching order, also foot inspection. Coys had Baths. 2LT R G FONTEYN returned from Bombing Course	

H. W. Guyther
for Lt Col
Commanding 12 Royal Fusiliers

Army Form C. 2118.

WAR DIARY
or
INTELLIGENCE SUMMARY

(Erase heading not required.)

12th Royal Fusiliers

Place	Date	Hour	Summary of Events and Information	Remarks and references to Appendices
HUTS NOEUX LES MINES	18-2-17		Mild. Dull. Coys training as per programme of work. 2LT C GILL 2LT E L MOODY proceeded on Course at 24th Divisional School	
"	19-2-17		Mild. Dull. Battalion commenced training under the new organisation scheme. 2LT E COHEN admitted to Hospital. 2LT J. CAMPBELL 2LT R N BENTAMIN 2LT A HOPE joined this Battalion, posted to No. 2 Coy, posted to No. 3 Coy	
"	20-2-17		Mild. Dull. Battalion spent the day training (Physical Drill, Musketry, Bombing etc) 2LT H PENROSE returned from Hospital	
"	21-2-17		Mild. Rain. Divisional Gas Officer inspected the Gas Equipment of the Battalion.	
"	22-2-17		Dull. Rain.	
"	23-2-17		Fine. Training carried out by Coys as laid down in programme of work. The Battalion eleven played the 13th Field Ambulance at NOEUX LES MINES in the Semi-Final for the Brigade Recreation Football Competition. Result 13th Field Ambulance 2 goals 12th Royal Fusiliers 1 goal	

H. W. Crysher Lt Col
Commanding 12th Royal Fusiliers

Army Form C. 2118.

WAR DIARY
or
INTELLIGENCE SUMMARY

12th Royal Fusiliers

(Erase heading not required.)

Place	Date	Hour	Summary of Events and Information	Remarks and references to Appendices
HUTS NOEUX LES MINES	24-2-19		Fine. Battalion Route march. Dress Fighting Order. MAJOR A.B. DICK-CLELAND proceeded on 20 days special leave.	
"	25-2-19		Fine. Church Parade. Captain L. Ventress returned from leave. 2nd Lt. A.H. Lee returned from course at 1st Army School.	
"	26-2-19		Fine. Battalion competed in the Divisional Cross Country Team Race. 4567 PTE BARHAM. T. No 1 Coy finished sixth and won a prize.	
"	27-2-19		Fine. Full Battalion Route march in full marching order.	
"	28-2-19		Fine. Battalion took part in an Aeroplane Contact Scheme at Inquerelles.	

H.W. Crupha Lt Col
Commanding 12th Royal Fusiliers

Army Form C. 2118.

WAR DIARY
or
INTELLIGENCE SUMMARY

(Erase heading not required.)

12th Royal Fusiliers   Vol. 19

Place	Date	Hour	Summary of Events and Information	Remarks and references to Appendices
NOEUX LES MINES	1-3-1917		Fine.	
	2-3-1917		Fine. 2 Lt B.I. Deakin proceeded on L.G. Course.	
	3-3-1917		Fine. Party of 1 Officer and 50 O.R. attached to 255th Tunnelling Coy.	
	4-3-1917		Fine. Battalion relieved the 1st Royal Fusiliers in BULLY-GRENAY in Brigade Reserve. Battalion in billets.	
BULLY-GRENAY	5-3-1917		Fine. Working parties of 2 Officers and 145 O.R. found for unloading ammunition.	
	6-3-1917		Fine. Large working parties found. 2 Lt H. Martin returned Battalion from Hospital (granted 10 days sick leave in England).	
	7-3-1917		Fine but cold. Very windy. Large working parties found.	
	8-3-1917		Snow fell early in morning. Large working parties found. 2 Lt H. Martin proceeded on Lewis Gun Course, 1st Corps.	
	9-3-1917		Fine. Snow fell during the afternoon. The Battalion relieved the 1st Royal Fusiliers in the Trenches (ANGRES SECTION). Enemy very quiet.	

Commd. Lt. W. Coughton, Lt. Col.
12 Royal Fusiliers

Army Form C. 2118.

WAR DIARY
or
INTELLIGENCE SUMMARY

(Erase heading not required.)

12th Royal Fusiliers

Instructions regarding War Diaries and Intelligence Summaries are contained in F. S. Regs., Part II. and the Staff Manual respectively. Title Pages will be prepared in manuscript.

Place	Date	Hour	Summary of Events and Information	Remarks and references to Appendices
TRENCHES ANGRES SECTION 10-3-1917	10-3-17		Dull. Usual enemy Trench Mortar Activity. 2/Lt A Penrose transferred to the 8th Royal Fusiliers. 2 Lt R.C. Cotton proceeded on L.G. Co. Course.	
"	11-3-17		Dull morning raining in the afternoon. Very quiet day. Captain S. L. Blackford left Battalion to take up appointment of actings TOWN MAJOR. SAINS EN GOHELLE. 2/Lt R.N. JENNINGS rejoined Battalion. Casualties Wounded. 1. O.R.	
"	12-3-17		Raining. Very little shelling. Quiet day	
"	13-3-17		Dull. Rain fell during the day. Enemy very quiet. 2/Lt R.G FONTEYN proceeded on Bombing Course. 2nd Army School Lieut 2/B HOME-GALL rejoined the Battalion	
"	14-3-17		Dull. Raining. Lieut W.B HOME-GALL attached to X/24 Trench Mortar Battery. Casualties. 1. O.R. Wounded	

H.W. Compton Lt Col
Commanding 12th Royal Fusiliers

Army Form C. 2118.

WAR DIARY
or
INTELLIGENCE SUMMARY
(Erase heading not required.)

12th Royal Fusiliers

Place	Date	Hour	Summary of Events and Information	Remarks and references to Appendices
TRENCHES ANGRES SECTION	15-3-1917		Dull, very cold. Battalion relieved in the trenches by the 1st Royal Fusiliers Battalion and proceeded to FOSSE 10 in Divisional Reserve. Battalion in billets. 2LT C GILL and 2LT E L MOODY returned from course of instruction at 24th Divisional School. 50308 PTE STADE N.W. died in hospital of accidental injuries received on the Light Railway. MAJOR E L NEYNOE performed the duties of 2nd in Command from 25-2-17 – 15-3-17.	
FOSSE 10	16-3-1917		Fine. Companies spent the day cleaning up and bathing.	
"	17-3-1917		Fine. Dummers carried out a few programmes. Lt Col H.W. Compton proceeded on leave (20 days). Major A.B. Dick-Cleland returned from leave 2 Lt H.D. DOUDNEY proceeded on leave. Major A.B. DICK CLELAND took over command of the Battalion.	
"	18-3-17		Fine. 2LT R C CUTTER, 2LT F T DEAKIN, CAPTAIN L VENTRESS proceeded on L.S. Course. CAMIERS, 2LT J. CAMPBELL proceeded on course of instruction at 24th Divl School.	
"	19-3-17		Very windy, rain fell in the afternoon.	

H.W. Compton Lt Col
Commanding 12th Royal Fusiliers

WAR DIARY or INTELLIGENCE SUMMARY

Army Form C. 2118.

Place	Date	Hour	Summary of Events and Information	Remarks and references to Appendices
FOSSE 10	20-3-17		2 Letters during the day 4796 Cpl. MOORE R.F. awarded Bar to Military Medal	
"	21-3-17		2 Letters. Battalion relieved 1st Royal Fusiliers in the trenches (ANGRES SECTION) 2 Lt. E. COHEN and 64 O.R. proceeded to 24th Div Training Battn	
	22-3-17		Snow fell during the night. Enemy attempted two raids on our left front Coy but was easily repulsed. Heavy enemy artillery fire. Enemy raid Casualties 4 O.R. Killed, 10 O.R Wounded	
	23-3-17		Enemy bombarded twice during the day, doing considerable damage to our trenches. Enemy aeroplanes very active. 1 O.R died of wounds received in action. Extract of letter received from the Brigadier General. "Will you kindly convey my appreciation to your Lewis gun team and the men who were in the post near Sap 22 on the morning of March 22nd of the excellent work they did in repelling the German raid. This is a very good example of what can be done if steady determined men hit under a heavy bombardment to the highest test of discipline and hang on under a heavy bombardment as long as our men did this. No German raid can ever be successful."	
	24-3-17		Enemy very quiet. 10 R. joined Battalion. 1 O.R. Died of wounds received in action.	

H.W. Compton Lt. Col.
Commanding 12 Royal Fusiliers

Army Form C. 2118.

WAR DIARY
or
INTELLIGENCE SUMMARY

(Erase heading not required.)

12th Royal Fusiliers

Place	Date	Hour	Summary of Events and Information	Remarks and references to Appendices
TRENCHES ANGRES SECTOR	25-3-17		Fine Sunny. Enemy quiet during the day but bombarded our lines very heavily at 8 p.m. for 3/4 of an hour. 2 Lt. R.G. FONTEYN returned from Bombing C'i. 2 LT R.W. JENNINGS proceeded on L.G. Course.	
	26-3-17		Raining. Dull. Gun Artillery very active from 8 a.m.–9 p.m.	
	27-3-17		Snowing. Battalion relieved by 1st Royal Fusiliers and proceeded to Billets in BULLY GRENAY. Battalion in Brigade Reserve. CAPTAIN L'VENTRESS returned from L.G. Course. 2LT A.F WATSON proceeded on Lewis Course at 1st Corps. 2LT E. COHEN and 41.O.B. rejoined from Divisional Innings 93 Battalion.	
BULLY GRENAY	28-3-17		Fine. Battalion spent the day cleaning up and bathing. Large working parties found 2 LT D BROWN 2LT A.L.P TANNER joined the B'Battalion. Casualties 1.OR wounded.	
	29-3-17		Raining. 2LT H.D DOUDNEY returned from how Battalion had B'thou. Large working parties found.	

M.W.Carpyhr Lt Col.
Commanding 12th Royal Fusiliers

Army Form C. 2118.

WAR DIARY
or
INTELLIGENCE SUMMARY
(Erase heading not required.)

12th Royal Fusiliers

Place	Date	Hour	Summary of Events and Information	Remarks and references to Appendices
BULLY GRENAY	30-3-19		Enemy shelled BULLY GRENAY. Large working parties found. 7938 PTE DOWNARD F. awarded the Military Medal	
	31-3-19		Enemy shelled BULLY GRENAY. Large working parties found. Casualties 1 OR Wounded.	

H.W. Crompton Lt Col
Commanding 12th Royal Fusiliers

12th ROYAL FUSILIERS

17th INFANTRY BRIGADE

24th DIVISION

APRIL 1917

Army Form C. 2118.

WAR DIARY or INTELLIGENCE SUMMARY

(Erase heading not required.)

12th Royal Fusiliers Vol 2

Place	Date	Hour	Summary of Events and Information	Remarks and references to Appendices
Bully Grenay	1-4-17		Fine in morning; snow fell during afternoon. Enemy shelled Bully Grenay during day and night. 2nd Lt. C. Gill proceeded to England on leave. 2nd Lt. R.F. Barlow & 4 O.R. proceeded to 34 Div Training Battn. Allouagne. 2nd Lt. V.C. Cornish returned from 255th Tunnelling Coy.	
Grenades (Angres Sect.)	2-4-17		Snow fell during the day. Bn relieved the 1st Roy. Inskn in the trenches. Enemy artillery very active.	
"	3-4-17		Raining. Enemy artillery active. 2nd Lt. R.F. Barlow appointed A/Quartermaster. No 32480 L/Cpl Wood A/S 3 Coy. Awarded the Military Medal. 1 O.R. joined the Battalion. 2nd Lt. Ew Jennings returned from Lewis Gun Course. Wounded in action 3 O.R.	
"	4-4-17		Rain & sleet all day. Enemy shelled Communication Trenches & back area.	
"	5-4-17		Fine. Enemy artillery activity continued. Major A.B. Dick-Lehman proceeded to England on Command Officers' Course. Major E.L. Neynoe took over command of the Battalion. Capt. J.W. Wilson took over 2nd in command. Major E.L. Neynoe appointed in command vice Major A.B. Dick - to Command 2nd/6 A&S Walker. returned from 100 Corps Sniping School.	

H.W. Compton Lt Col
Commandg 12th Royal Fusiliers

WAR DIARY
or
INTELLIGENCE SUMMARY

(Erase heading not required.)

Army Form C. 2118.

12th Bn Royal Fusiliers

Place	Date	Hour	Summary of Events and Information	Remarks and references to Appendices
Trenches (Angres Sect.)	6-11-17		Fine. Enemy fairly quiet. 3 O.R. Jones Battalion. 2 No/s R. Richardson transferred to 1st Field Survey Coy. 2 No/s R.N. Benjamin relieved from 1st Army School of Instruction. Wounded in action 1 O.R.	
"	7-11-17		Fine. Battalion relieved in the trenches (Angres Section) by the 1st Royal Marine Light Infantry & proceeded to billets in Marqueffles Farm in Divisional Reserve.	
Marqueffles Farm	8-11-17		Fine. Lt. Col. W.S. Bompton returned from leave. Battalion spent the day cleaning up. Wounds in action 1 O.R.	
Do	9-11-17		Fine. (8 hours sunshine.) 2 No/s D. Brown admitted to hospital. Battalion attached to 73rd Inf. Bde. during operations.	
Do	10-11-17		Showing. Wounds in action 1 O.R.	
Do	11-11-17		Snowing & free during day. Snow lay about 6" deep. No/s 3 + 4 Companies	
Do	12-11-17		Fine day. Snow lay about 6" deep. No/s 3 + 4 Companies under Comm and of Major L.H. Neynoe proceeded to trenches on the BOIS EN HACHE + ARRAS ROAD in close support for the attack from 24th Divisional Training Batt. Allonagne. 2.O.R. James Battalion Killed in Action 1 O.R. Wounded in Action 8 O.R.	

H.W. Crayson Lt Col
Command 12th Bn Royal Fusiliers

Army Form C. 2118.

WAR DIARY
or
INTELLIGENCE SUMMARY
(Erase heading not required.)

12th Bn Royal Fusiliers

Place	Date	Hour	Summary of Events and Information	Remarks and references to Appendices

13-4-17 — Fine. At 9.30 am the enemy was seen shelling Roeux from 3rd line, + Lt Col 17oBks, 7th Northants & Major E.L. Negmor proceeded to the 3rd line of the enemy trenches NE of Sunday Jump, then visibly damaged by our shell fire + unoccupied. Information reported to 73rd Inf Bde. At midnight Nos 3 & 4 Coys under Major Negmor undertook to take over forward positions held by 2 Coys each of 9th Sussex + 2nd Leinsters + Nos 1 + 2 Coys moved up in support to take over from the other 2 Coys of the 9th Sussex + 2nd Leinsters. Owing to the creeping darkness of the night + difficult country, the relief was not complete until 8 am on the 14th inst. 2nd Lt C.N. Ratten hasch continues on his appointment as Transport Officer. 2nd Lt J. Campbell returned from 34th Divisional School, and of Toronto received no action.

H.W. Anspach Lt Col
Commanding 12th Royal Fusiliers

Army Form C. 2118.

WAR DIARY
or
INTELLIGENCE SUMMARY
(Erase heading not required.)

12th Bn Royal Fusiliers

Place	Date	Hour	Summary of Events and Information	Remarks and references to Appendices
	14th April 17		Same. Position held at 6 a.m. this date was through the crater running from N.T.S. through ANGRES village to. Patrols were immediately sent out E. to the CHALK PIT on the SOUCHEZ RIVER - CITE DE ROLLENCOURT. ROAD to the CITE DE GAUMONT. The patrols reported all clear. So No 3 Coy proceeded through CALVARY TRENCH to No 4 Coy proceeded under cover in the BOIS DE ROLLENCOURT, & occupied the Sunken Road from 400 yards E. of the CITE DE GAUMONT, to the RED MILL in the outskirts of LIEVIN. This line was occupied by midday. After continuing to push forward, lateral SOUCHEZ RIVER running N to S. through LIEVIN to the CITE DE L'ABATTOIR. No. 3 & 4th Companies at 2 pm pushed forward through LIEVIN to BRICKFIELD west of CITE DE L'ABATTOIR & occupied the line of the SOUCHEZ RIVER mentioned above, the patrols were pushed to the BOIS DE RIAUMONT & the CITE DES SABENNES, and.	

H.W. Aughen Lt Col.
Comm of 12th Royal Fusiliers.

Army Form C. 2118.

WAR DIARY
or
INTELLIGENCE SUMMARY
(Erase heading not required.)

12th Bn. Royal Fusiliers

Place	Date	Hour	Summary of Events and Information	Remarks and references to Appendices

finding the area clear of the enemy, Nos 3 & 4 Coys again advanced, & at 4-30 pm had established themselves on the Eastern edge of the BOIS DE RIAUMONT & in the trenches in the CITE DES GARENNES. Patrols debouching from the Eastern edge of the wood to reconnoitre the CITE DE RIAUMONT came under heavy Machine Gun fire & had to retire, as they found the CITE DE RIAUMONT, & the trenches immediately to the East of it strongly held by the enemy. The enemy put up a strong barrage between the BOIS DE RIAUMONT and the CITE DE RIAUMONT, BOIS itself was searched from 5 pm until midnight with S.G's but, by careful distribution, our losses were very slight. Meanwhile No 3 & 4 Coys advanced through ANGRES to the QUARRIES EAST of LIEVIN, coming under heavy shell fire the whole time, especially on the high ground S.E. of the BOIS DE ROLLENCOURT. The various patrols under 2nd/Lt F.J. Deakin, 2nd/Lt S.M. Lawhorne & 2nd/Lt Little were especially thorough in their work,

Commdg. 12 Royal Fusiliers
2nd/Lt W. Crispin Lt/Col

Army Form C. 2118.

WAR DIARY
or
INTELLIGENCE SUMMARY

(Erase heading not required.)

1st Bn Royal Fusiliers

Place	Date	Hour	Summary of Events and Information	Remarks and references to Appendices

& the advance" of No 3 & 4 Coys was skilfully managed by Capt R Venturi & Capt H.D. Donohey, all available cover & trenches being made use of. Enemy aeroplanes flying low, observed our occupation of the Bois de RIAUMONT as the advance from LIEVIN to the Western edge of the Bois was over open country, & they were consequently under heavy shell fire the whole time. Contact with the 3rd Rifle Brigade on the left, & with the 5th Division on the right was continually maintained by patrols & at the close of the day we joined up with the 17th In. F. Bde at the N corner of the BOIS DE RIAUMONT & with the 5th Division at the bridge on the SOUCHEZ RIVER in the CITE DE L'ABATTOIR. Our right flank was somewhat drawn back owing to the inability of the 5th Division to occupy the CITE DES. PETITS BOIS.

H.W. Anjohn Lebue.
Comm'g 12th Bn Royal Fusiliers

Army Form C. 2118.

WAR DIARY
or
INTELLIGENCE SUMMARY
(Erase heading not required.)

12th Royal Fusiliers

Place	Date	Hour	Summary of Events and Information	Remarks and references to Appendices
	14/4/17		During the advance, much booty was captured including the Field Guns by No 2 Company. The following Officers from London Gazette dated 14/4/17 are published for information:— 2nd/Lt H.D. Dorsney to be Lieutenant 8-6-16. 2nd/Lt A.E. Hughes to be Lieutenant 8-6-16. 2nd/Lt N.G. Gibson to be Lieutenant 29-6-16. 2nd/Lt C.N. Walter back to be Lieutenant 6-3-17. Capt R. Hare proceeded to 39th I.B. Depot no longer constructing Officer. 2nd/Lt _____ in Action 3. O.R. Wounded.	
	15-4-17		Fine. At about 9 a.m. 2 Fighting Platoons under 2nd/Lt A.M. Lee & 2nd/Lt J.G. Deaton Banks pushed forward into the CITÉ DE RIAUMONT. The left platoon established themselves in spite of heavy Machine Gun fire in the Brewery cutting between the CITÉ DE RIAUMONT & the CITÉ DE BOIS DE LIEVIN. The right platoon were sorry to establish themselves in the Western houses of the CITÉ DE RIAUMONT owing to the Machine Gun fire, and	

19th Lumpton Lt Col
Commdt 12th Royal Fusiliers

Army Form C. 2118.

12th Royal Fusiliers

WAR DIARY
or
INTELLIGENCE SUMMARY
(Erase heading not required.)

Place	Date	Hour	Summary of Events and Information	Remarks and references to Appendices
	15-4-17		Trench mortars from FOSSE 3. DE LIEVIN & from the houses in the S.E. corner of the CITE DE RIAUMONT. During the night, orders were received from the G.O.C. to withdraw these Platoons to the BOIS DE RIAUMONT as he did not wish them to be seriously engaged with the enemy. This withdrawal was completed by midnight all our casualties being brought in. All day the BOIS DE RIAUMONT & the town of LIEVIN were heavily shelled by the enemy. 2ndLt R^d Cutler, 2ndLt S.E. Davies 2ndLt J.J. Scallion wounded in action & (still at duty). Killed in action 5. O.R. wounded in action 12 O.R.	RIAUMONT.
	16-4-17		Raining. BOIS DE RIAUMONT and LIEVIN heavily shelled. The Battn were relieved by the 7th Northants & went into Brigade Reserve. 3 Companies in ANGRES village & 1 Company in LIEVIN.	

H.W. Campbell Col.
Commdt. 12 Royal Fusiliers

15
12 Royal Fusiliers

WAR DIARY or INTELLIGENCE SUMMARY

Army Form C. 2118.

(Erase heading not required.)

Instructions regarding War Diaries and Intelligence Summaries are contained in F. S. Regs., Part II. and the Staff Manual respectively. Title Pages will be prepared in manuscript.

12th Royal Fusiliers

Place	Date	Hour	Summary of Events and Information	Remarks and references to Appendices
	16-4-17		2nd/Lt H. Markin returns from 1st Army Signalling School. 2nd/Lt V.C. Cornish wounded in action.	10 O.R. wounded in action.
	17-4-17		2nd Lts T. Steel, 2nd/Lt R. Boscoby & 2nd/Lt H.E. Lampber joined the Battalion. 1st O.R. joined the Battalion. 2nd/Lt A. Hope wounded in action. 3 O.R. wounded in action.	
	18-4-17		12th Batt. Battalion relieved by the 6th Notts & Derby Regt. & proceeded to Marqueffles farm in lieu, billets, relieved from London Gazette dated 18-May. Lt J.D. Stewart from Scottish Rifles (Andrews) to be temp. Lieutenant (Royal Fusiliers) March 23 - also with seniority from 5-1-1916.	
Marqueffles Farm	19-4-17		Battalion marched to MARLES LES MINES (in billets). Capt J.V. Wilson appointed Acting Adjutant vice 2nd/Lt Z.F. Cooper. Lt J.D. Stewart took over command of No.1 Company vice Capt J.V. Wilson.	
MARLES LES MINES	20-4-17		9am. Battalion marched to billets in ECQUE DECQUES.	

A.W. Cupher Lt Col
Commdt 12 Royal Fusiliers

Army Form C. 2118.

WAR DIARY
or
INTELLIGENCE SUMMARY

(Erase heading not required.)

12th Royal Fusiliers

Instructions regarding War Diaries and Intelligence Summaries are contained in F. S. Regs., Part II. and the Staff Manual respectively. Title Pages will be prepared in manuscript.

Place	Date	Hour	Summary of Events and Information	Remarks and references to Appendices
ECQUEDECQUES	21-4-17		Fine. 2/Lt W.J. Cox & 2nd/Lt R.G. Fonteyn returned from Hospital.	
D°	22-4-17		Fine, Sunny. 1 O.R. dies of wounds received in action.	
D°	23-4-17		Fine.	
D°	24-4-17		Fine. Battalion marched to LISBOURG. Battalion in billets.	
LISBOURG	25-4-17		Fine. Rain free during the day.	
D°	26-4-17			
D°	27-4-17		Fine. Battalion marched to ECQUEDECQUES in billets.	
D°	28-4-17		Fine. Battalion proceeded to BETHUNE. Battalion in MONTMORENCY BARRACKS.	
BETHUNE	28-4-17		Fine. Sunny. 2nd/Lt E. Cohen proceeds to England on leave.	
D°	29-4-17		Fine. Sunny. Battalion proceeded to ALLOUAGNE. Battalion in billets. 2nd/Lt 2nd Coper, 2nd/Lt A.H. Lee, 2nd/Lt A.H. Walton proceeded to BOMY for Lewis Gun training under Staff Officer of the 34th Division. 2nd/Lt C. Gill proceeded on L.G. Course. 2/Lt TOUQUET Gunnery 1000yds N/ of LA BASSEE canal — 1000 yds W/ of GIVENCHY LES LA BASSEE. Motor key recommended.	
ALLOUAGNE	30-4-17		Fine. 2nd/Lt A.P. Yapner proceeds on Bugger Course at AIRE. Battalion started training.	

H.W. Compton Lt Col.
Comm'd'g 12th Royal Fusiliers.

SECRET
O.O.136/1.

Officer Commanding

   12th Royal Fusiliers
   ----

1. On the 7th April Officers of the 12th Royal Fusiliers will reconnoitre routes as under :-

   (a) From MARQUEFFLES FARM to that portion of the MAISTRE LINE adjoining the ARRAS ROAD (Squares R.23.a., R.23.c., R.22.d.).

   (b) From the MAISTRE LINE to the area M.31.d., M.32.c., S.1.b, S.2.a (Communication trenches for this reconnaissance are ARRAS RD, RATION TR and COOKER ALLEY).

2. The 12th Royal Fusiliers will be required to move after dark on the 8th April to the MAISTRE LINE near the ARRAS RD.

3. Acknowledge.

5/4/17

                                              Captain for

                          Brigade Major 17th Infantry Brigade.

Operation Orders. No. 100.

By Lt-Col. H.W.Compton,
Commanding 12th. Battalion Royal Fusiliers.   April 27th.1917.

The Battalion will move to MONTMORENCY BARRACKS, BETHUNE today the 27th. inst.

Route - LILLERS - CHOCQUES - BETHUNE.

Head of Column will be outside Battalion Headquarters facing East. Companies will parade ready to move off at 1.15 pm.

Dress - Full Marching Order. Caps will be worn.

Order of march - H.Q., Drums, Nos. 1,2,3 and 4 Companies. Transport will accompany battalion.

All men unfit to march will parade outside Orderly Room at 11.45 am. Dinners at 12 noon.

Blankets will be stacked in bundles of 10 outside the Church by 11.30 am.

Officers Mess Kit and valises will be stacked outside the Church by not later than 12 noon. A small box per Company can be placed outside H.Q. Mess by 12.45 pm. The Mess Cart will call at Battn. H.Q. at 12.45 for H.Q. Mess Kit, and will collect this also.

Lewis Guns will remain in the Lewis Gun Limbers. Lewis Gun handcarts will accompany transport, and will follow in rear of Battalion, and in front of the transport.

A guard of men unfit for marching, will be detailed to remain with blankets etc. The 2 lorries will call and collect these about 3 pm.

Arrangements are being made for conveying extra kit left in the BOMY area. These will be notified in due course.

Before marching off, Company Commanders will send in a certificate that all billets are left clean, and all claims satisfied.

Brigade Headquarters will be at 4 Rue de College, BETHUNE.

Whilst in Corps Support, the Battalion will be ready to move off at 6 hours notice.

Captain Blackford proceeded with the 4 C.Q.M.Sgts and A/Sgt Horne in advance at 10 am. to report to Brigade H.Q. and arrange Billets for H.Q. and Companies.

Rations will be issued to Company Cookers at 11.30 am. to day.

(sd) J.V.Wilson, Capt.,
A/Adjutant, 12th. Battalion Royal Fusiliers.

COPIES ISSUED AS FOLLOWS :-

1. C.O.   7. O.C. No. 1 Coy.
2. 2nd. in Command.   8. O.C. No. 2 Coy.
3. Adjutant.   9. O.C. No. 3 Coy.
4.) Capt. Blackford.   10. O.C. No. 4 Coy.
5.) Q.M.   11. R.S.M.
6. T.O.

Confidential. Vol 21

War Diary
of
12th Battalion Royal Fusiliers
for
May 1917.

VOL 21

June 3rd/1917   H.W. Compton Lt Col
                Commanding 12th Royal Fusiliers

Army Form C. 2118.

WAR DIARY
or
INTELLIGENCE SUMMARY

(Erase heading not required.)

VOL. 21.   12th Royal Fusiliers

Place	Date	Hour	Summary of Events and Information	Remarks and references to Appendices
ALLOUAGNE	1.5.17		Sunshine. 2nd Lt. D. Brown to England. Sick leave.	
"	2.5.17		Sunny. 10 hours Sunshine. No. 1 and 2 Companies used Rifle Range. 2Lt. W. J. Cooper, 2Lt. Ashlee and 2Lt. A. J. Watson returned from BOMY Training Area.	
"	3.5.17		No. 3 and 4 Companies used the Rifle Range. 2 Lt. to L. Moody returned from Hospital.	
"	4.5.17		The B.G.C. inspected the Battalion and expressed entire satisfaction at the good turn out of the Battalion. 2 O.R. joined the Battalion. 2Lt. J. Aickers. 2Lt. A. M. Rawbone proceeded	
"	5.5.17		Lt. J.A. Stewart, 2Lt. J.A. Stewart to BOMY for instruction in Tactical Exercises under a Staff Officer.	
"	6.5.17		Force between 1st R.J. and 12th R.J. The G.O.C. and B.G.C. were present. 12th R.J. won by 9 events to 5.	
"	7.5.17		Sunny fell during morning. 3 me in the afternoon. Lt. J.A. Stewart	
"	8.5.17		Rain fell during morning. 3 me in the afternoon. Lt. J.A. Stewart 2Lt. J. Aickern and 2Lt. A.M. Rawbone returned from Bomy.	

H. W. Lupton Lt-Col.
Commanding 12th Royal Fusiliers

Army Form C. 2118.

WAR DIARY
or
INTELLIGENCE SUMMARY
(Erase heading not required.)

12th Royal Irish Rifles

Instructions regarding War Diaries and Intelligence Summaries are contained in F. S. Regs., Part II. and the Staff Manual respectively. Title Pages will be prepared in manuscript.

Place	Date	Hour	Summary of Events and Information	Remarks and references to Appendices
ALLOUAGNE	9.5.17		2Lt L. Cohen returned from leave. 2Lt A. L. Rice struck off the strength of this Battalion and taken on the strength of the 17th L.T.M. Battery	
ST FLORIS	10.5.17		Battalion moved to ST. FLORIS. Battalion in Billets.	
"	11.5.17		The Surgical Commander inspected the Battalion and told the Colonel he had a Battalion that he might be proud of. The Battalion marched to HAZEBROUCK. Battalion in Billets. 1 O.R joined Battalion, 9 O.R transferred to the Base (unfit for Service at the front).	
HAZEBROUCK	12.5.17		Battalion marched to Steenvoorde. Battalion in Billets. 111 O.R joined Battalion.	
STEENVOORDE	13.5.17		Battalion attended Church Parade. Showers fell during afternoon. 88 O.R joined Battalion.	
"	14.5.17		2Lt R. N. Benjamin admitted to Hospital having been thrown from his horse.	
"	15.5.17		Battalion moved to ST LAURENT in Billets.	
ST LAURENT	16.5.17		7 O.R joined Battalion.	

H.W. Crispin Lt. Col.
Commanding 12th Royal Irish Rifles

Army Form C. 2118.

WAR DIARY
or
INTELLIGENCE SUMMARY

(Erase heading not required.)

12th Royal Fusiliers

Instructions regarding War Diaries and Intelligence Summaries are contained in F. S. Regs., Part II. and the Staff Manual respectively. Title Pages will be prepared in manuscript.

Place	Date	Hour	Summary of Events and Information	Remarks and references to Appendices
ST LAURENT	17.5.17		Rain fell during morning. Dryde during afternoon. No 1, 2 and 3 Coys. moved into new billets in the same area.	
"	18.5.17		Fine. Windy.	
"	19.5.17		Bn.H.Q. Battalion practised a Tactical Scheme. Lt. and Q.M. to. Lacey joined Battalion from 24th Div. H.Q.'s and was appointed Assistant Adjutant. 3 O.R. joined this Battalion.	
"	20.5.17		3 O.R. joined Battalion.	
"	21.5.17		2Lt R.C. Cruter, 2Lt. G. L. Davis returned from 1st Army School. Capt. Gibson proceeded to England on leave.	
"	22.5.17		Raining. She Colonel and 4 officers reconnoitred the trenches in the ST ELOI org. Major A.B. Buck-Ulland, Major R.C. Haynes 8th Bn. C.S. M. Dunken (R. mentioned on Sir D. Haig's despatch dated April 9th 1917)	
"	23.5.17		2 O.R. joined the Battalion	

H.W. Gough Lt. Col.
Commanding 12th Royal Fusiliers

Army Form C. 2118.

12th Royal Fusiliers

WAR DIARY
or
INTELLIGENCE SUMMARY

(Erase heading not required.)

Place	Date	Hour	Summary of Events and Information	Remarks and references to Appendices
ST LAURENT BLANGY	24.5.17		Windy. General H. Plumer Commanding 2nd army inspected the Battalion. 2 Lt. N. Bollason returned to the Battalion.	
"	25.5.17		Very hot. 2 Lt. W.S. Nattrass relinquished the appointment of Assistant Adjutant. 2 Lt. N. Bollason appointed Assistant Adjutant. 2 Lt. R.W. Fanning proceeded to England on leave. Lt. & Q.M. Stewart proceeded to PARIS on leave.	
"	26.5.17		Very warm. Battalion proceeded to Camp S. of POPERINGHE and bivouacked for the night. Capt & Adj. Gordon-Ingram the Battalion. Left. Lt. J. Watson relinquished the appointment of Acting Adjutant. 2 Lt. J.F. Deakin, 2 Lt. R.W. Goodwyn, 2 Lt. W.J. Watson proceeded to PARIS on leave.	
CAMP S. OF POPERINGHE	27.5.17		2 Lt. H.G. Putnam, 2 Lt. H.W. Hughes, 2 Lt. H.A. Bayley joined the Battalion. 1 O.R. joined Battalion.	
"	28.5.17		The Battalion relieved the 8th Middlesex Regiment in the DICKEBUSCH HUTS.	

H.W. Cooper Lt. Col.
Commanding 12th Royal Fusiliers

Army Form C. 2118.

12th Royal Inniskilling

WAR DIARY
or
INTELLIGENCE SUMMARY

(Erase heading not required.)

Place	Date	Hour	Summary of Events and Information	Remarks and references to Appendices
DICKEBUSCH HUTS.	29.5.17		June. The Battalion found large working parties. Trenches and approaches to trenches in the ST ELOI area thoroughly reconnoitred.	
	30.5.17		June. The Battalion found large working parties. Trenches and approaches to trenches in the ST ELOI area thoroughly reconnoitred.	
	31.5.17		June. Battalion moved to Camp S. of POPERINGHE. Wounded in action 1 O.R.	

H. W. Crispin Lt. Col.
Commanding 12th Royal Inniskilling

Operation Orders.

By Lt-Col. H.W.Compton,
Commanding 12th. Battalion Royal Fusiliers.   May 9th. 1917.

<u>Move</u>. The Battalion will move to ST FLORIS today at 1.30 pm. Route - HAUT RIEUX - LILLERS.

Companies will parade on road outside Orderly Room ready to march off at 1.25 pm. Head of column to be at Cross Roads by Battalion H.Q. Dress - Marching Order. Shrapnel helmets will be carried on packs. Officers will wear Sam Brownes and Box Respirators. Order of March, H.Q., Drums Nos. 3, 4, 1 and 2 Companies.

<u>Brigade H.Q.</u>   New Brigade H.Q. at St. VENANT.

<u>Dinners</u> will be at 12 noon.   Teas at St. FLORIS.

<u>Transport</u>. Transport will follow in rear of Battalion.   Blankets and all kits which cannot be carried will be stacked in Q.M. Stores by 11 am. Officers valises will be stacked ready for handing in Q.M. Stores by 11.15 am.   Lewis Gun Handcarts will follow Battalion and will march in front of transport.

<u>Mess Kit</u>. Officers Mess Kit will be stacked in Q.M. Stores with valises, but each Company will retain a small box which can go on Mess Cart. This will be placed outside Battn. H.Q. Mess not later than 1 pm. Mess Cart will call at the Battn. H.Q. Mess at 1.15 pm.

Maltese cart will move under arrangements to be made by the M.O.

Company Commanders will each detail 8 men to report to Lewis Gun Officer who will arrange for them to draw Hand Carts and be responsible for them on the line of march.

Company Commanders will render a certificate to the Orderly Room by 10.30 am. stating that all claims have been settled.

Company Commanders and 2nd. Lt. H.Martin will hand in to Orderly Room by 10.30 am a parade state.

Men considered likely to fall out on the line of march, will parade outside Orderly Room at 11 am. for inspection under M.O.

The Q.M. will hand in to Orderly Room by 12 noon a certificate from the Maire, stating that all claims have been settled.

<u>Billeting Party</u>. Capt. Blackford will take the 4 C.Q.M.Sgts. and A/Sgt Horne forward to St. FLORIS at 8.30 am.

A lorry will call at Church, ALLOUAGNE for blankets etc. *About 10 a.m.* The Orderly Officer will supervise the loading and see that it is not delayed more than half an hour.

All practice bombs will be handed over to the 46th. Div. and receipts obtained.

(sd) J.V.Wilson, Capt.,
A/Adjutant 12th. Battalion Royal Fusiliers.

<u>Copies issued as follows.</u>

1. C.O.
2. Second in Command.
3. O.C. No. 1 Coy.
4. O.C. No. 2 Coy.
5. O.C. No. 3 Coy.
6. O.C. No. 4 Coy.

7. M.O.
8. Q.M.
9. T.O.
10. Capt. Blackford.
11. 2nd. Lt. H.Martin.

Operation Orders No. 104.

By Lt.-Col. H.W. Compton,
Commanding 12th. Battalion Royal Fusiliers.   May 10th. 1917.

Move. The battalion will move to HAZEBROUCK tomorrow.

Route – St. VENANT – HAVERSKERQUE – MORBECQUE – HAZEBROUCK.

Parade. Companies will parade ready to move off at 8.15 am. Head of column to be outside Church near Orderly Room. Order of march – H.Q., Drums, Nos. 4, 1, 2 and 3 Coys, Lewis Gun Handcarts and Transport.

Meals. Breakfasts 6.30 am. Dinners at HAZEBROUCK.

Transport. Blankets will be stacked in bundles of 10 properly labelled, outside Q.M. Stores by 7 am. Officers Valises and Mess Kit by 7.30 am. Spare Kit not required on Transport by 8 am. Transport Officer will see that only Kit allowed on 1st line Transport is taken.
Mess Cart will collect H.Q. Mess Kit and 1 box per Company from H.Q. Mess at 8 am. and will follow in rear of battalion.
Mess Cart will move under arrangements to be made by M.O.
A lorry will call on Q.M. Stores to collect spare kit at 9 am.
The Adjutant will detail a guard of men unfit to march who will remain with lorry and assist to load. They will then accompany lorry.

Returns. Company Commanders, Q.M., T.O. and 2nd. Lt. Martin will hand in to Orderly Room not later than 7.30 am following returns :-
  1. Parade State.
  2. Certificate that all billets are left clean and all claims settled.
The Quartermaster will receive from the Maire a certificate that all claims have been settled.

Billeting Party. The following billeting party will proceed in advance, and take over billets from the Town Major at HAZEBROUCK. Capt Blackford the 4 C.Q.M. Sgts, A/Sgt Horne for H.Q. and a representative for Transport to be detailed by the Transport Officer. They will report to the Staff Captain at the Town Majors Office at 9.30 am. Capt. Blackford will arrange to obtain copies of the Town Orders.
Billeting Party will arrange to meet Battalion outside HAZEBROUCK.

Men unfit to march. All men considered unfit to march will parade outside Orderly Room at 6.30 am for inspection by Medical Officer.

Headquarters. Divisional Headquarters will remain at NORRENT FONTES. 17th. I.B. H.Q. move to HAZEBROUCK. Location and arrival of unit will at once be communicated to Brigade H.Q. by runner.

Dress. On arrival men will not move out of billets unless properly dressed. All ranks will wear belts – Sergeants sidearms.
Company Commanders will make themselves acquainted with the Town Orders, and see that they are strictly adhered to.

                              (sd) J.V. Wilson, Capt.,
                         A/Adjutant 12th. Battalion Royal Fusiliers.

VOLUME. No 22.

12ᵗʰ Royal Fusiliers.

War Diary for June 1917.

July 1ˢᵗ/1917   H. W. Hope Johnstone Lt Col
Commanding 12ᵗʰ Royal Fusiliers

Vol 22

Army Form C. 2118.

WAR DIARY or INTELLIGENCE SUMMARY

(Erase heading not required.)

VOL. 22

12th Royal Fusiliers.

Place	Date 1917	Hour	Summary of Events and Information	Remarks and references to Appendices
CAMP S. OF POPER-INGHE	June 1		Capt. A.J. Gibson admitted to Hospital. 30 O.R. joined Battn.	
"	2		Battalion proceeded to N. of STEENVOORDE. Battn. in Billets. 2Lt. S.G. BREALY joined Battalion.	
N. OF STEENVOORDE	3		Battalion practised attack scheme in conjunction with 1st R.F. 3RD R.B. 6th Buffs. 150 O.R. joined	
"	4		Very hot. Battn. moved to camp at HEKSKEN.	
HEKSKEN	5		Battalion.	
HEKSKEN	6		Battalion moved to ALBERTA CAMP, RENINGHAELST. REYNOLDS. B. awarded the Distinguished Conduct Medal 5156 C.S.M.	
ALBERTA CAMP RENINGHAELST	7		Battalion proceeded to trenches at Bund of the Etang de Dickebusch and arrived there at 1.10 am 3.10 am Huns. mines exploded barrages and intense bombardment simultaneously opened. 12.29 pm orders received from 17th I.B. to proceed to Gt.H.19. Battalion left Etang de Dickebusch for G.H.Q. advanced 2nd Line. 1 pm. Battalion left Etang de Dickebusch for G.H.Q. advanced 2nd Line.	

A.M. Mackenzie
Lt Col.
Commanding 12th Royal Fusiliers

Army Form C. 2118.

WAR DIARY
or
INTELLIGENCE SUMMARY

(Erase heading not required.)

12th Royal Fusiliers

Place	Date	Hour	Summary of Events and Information	Remarks and references to Appendices
	June 7	2 p.m.	The Battalion in position in the G.H.Q 2nd line (advanced).	
		3.10 p.m.	Second Zero. 24th Div. attack the Green Line.	
		5 p.m. (approx)	Battalion left G.H.Q advanced 2nd Line by Red-flagged tracks for our old front and support lines between ST ELOI and the BOIS CONFLUENT.	
		6.45 p.m.	Battalion in position in our old front and support lines between ST ELOI and the BOIS CONFLUENT.	
		at 6.45 p.m. (approx)	heavy barrage fire opened by our field artillery Battalion advanced to take over the positions vacated by 8th Buffs	
		11.40 p.m.	in the neighbourhood of the DAMMSTRASSE near HIELE FARM.	
			Casualties 4 O.R wounded.	
			During the night 7th/8th Battalion carried rations and supplies to the 1st. R.F. and the 3rd R.B in the front line.	
DAMMSTRASSE 8.		2 am (approx)	Battalion dug-in in position East and West of Dammstrasse. No. 3 & 4 Companies situated East. H.Q. situated in OASIS trench at point No 1 + 2 - West.	
			O. 8. b. 8. 4.	
		9 pm to 10 pm	Intense barrage opened by our field artillery.	

Sgd W Winterton Lt. Col.
Commanding 12th Royal Fusiliers

Army Form C. 2118.

WAR DIARY
or
INTELLIGENCE SUMMARY
(Erase heading not required.)

12th Royal Fusiliers

Place	Date 1917	Hour	Summary of Events and Information	Remarks and references to Appendices
DAMSTRASSE	June 8	10.30 p.m.	2Lt. A.H. LEE commanding no 4 Coy wounded by shell-fire. 2Lt. R.G. FONTEYN took over command of the Coy pending approval of Capt Ventress. Casualties 2 O.R. wounded 1 O.R. died from illness.	
"	9		Capt L. VENTRESS arrived about 5 p.m. and took over command of no 4 Coy. During the night 8th/9th and this day, Battalion carried rations etc as on the previous day.	
		9.30 p.m.	Battalion proceeded to relieve H.Q. and the left front line company of the 1st. R.F. and the Right company of the 9th Royal Sussex about the ROOZEBEEK Stream and BIG wood and ROSE wood.	
		9.45 p.m.	LT.COL. H.W. COMPTON, CAPT G.M.GORDON, CAPT J.V. WILSON and CAPT C.A. WHITTINGHAM (R.A.M.C) were wounded by a shell while approaching new Battn. H.Q. at O. 15. b. 2.7.	
		10 p.m.	Capt L. VENTRESS took over command of the Battalion pending arrival of Major E.L.NEYNOE. 2Lt. W.S. NATHAN assumed duties of Adjutant temporarily. 2Lt. R.G. Fonteyn assumed command of no 4 Coy.	
		12 M.N. (approx)	Capt G.M. GORDON and CAPT C.A. WHITTINGHAM (RAMC) died of wounds. Casualties 3 O.R. missing 1 O.R. wounded.	

Lymp Freeman Lt/Col
Commanding 12th Royal Fusiliers

Army Form C. 2118.

WAR DIARY
or
INTELLIGENCE SUMMARY
(Erase heading not required.)

12th Royal Fusiliers

Instructions regarding War Diaries and Intelligence Summaries are contained in F. S. Regs., Part II. and the Staff Manual respectively. Title Pages will be prepared in manuscript.

Place	Date 1917.	Hour	Summary of Events and Information	Remarks and references to Appendices
	June 10	1.30am	Our line fairly heavily bombarded.	
		2am	No. 1 Coy sent out patrols along ROOZEBEEK Stream, nothing to report.	
		3.30am	Major R. L. Reynolds arrived and took over Command of the Battalion. Capt. L. Ventress assumed duties of Second in Command.	
		6.30am	Capt. J. P. Lahiri arrived and assumed duties of M.O. until midday when relieved by Capt. Peux.	
			During the day, the area held by the battalion was subjected to a considerable amount of shelling.	
		9.35pm	Relief of Battalion by 9th Welsh Regiment commenced.	
		10.30pm	S.O.S. were sent up and very intense barrage opened up along the whole Corps front. The enemy shelled us very heavily retarding the relief.	
		12.30am	Relief complete. Battalion moved by platoons to MICMAC CAMP SOUTH. Casualties: 3 O.R. Killed 48 O.R. Wounded. 1 O.R. died of wounds.	
MICMAC CAMP SOUTH.	11		June. Major Iden-Johnstone 1st Royal Fusiliers took over temporarily Command of the Battalion. Capt. A. Silkmore 1st Royal Fusiliers took over duties of Adjutant temporarily. Capt L. H. Skeene R.A.M.C. joined Battalion and took over duties of M.O.	

Major Iden TMC Lt Col
Commanding 12th Royal Fusiliers.

Army Form C. 2118.

WAR DIARY
or
INTELLIGENCE SUMMARY

12th Royal Fusiliers

(Erase heading not required.)

Place	Date 1917	Hour	Summary of Events and Information	Remarks and references to Appendices
	June 11.		Funeral Service at RENINGHELST Military Cemetery of Capt G. M. Gordon and Capt G. A. Whittingham R.A.M.C. with full Military Honours. Service performed by D.A.C.G. 10th Corps and the Rev Kennedy C.F. attached 1st Royal Fusiliers. Capt G. M. Gordon was buried in Grave no 33 and Capt G. A. Whittingham was buried in Grave no 34. 2 Lt W. Hughes admitted to hospital. 1 O.R joined Battalion.	
MICMAC CAMP SOUTH.	12.		Battalion relieved the 13th D.L.I. in trenches at 11 pm. Relief very bad owing to enemy shelling. Relief completed by 3.30 am.	
IMPARTIAL TRENCH	13		1 man. Battalion occupied Assembly position ready to launch an attack on the Aug. onto north of Railway.	
"	14		BATTLE WOOD, in conjunction with the 8th Buffs on our right. 2Lt A.L.P TANNER & 2Lt H.J. CAMPBELL wounded in action. The Battalion attacked at 7.30 pm. in a two-company front, in conjunction with the 8th Buffs on our right. All objectives gained and the attack was highly successful. 28 Prisoners were captured together with a machine gun.	

M.M.P. Finn Lt Col
Commanding 12th Royal Fusiliers.

WAR DIARY or INTELLIGENCE SUMMARY

Army Form C. 2118.

Place	Date	Hour	Summary of Events and Information	Remarks and references to Appendices
12th Royal Fusiliers	14/6/19		At Zero hour the 1 Coy on the left and the 4 Coy on the right, formed up under barrage from IMPARTIAL TRENCH with No 3 Coy in close support (this company supplying mopping up parties for the two preceding companies) No 2 Company being in Reserve. All objectives were gained after very stiff fighting and a line of 6 outposts established and consolidated. Details of 3 fightings. On reaching line of outposts in RAILWAY EMBANKMENT the Right Company came under intense machine gun fire from the Right flank which made the advance very difficult. The Outposts were well garrisoned by the enemy who offered strong resistance to our advance. All the Outposts were found to be entrenched by our bombardment and in very good condition. It was only owing to the great determination and dash all shown by this Company that the objectives were gained. M. McPherston Lt Col Commanding 12 Royal Fusiliers	

WAR DIARY
or
INTELLIGENCE SUMMARY

Army Form C. 2118.

12th Royal Inniskilling

Place	Date	Hour	Summary of Events and Information	Remarks and references to Appendices
	14-6-1917		The first dugout encountered contained 20 of the enemy, including an Officer and a machine gun. The Platoon held off to clear this, did splendid work, the enemy offering strong resistance to the last, and nearly the whole of the Germans were killed in hand to hand fighting before the remainder finally surrendered. This machine gun was captured together with a few remaining Germans left alive, its Officer was badly wounded in the fighting and died during the night. The next dugout encountered, containing about 40 of the enemy, also held out to the last and the mopping up Platoon which cleared this had a very stiff fight. On the enemy turned out and made a determined fight in the open. My men however finished the dugout and very soon finished all opposition capturing about 20 of the enemy and killing the remainder severely. The Platoon lost rather severely.	

Commanding 12 Royal Inniskilling Lt Col

Army Form C. 2118.

WAR DIARY
or
INTELLIGENCE SUMMARY
(Erase heading not required.)

Place	Date	Hour	Summary of Events and Information	Remarks and references to Appendices
	14-6-17		12th Royal Fusiliers further had to send back for reinforcements before proceeding. Two Platoons were sent up from the Reserve Company. Their advance was made very difficult owing to the barrage of 5"9 which the enemy put up just in front of IMPARTIAL TRENCH. It was owing to good leadership and dash that these reinforcements were able to help the leading Company so effectively and thus enabled the final objective to be taken. The Left Company met with very little opposition and soon gained its objective, the only opposition being a post in the Ravine in IMPARTIAL AVENUE. This was soon cleared of the enemy. This Ravine was originally the objective of the Right Platoon of the Left Company. The Platoon Commander soon realized so further position for strongpoint	

Reinholt Drewitt Col.
Commanding 12 Royal Fusiliers

Army Form C. 2118.

WAR DIARY
or
INTELLIGENCE SUMMARY

(Erase heading not required.)

Instructions regarding War Diaries and Intelligence Summaries are contained in F. S. Regs., Part II. and the Staff Manual respectively. Title Pages will be prepared in manuscript.

Place	Date	Hour	Summary of Events and Information 12th Royal Fusiliers	Remarks and references to Appendices
	14-6-1917		would be in another Ravine which ran along the road 100 yards further South, he determined to push his men forward and take advantage of the further observation this he did under very heavy machine gun fire. Consolidation. The work of consolidation was carried on under the greatest difficulty, the enemy kept up an intense machine gun fire from OAF KEEP and from the North side of the RAILWAY EMBANKMENT, in spite of this my men dug in and consolidated the fire strong points so obtained, in full view of the enemy and before darkness the post were in a position to offer a determined resistance to any counter attack the enemy might make.	

M?? ??? ??? Lt Col
Commanding 12th Royal Fusiliers

WAR DIARY
INTELLIGENCE SUMMARY

Army Form C. 2118.

Place: 12th Royal Fusiliers

Date	Hour	Summary of Events and Information	Remarks and references to Appendices
14-6-1917		**Artillery**	
		The enemy's artillery after Zero hour put up a strong barrage of 5:9" on IMPARTIAL TRENCH and Support Trenches, the barrage was very unpleasant owing to it being flanking fire; in fact, during the whole operations and during the work of consolidation "this fire was kept up by the enemy", it appeared to be coming from the direction of HOOGE.	
		Machine Gun Fire	
		The enemy kept up continuous fire from OAF KEEP and North of the RAILWAY EMBANKMENT, these machine guns were in concrete dugouts and untouched by the bombardment, and naturally made our advance difficult.	

Commanding 12 Royal Fusiliers Lt Col

Army Form C. 2118.

WAR DIARY
or
INTELLIGENCE SUMMARY
(Erase heading not required.)

Summary of Events and Information 12th Royal Inniskilling

Place	Date	Hour	Summary of Events and Information	Remarks and references to Appendices
	14.6.1917		**Runners** The work of the Runners during the operations was exceptionally good. They had to take risks which they did, in performance of their duties, and all messages brought back from the line of outposts had to be carried in full view of the enemy. It was owing to them good work that information was sent through 40 minutes after Zero, and from that time to the time of relief the Runners did splendid work. **Signals** One hour after the objective was taken telephone communication was established with the left front Company. A line was also run out to the Right front Company, but was continually being broken by enemy artillery fire and thus	

M. J. F. Murphy Lt Col
Commanding 12 Royal Inniskillings

Army Form C. 2118.

WAR DIARY
or
INTELLIGENCE SUMMARY

(Erase heading not required.)

Place	Date	Hour	Summary of Events and Information	Remarks and references to Appendices
	14.6.1917		12th Royal Fusiliers forward direct communication. A forward relay post was established in IMPARTIAL TRENCH and direct communication with Battalion HQrs was kept up throughout the operation in spite of the enemy heavy fire kept up by the enemy in this quarter. A Lamp which proved of enormous value was located from the forward post to Battalion HQrs and thence on to the Brigade Station this helped wonderfully in the work of the Stretcher Bearers and the Runners and also enabled walking cases to get down without guides. 2LT W.S. NATHAN, 2LT H.A. BAYLY Killed in action. CAPTAIN H.D. DOUDNEY, 2LT D.M. RAWBONE, 2LT E.L. BESCOBY, 2LT F.J. DEAKIN, Wounded in Action. 2LT G.E. DAVIS Wounded in Action and remained at duty. 8 O.R. Killed in action. 84 O.R. Wounded in action. Mammott Freestone Lt Col. Commanding 12 Royal Fusiliers	

Army Form C. 2118.

WAR DIARY
or
INTELLIGENCE SUMMARY
(Erase heading not required.)

Instructions regarding War Diaries and Intelligence Summaries are contained in F. S. Regs., Part II. and the Staff Manual respectively. Title Pages will be prepared in manuscript.

Place	Date	Hour	Summary of Events and Information	Remarks and references to Appendices
	15-6-1917		Sirs The Battalion was relieved by the 7 Northants and proceeded to MICMAC CAMP SOUTH. 2Lt D BROWN admitted to Hospital. Following was dated 15th June was received from the 2nd Army Commander:— "Second Army Commander wishes to congratulate all concerned on the success of last night operations which have succeeded in substantially advancing our whole line. The operations reflect much credit on all concerned" Following was from 17th I.B was received:— The G.O.C. 24th Division congratulates you on your success tonight"	12th Royal Fusiliers
			4 O.R. Killed in Action 5 O.R. Missing in Action 31 O.R. Wounded in Action	
MICMAC CAMP 6-1917 SOUTH			Sirs The Battalion returned to MICMAC CAMP "SOUTH" after being relieved by the 1st Northants Relief completed by 6 am Battalion rested during the day 1 O.R. Joined Battalion	

Commanding 12 Royal Fusiliers Lt Col

2449 Wt. W14957/M90 750,000 1/16 J.B.C. & A. Forms/C.2118/12.

Army Form C. 2118.

WAR DIARY
or
INTELLIGENCE SUMMARY
(Erase heading not required.)

12th Royal Irish Rifles

Place	Date	Hour	Summary of Events and Information	Remarks and references to Appendices
MICMAC CAMP SOUTH	17/6/1916		The G.O.C. 24th Division saw the Battalion at 9-30 a.m. congratulated it on its success and thanked everyone concerned. Battalion warned that the 17 I.B. will relieve the 72 I.B. on the night 19/20. B. Battalion to relieve the 8th Bn. The Queens.	
"	18/6/1916		Divine service shown in the afternoon. 6 Officers reconnoitre line. Impossible to get up in daylight on account of shelling. Major E. L. Heyman goes on and reconnoitred. 2 Lieut E. L. Beacaby died of wounds at 2-30 a.m. at no 3 C.C.S. (POPERINGHE) Buried at 2 p.m. 6 Officers of B. Battalion were present.	
"	19/6/1916		Bn. Battalion moved from MICMAC CAMP SOUTH at 8-45 p.m. in order to relieve 8th Batt. "Queens" in HILL 60 Area (Squared (.30 b, c, d.) Battalion in Support, distributed as follows — Battn HQr + no 1 Coy "CRAB CRAWL TUNNEL" no 2 Coy "RUDKIN HOUSE" no 3 Coy "MOUNT SORRELL TUNNEL" no 4 Coy "METROPOLITAN TUNNEL" Commanding 12th Royal Irish [signature] Lt Col	

Army Form C. 2118.

WAR DIARY
or
INTELLIGENCE SUMMARY
(Erase heading not required.)

12th Royal Fusiliers

Place	Date	Hour	Summary of Events and Information	Remarks and references to Appendices
	19/6/1917		The relief was not completed until 4-30 am 20/6/17 owing to heavy guns and shelling, especially in Back Areas. All Coys and Battn. H.Q. suffered casualties viz.— 4. O.R. Killed in Action. Captain L.V. Ventress admitted to Hospital. 15. O.R. Wounded in Action. Lt M.S. Cox proceeded on leave.	
"HILL 60 AREA"	20/6/1917		Fine Day fairly quiet. Enemy shells the Back Areas during the evening. Transport unable to bring up Rations to DUMP and rations had to be dumped at MANOR FARM. Wounded in Action 5 O.R.	
	21/6/1917		Fine. Enemy shelled heavily about 12.30 am. At 1-15 am a heavy shell (probably a 8" shell) got a direct hit, completely smashing and blocking up Gallery about 4 yards from Battn. HQ. Lt M. Marten partially buried. Explosion caused Gas Captain L.M. Skene (R.A.M.C.) and Lieut M Marten and After a Similar conveniences and were badly gassed Oxygen was used to bring them round. All three Officers went down to the 10. C.C.S. Remainder of Battalion of Battalion &	

J M Kington Lt Col
Commanding 12th Royal Fusiliers

Army Form C. 2118.

WAR DIARY
or
INTELLIGENCE SUMMARY.
(Erase heading not required.)

Instructions regarding War Diaries and Intelligence Summaries are contained in F. S. Regs., Part II. and the Staff Manual respectively. Title pages will be prepared in manuscript.

Place	Date	Hour	Summary of Events and Information	Remarks and references to Appendices
			12th Royal Fusiliers	
	21-6-1917		Major H.M. Hope-Johnstone M.C., Major E.L. Hughes, and 2Lt R.G. Intsyn slightly gassed but remained at duty. Batt. HQ moved to No 1 Coy HQ. Gas helmets found ineffective against the C.O. of shell. Enemy attitude more active. 2 O.R. in Cellizon wounded at 5 P.M. from Trench Mortar fire and took over the duties of acting Adjutant vice Captain A. Tomkins. 2nd Lt E.L. Moody proceeded on course of Instruction at Second Army Central School. 2.O.R. gained Battn. 2.O.R. Wounded in action	
	22-6-1917		Company Commanders reconnoitred Front Line held by 1st ROYAL FUSILIERS. Enemy shelled Front Line for 3 hours. Calm in Back Areas.	

Hopeol Hughes Lt Col
Commanding 12th Royal Fusiliers

A.5834 Wt. W4973/M687 750,000 8/16 D. D. & L. Ltd. Forms/C.2118/13.

Army Form C. 2118.

WAR DIARY
or
INTELLIGENCE SUMMARY
(Erase heading not required.)

Instructions regarding War Diaries and Intelligence Summaries are contained in F. S. Regs., Part II. and the Staff Manual respectively. Title Pages will be prepared in manuscript.

Place	Date	Hour	Summary of Events and Information	Remarks and references to Appendices
			12th Royal Fusiliers	
	22/6/1917		3 men dug by Battalion when knocked in by enemy shelling. 8449 L/Sgt C. Price, 9745 Pt J Griffiths awarded the Military Medal. 2 Lt W.J. Cooper returned from Hospital. Captain D L Blackford to be Aide-de-Camp to G.O.C. 24th Division. Lieut C.V. Matthew proceeded on leave.	
	23/6/1917		Four of the Company's officers saw Company Commander at 2 a.m. to discuss new dispositions and all went over the new line. The line was in a very bad condition and extremely muddy (Knee deep). At 10 P.M. the Battalion moved up to relieve the 1st ROYAL FUSILIERS in the front line. Enemy shelling fairly active during night. During the day a working party by No 2 Coy were recovering entrenching work to the Stone Causeway from RE's. found by a shell fire amongst them causing the following casualties. Killed 5 O.R. Wounded 14 O.R.	

D. M. M. Franklin Lt Col
Commanding 12th Royal Fusiliers

Army Form C. 2118.

WAR DIARY
or
INTELLIGENCE SUMMARY.
(Erase heading not required.)

Instructions regarding War Diaries and Intelligence Summaries are contained in F.S. Regs., Part II. and the Staff Manual respectively. Title pages will be prepared in manuscript.

Place	Date	Hour	Summary of Events and Information	Remarks and references to Appendices
			12th Royal Fusiliers	
	24/6/1917		Sine. Relief was completed by 2-35 a.m. was satisfactorily with no casualties. At 5 a.m. Lieut J D Stewart went to Hospital sick. Coy Commanders sent in their dispositions. There were sent to the Brigade. Day passed quiet. Enemy quiet. Ration arrived about 12 midnight. Enemy artillery more active. 2 Lt A. Hope went down to Transport lines. Wounded in Action 9. O.R. Major H M Hope Johnstone in C hosted to the Battn and to be intemporary Command. 285 L/Sgt J S Smith, 1462 Pte H Etheriolge, 4093 Pte A P Lavemon, 5381 Pte W Trafford are awarded the Military Medal.	
	25/6/1917		Sine. At 12-15 am enemy heavily Bombarded our Right Front and Left Front Coys (no 2 + 4 Coys) with everything up to 5.9's. This continued until 2-15 a.m. when normal state was resumed. No 2 Coy were cut off as soon as the Minnisfournitur Lt Col Commanding 12 Royal Fusiliers	

A 5834 Wt. W4973/M687 750,000 8/16 D. D. & L. Ltd. Forms/C.2118/13.

Army Form C. 2118.

WAR DIARY
or
INTELLIGENCE SUMMARY.
(Erase heading not required.)

Instructions regarding War Diaries and Intelligence Summaries are contained in F. S. Regs., Part II. and the Staff Manual respectively. Title pages will be prepared in manuscript.

Place	Date	Hour	Summary of Events and Information	Remarks and references to Appendices
			12th Royal Fusiliers	
"	25/6/1917		Bombardment started but communication was kept up the whole time with the remaining 3 Companies. "C" 2 Coy Front heavily shelled between 10 am and 1.30 pm. Retaliation asked for and results satisfactory. Major E.L. Huyton and 2nd Lt W.J. Cooper arrived up from transport lines at 1 pm. Night very calm. Wounded in action 2 O.R.	
"	26/6/1917		Fine. The Battalion will be relieved on night of June 27/28 by 9th York and Lancs Regt. Day calm. 2 Lt R.G. J'onteyn left the trenches to proceed on leave to England. Captain A. Lindsay and Captain L.A. Thorne (R.A.M.C.) returned from hospital and M. Mathew went to the Base.	

M Mepemston Lt Col
Commanding 12th Royal Fusiliers

Army Form C. 2118.

WAR DIARY
or
INTELLIGENCE SUMMARY.

(Erase heading not required.)

Instructions regarding War Diaries and Intelligence Summaries are contained in F. S. Regs., Part II. and the Staff Manual respectively. Title pages will be prepared in manuscript.

Summary of Events and Information 12th Royal Fusiliers

Place	Date	Hour	Summary of Events and Information	Remarks and references to Appendices
	27-6-19.		Fine. The Battalion was relieved by 9th Battn York and Lancs. Officers and NCOs arrived to reconnoitre and remained until relief was completed. Wounded in Action 4 O.R. Missing 3 O.R.	
MICMAC CAMP SOUTH	28/6/1917		Wt. Relief complete by 6am. Battn. returned to MICMAC CAMP SOUTH. No 2 Coy remaining at DICKEBUSCH for baths, the remainder of the Battn. had baths during the day. Clean change of clothing issued to the Battalion	
"	29/6/1917		Wt. 2 Lt W. J. Cooper, 2 Lt N. C. Putman, 2 Lt S. G. Bready and 3 NCOs attended to a demonstration of a "Company in the attack" at 2nd Army Musketry School. The Battn. left MICMAC CAMP SOUTH at 1-30 pm and marched to RENINGHELST SIDING at 2-30 pm and entrained for LUMBRES at 5 pm arriving at LUMBRES at 7 pm.	

Mmofpungtus Lt Col
Commanding 12th Royal Fusiliers

Army Form C. 2118.

WAR DIARY
or
INTELLIGENCE SUMMARY.
(Erase heading not required.)

Summary of Events and Information 12th Royal Fusiliers

Place	Date	Hour	Summary of Events and Information	Remarks and references to Appendices
	29/6/1917		After detraining the Battn were encamped just outside the station for the night. 6 officers being billetted in LUMBRES. 2 Lt R.G. Fortnum proceeded on leave.	
LUMBRES	30/6/1917		Very Wet. Battn left camp at 8-30 a.m and marched to HENNEVEUX. The men marched splendidly, no one falling out. Arrived at HENNEVEUX at 1-30 p.m. 9 m Billets. Billets very good.	

Reynolds Fummens Lt Col
Commanding 12th Royal Fusiliers

"A" Form.
MESSAGES AND SIGNALS.

Army Form C.2121.
(In pads of 100.)

TO: All Coys.

Sender's Number: A.S.20
Day of Month: 13

AAA

Batt<u>n</u> Operations Orders.
To be read in conjunction with
Brigade Operation Orders issued to Coys
this morning

(1) At ZERO hour Nos. 1 & 4 Coys will
get into position under barrage
which will be 150 yds in advance
of assembly position.

(2) No 3 Coy taking up position in
IMPARTIAL TRENCH.

(3) No 2 Coy being ready to move if
required in DURHAM LANE

(4) No 4 Coy will attack on right
their objective being RAILWAY
EMBANKMENT on RIGHT at O6A 30.80
their left resting on RAVINE at 9 36 c 85.40

"A" Form.
MESSAGES AND SIGNALS.

Prefix........ Code......... m	Word.	Charge.	This message is on a/c of:	Recd. at .... m
Office of Origin and Service Instructions.				
	Sent		..........Service.	Date...........
No 2	At........m.			From ....
	To........			
	By........		(Signature of "Franking Officer.")	By........

TO

| Sender's Number. | Day of Month. | In reply to Number. | AAA |

(5) No 1 Coy. will attack on left. their ~~RIGHT~~ resting on RAVINE at 9 36 c 85.40 and their left resting on road at 9 36 B 20.30

(6) No 3 Coy will act as "Moppers Up" to the two attacking Coys

(7) No 2 Coy will be in RESERVE at DURHAM LANE

(8) <u>Coy DISPOSITIONS</u>
The two attacking Coys will form up under the barrage in front of present line at ZERO hour. as per attached sketch, with two platoons of No 3 Coy as "Moppers Up" at 25 yds in rear

(9) The duties of "Moppers Up" will be to clear line of dugouts in RAILWAY

From
Place
Time

The above may be forwarded as now corrected. (Z)

Censor. Signature of Addressor or person authorised to telegraph in his nam

* This line should be erased if not required.

"A" Form.
MESSAGES AND SIGNALS.

Army Form C. 2121.
(In pads of 100.)

3/

EMBANKMENT. Coy Com of No 3 Coy will detail one section at least to advance over the EMBANKMENT to clear those dugouts & prevent surprise from the right flank, the other platoon of "Moppers Up" clearing any dugouts during advance & making their main objective the RAVINE at J 36 c 80.40 to J 36 D 00.50

(10) The 3rd platoons of Nos 1 & 4 Coys will follow Moppers Up 50yds distance together with Coy HdQrs in line of Sections & will act as the mobile reserve under the immediate orders of the Coy Commanders.

(11) The 3rd platoon & Coy Hd Qrs of No 3 Coy

"A" Form.
MESSAGES AND SIGNALS.

Army Form C. 2121.
(In pads of 100.)

will follow 50 yds in rear of the 3rd platoons of the leading Coys & will be ready to fill gaps or supply extra "Moppers Up" if occasion demands

They will take up a central position to support any gaps that may occur in the centre of attacking line

(12) Men when extended will extend to not less than four paces & will maintain this distance throughout

(13) The 72nd Brigade will work in conjunction on our immediate left & will send out strong patrol to occupy knoll at J36B30.30.

"A" Form.
MESSAGES AND SIGNALS.
Army Form C. 2121.
(In pads of 100.)

5/

(14) Coys will move into assembly positions to night 13th No 2 Coy moving direct to DURHAM LANE & not as arranged this afternoon

(15) Coys will notify Battn HQ Qrs when they are in position by runner

(16) Battn Head Qrs will remain the same unless notified otherwise

(17) Advanced relay stations for stretcher bearers will be at dugouts where No 2 Coy is at present also one advanced station in present FRONT LINE Tapes will be put out tonight overland to guide stretcher bearers to relay stations

(18) ZERO time will be notified later

"A" Form.
MESSAGES AND SIGNALS.

Army Form C. 2121.
(In pads of 100.)

(10) Coys will reorganise as soon as possible after the objective has been gained

A. Simkins Capt.
act adjt.
12th Royal Fusiliers.

Confidential

12th BATTALION ROYAL FUSILIERS.

WAR DIARY FOR MONTH OF JULY 1917. VOLUME No. 23.

August 5th/1917.   ......A Junkins...... Captain.

                    Commanding 12th Battalion Royal Fusiliers.

VOLUME 23

Army Form C. 2118.

WAR DIARY
or
INTELLIGENCE SUMMARY.

13th Royal Fusiliers

(Erase heading not required.)

Instructions regarding War Diaries and Intelligence Summaries are contained in F.S. Regs., Part II. and the Staff Manual respectively. Title pages will be prepared in manuscript.

Place	Date	Hour	Summary of Events and Information	Remarks and references to Appendices
HENNEVEUX	July 1/17		Fine. Battalion attended Church Parade. B.O. Conference held at 17th Bde H.Q. — Report rendered on Operation of 14–6–17. Lt C. Every proceeded on leave.	
Do	July 2/17		Fine.	
Do	July 3/17		Fine. Major A.B. Birk-Clemens rejoined Battalion. 80 O.R. joined Battalion. Lt H.J. Cox returned from leave.	
Do	July 4/17		Wet day. — 3 O.R. joined Battn. Lt C.V. Wakenbach returned from leave.	
Do	July 5/17		Fine. — Major A.B. Birk-Clemens attached to 12th Royal Fusiliers.	

J. Leinken Capt.
Commanding 13th Royal Fusiliers

WAR DIARY
or
INTELLIGENCE SUMMARY.
(Erase heading not required.)

15th Royal Fusiliers

Army Form C. 2118.

Place	Date	Hour	Summary of Events and Information	Remarks and references to Appendices
HENNEVEUX	July 6/17		Fine. Battalion route march. Proceed on leave. 2nd Lt A.F. Walton proceeded on leave.	
"	July 7/17		Fine. Lt Col H.N. Compton died of wounds received in action at No 20 General hospital Camiers.	
"	July 8/17		Raining during morning, fine afternoon. Capt A. Sinkin proceeded on leave.	
"	July 9/17		Fine. Capt H.D. Soudrey returned from hospital.	
"	July 10/17		Fine. 96 O.R. joined Battn	
"	July 11/17		Fine. The Battalion practised "the attack". Capt R.E. Fordyn returned from leave.	
"	July 12/17		Fine. Battalion practised "the attack". Major Steward proceeded on leave.	
"	July 13/17		Fine. Battalion attended the 17th Bn Sports.	

J. Steadman Capt
Commanding 15th Royal Fusiliers

Army Form C. 2118.

WAR DIARY
or
INTELLIGENCE SUMMARY.
(Erase heading not required.)

13th Royal Fusiliers

Place	Date	Hour	Summary of Events and Information	Remarks and references to Appendices
HENNEVEUX	July 14/17		2nd Lt. N.P. Nussbaum - 2nd Lt. A.G. Bank - 2nd Lt. R. Cornish - 2nd Lt. C.G. Rose joined this Batln. 2nd Lt. Crecy returned from leave.	
"	July 15/17		2nd Lt. D. Brown returned from Hospital.	
"	July 16/17		Fine	
"	July 17/17		Fine. The Battalion marched to billets at FROMENTEL. 2nd Lt. W.F. Walton returned from leave.	
FROMENTEL	July 18/17		Battalion marched to billets at DAVENGHEM.	
DAVENGHEM	July 19/17		Fine - having. Battalion marched to billets at RENESCURE. Capt. D.G. Gibson returned from Hospital.	

J. Leushin Capt.
Commanding
13th Royal Fusiliers

Army Form C. 2118.

WAR DIARY
or
INTELLIGENCE SUMMARY

(Erase heading not required.)

Instructions regarding War Diaries and Intelligence Summaries are contained in F. S. Regs., Part II. and the Staff Manual respectively. Title Pages will be prepared in manuscript.

Place	Date	Hour	Summary of Events and Information	Remarks and references to Appendices
RENESCURE	July 20/17		Fine. Battalion marches to billets at CAESTRE. Capt. A. Sinkins returned from leave.	
CAESTRE	July 21/17		Fine. Battalion marched to EECKE. (in billets) 2nd Lt R.C. Cutler from leave.	
EECKE	July 22/17		Fine. Battalion marched to STEENVOORDE. E. in billets 31 O.R. joined Battalion	
STEENVOORDE E.	July 23/17		Fine. 2nd Lt A.L. Banks proceeded on Stokes Rigue Mortar Course. 30 O.R. joined Battalion	
Do	July 24/17		Fine. The Battalion addressed by the Archbishop of York. 2nd Lt Z.F. Cooper returned from 2nd Army Shipping School.	
Do	Aug 25/17		Rain. Free during the day. Battalion marched to MICMAC SOUTH CAMP. 2nd Lt J.D. Stewart returned from leave. Capt. F.C. Say - 2nd Lt K.B. Santana - 2nd Lt T. Kerry - 2nd Lt J. Tripp joined Battalion	

A Sinkin Capt
Commanding 12th Batt. Royal
Fusiliers

Army Form C. 2118.

WAR DIARY
or
INTELLIGENCE SUMMARY   13th Royal Fusiliers.
(Erase heading not required.)

Instructions regarding War Diaries and Intelligence Summaries are contained in F. S. Regs., Part II. and the Staff Manual respectively. Title Pages will be prepared in manuscript.

Place	Date	Hour	Summary of Events and Information	Remarks and references to Appendices
MICMAC CAMP	May 26/17		Fine. Officers reconnoitred Approaches & Assembly positions. 2nd Lt. R.C. Cull wounded in action. Lt. Winall returned from hospital. Lt. 2/13 Home-Gree re-joined Battn from X/34th Batt. M Bty.	
"	May 27/17		Fine. Officers reconnoitred Approaches & Assembly positions	
"	May 28/17		Fine. 2nd Lt. F.K. Moody returned from 4th Army Centre School.	
"	May 29/17		Fine.	
"	May 30/17		Fine. The Battalion moved from Micmac Camp at 9-1 a.m. in 5 parties. Nos 1, 2, 3 & 4 Coys to G.H.Q. 2nd line H.Q's with Q.M. Transport party were reported to be all in at 10-45 a.m. 1 Officer & O.R per Coy moved up to Assembly position at 3-30 p.m. The Battn moved from G.H.Q. 2nd line up to Assembly positions at 5-30 p.m. in the following order. H.Q., Nos 1 2 3 & 4 Coys. 5 minutes interval between each platoon. Assembly postions	

H. Trenchie Capt.
Commanding 13th Royal Fusiliers

WAR DIARY
or
INTELLIGENCE SUMMARY.
(Erase heading not required.)

Army Form C. 2118.

Place	Date	Hour	Summary of Events and Information	Remarks and references to Appendices
	July 30/17		Continued	
			No 1 Coy in RUM TRENCH	
			No 2 Coy in HALIFAX ST. (left)	
			No 3 Coy. in HALIFAX ST. (right)	
			No 4 Coy in THE BELT.	
			Batt. Headquarters were in Canada St Tunnels.	
			2/Lt. Putman & 2 O.R.s were killed &	
			2/Lt Campbell & 3 O.R's were wounded	
			in assembly positions	
	July 31/17		And. Orders were received at 1.45 PM that zero hour	
			would be at 3.50 AM	
			At 3 am Coys No 1, 2 & 3 Coys were formed up to go	
			over the top & they too in Artillery formation No 4 Coy	
			being in reserve also No 1 Coy on the same formation.	
			No 1 Coy on left, No 2 Coy in centre, & No 3 Coy on right	
			No 1 Coys left resting on ST PETERS ST & No 3 Coys right	
			over Hunhin Crapet	
			Commanding 12th RI Fusiliers	

Reference trench map sheet
M.C.1 Zy Belgrave & NE 3 (part of)
[illegible] of N.W. & N.E. 3 (part of)

Army Form C. 2118.

WAR DIARY
or
INTELLIGENCE SUMMARY.
(Erase heading not required.)

Instructions regarding War Diaries and Intelligence Summaries are contained in F. S. Regs., Part II. and the Staff Manual respectively. Title pages will be prepared in manuscript.

Place	Date	Hour	Summary of Events and Information	Remarks and references to Appendices
	July 31/7		Continued. Infantry on "F" Sap. Company remained in three sections until Zero plus 5 minutes, when they advanced to the attack. 2/Lt. B. Gill was killed at the jumping off place. The Batt. advanced about 200 yds in rear of 1st Royal Fus, to JEFFERY AVENUE where they were held up by Stony points at J19 c 90.10, + in WOOD between T25 b 05.80 + T19 c 90.15 + Stony point at T25 t 15.91. (Capt. H.J. Gose, Capt. H.B. Burtt, 2/Lt. E.G. Chu (mortally) 2/Lt. C. Day, + Capt. J.C. Day, 2/Lts were killed. 2/Lt. Ashcroft severely wounded from these points. Lt Martin was killed.)	
		4.10 A.M.	Signallers advanced at zero + 10 with two (2) MLG Stoney points were cleared by the 1st Royal Fusiliers + the 12th Royal Fusiliers passed through the 1st Royal Fusiliers at 4.15 A.M. in JEFFERY AVENUE + were again held up by Stony points at T19 a 2.6, who being now observed by no. 3 Coy + then advanced continued through BODMIN COPSE to the front.	

Kirschner Capt.
Commanding 12th Royal Fus
Fusiliers

Army Form C. 2118.

WAR DIARY
or
INTELLIGENCE SUMMARY.
(Erase heading not required.)

Instructions regarding War Diaries and Intelligence Summaries are contained in F.S. Regs., Part II. and the Staff Manual respectively. Title pages will be prepared in manuscript.

Place	Date	Hour	Summary of Events and Information	Remarks and references to Appendices
	July 3/17		*Continued* left of the O.P.S.E. but moving met a strong enemy field of wire & heavy machine gun & rifle fire. He was detained from T19 b 57.00 T19 d 45 85 thence to T19 d 50.57. T19 d 23.33 the south west of B.9. in O.P.S.E. where we held in touch of T19 d 6.05. (Lt. N.P. Musbaum was wounded there) Company pushed on right towards ... ... T19 d 37 40 No 3 Coy in C from T19 a 60.41 to T19 b 47 64. No 4 Coy in Right from T19 a 77 34 South East edge of B19 in O.P.S.E. The Batt. was in touch with the 2nd Yorks. Regt. on left & the 3rd Rifle Brigade on Right.	

A. Nisbet Captn.
Commanding 12th Royal Fusiliers

WAR DIARY or INTELLIGENCE SUMMARY

Army Form C. 2118.

Place	Date	Hour	Summary of Events and Information	Remarks and references to Appendices
[In trenches]	July 3/17	5.30 a.m.	Batt No 20 arrived from CANADA ST TUNNELS at 5-30 a.m. to T.19 c 50.12. Capt Colonel N.H. M'C Johnston was mortally wounded on the way up. Capt. A. Simpkins took over command of the Battalion. Batt Hdqrs moved again owing to heavy artillery fire & was finally established at T.25 a 10.90 in THIRD RESERVE. This position was about 60 x [?] & was situated in a deep [?] [?] & was almost in [?] my Company position. Several messages had been sent from [?] to remainder to Batt Hd Qrs but none [?] [?] to the [?] men having been killed or wounded. It started to rain heavily about 10.15 PM until the Batt remained [?] [?] [?] [?] [?] [?] [?] [?] [?] [?]	
		1.0 PM	At about 11- 0 AM, two companies of the 2nd Yorks Regt [?] [?] [?]	

A. Leviston Capt.
Commanding 12th Royal Fusiliers.

Army Form C. 2118.

WAR DIARY
or
INTELLIGENCE SUMMARY.
(Erase heading not required.)

Place	Date	Hour	Summary of Events and Information	Remarks and references to Appendices
	July 31st	Continued	came up & relieved the 12th Royal Fusiliers in front line. This portion of the trench was handed over, & the 12th Royal Fusiliers moved back to CANADA ST TUNNELS, but the Bn remained in the same position. ILIAD RESERVE. Casualties O.R. Killed 30 O.R. Wounded 130.	

K. Tomkinson Capt.
Commanding 12th Royal Fusiliers

REPORT ON ATTACK ON JULY 31st. 1917.

The Battalion moved from G.H.Q. 2nd Line at 5-30 p.m. and reached the following Assembly Positions by 11 p.m.
All ranks had a hot meal before moving up.
No.1 Company in RUM TRENCH.
No.2 Company in HALIFAX ST.(Left)
No.3 Company in HALIFAX ST.(Right)
No. 4 Company BELT.

At 3 a.m. the leading Companies Nos. 1.2 and 3, moved up in 200 yds in rear of the 1st Royal Fusiliers in artillery formation. No.4 Company in 20 yds in rear of No.1 Company.

The Battalion was distributed as follows :-
No. 1 Company.......LEFT.........Capt.H.J.Cox.
No.2 Company.......CENTRE.......Capt.D.G.Gibson.
No. 3 Company.......RIGHT........Capt.H.D.Doudney.
No. 4 Company.....200 yds in rear of No.1 Company.....
                                    ....Capt.R.G.Fonteyn.
Battalion H.Qrs in CANADA ST. TUNNELS.
No.1 Coy's Left rested on ST PETERS ST. and No.3 Coy's RIGHT on "F" Sap.

The night was very dark and the weather had been very wet, making the ground sodden, and difficult for troops to advance over.
Whilst in Assembly Positions, 2nd Lt.H.G.PATMAN was Killed and 2nd Lt.J.CAMPBELL was Wounded.

At ZERO plus 5 minutes, leading Companies advanced to the Attack following 200 yds in rear of the 1st Royal Fusiliers to JEFFEREY AVENUE.
2nd Lt.C.Gill was Killed when just over our parapet.
The Battalion were held up by strong points situated at J.19.c.90.10, in Wood between J.25.b.95.80 and J.19.c.90.65 and strong point at J.25.b.05.90. This caused the leading Companies to swerve to the left thereby getting out of the Brigade Area.
Capt.H.J.Cox, Capt.H.D.Doudney, Lt.A.J.Waley, Lt.H.Martin, 2nd Lt.W.F.Cooper were Killed, and Capt.F.C.Day, 2nd Lt.E.Cohen were Wounded just about here.
These strong points were cleared by the 1st, Royal Fusiliers.
The 12th Royal Fusiliers passed through the the 1st Royal Fusiliers about 4 a.m. in JEFFEREY AVENUE, but were again held up by strong points J.19.d.20.60. This point was cleared up by a party of No.3 Coy under 2nd Lt.G.F.Watson and the advance continued through BODMIN COPSE to the forward edge of the COPSE. The Companies could not advance farther owing to the heavy Machine Gun and Rifle fire, so halted and started to consolidate and the line was established from J.19.d.56.90 - J.19.d.48.85 thence to J.19.d.50.67 - J.19.d.40.33 the S.E. edge of BODMIN COPSE. A block in communication trench was built at J.19.d.60.95.
Whilst consolidating this line Companies had several casualties and were worried very much by snipers and machine guns, making it extraordinarly difficult for the men to dig, the ground was also very sodden and the trench had about a foot of water when finished.
Capt.D.G.Gibson took over command of Nos 1.2 and 3 Companies.
Companies were very mixed up in this trench, but Capt.Gibson reorganised and the final dispositions were :-
Nos 1 and 2 Coys.........on the Left, from J.19.d.56.90 to J.19.d.50.76.
No. 3 Coy......Centre, from J.19.d.50.76 to J.19.d.47.54.
No. 4 Coy (under Capt.R.G.Fonteyn)...on Right from J.19.d.47.54 to J.19.d.40.33.
On the Left No. 1 Company were in touch with 2nd Yorks and No.4 Company on the Right in touch with the 3rd Rifle Brigade.
Battn H.Qrs moved from CANADA ST TUNNELS at 5-30 a.m. to J.19.c.50.15.
Colonel H.M.Hope-Johnstone was mortally Wounded on the way up.
Capt.A.Simkins took over command of the Battalion.
BattnH.Qrs again moved owing to very heavy shell fire and

continued :-

were finally established at J.25.a.60.90 in ILIAD RESERVE.
Battalion H.Qrs was subjected to very heavy bombardment being situated in a dangerous place.
The Commanding Officer not having received any messages stating what was happening, 2nd Lt.A.Hope went up to the Front Line and found the exact dispositions of the line being consolidated.

REMARKS.

1. The greatest difficulty was experienced in getting back back information, nearly all Company and Battalion having become casualties.

2. Great difficulty was experienced in evacuating Wounded owing to bad state of ground.

3. Suggest that a few more stretchers should be taken forward and dumped at a known place in the forward area.

4. Rifle Grenades proved invaluable against enemy strong points.

CASUALTIES.

OFFICERS KILLED
Capt.H.J.COX.
Capt.H.D.Doudney.
Lieut.A.J.Waley.
Lieut.H.Martin.
2nd Lt. E. Cohen.
2nd Lt.W.F.Cooper.
2nd Lt. C. Gill.
2nd Lt. H.G.Patman.

WOUNDED IN ACTION

Lt.Col.H.M.Hope-Johnstone. (since Died of Wounds)
Capt.F.C.Day.
Lt.N.P.Nussbaum.
2nd Lt. J. Campbell.

OTHER RANKS.

KILLED............... 43
WOUNDED..............166
MISSING.............. 60

TOTAL ALL RANKS......KILLED   52
           ......WOUNDED 169
           ......MISSING 60
                         ___
                         281
                         ___

PRISONERS OF WAR

---- N I L ----

RECOMMENDATIONS.
I would like to bring to notice the names of the Officers, Warrant Officers and N.C.Os for distinguished conduct in the field.

RECOMMENDATIONS.

OFFICERS.

2nd Lt. A.F. Watson.
2nd Lt. A. Hope.
A/Capt. D.G. Gibson.
2nd Lt. S.G. Brealy.
Capt. A.L.H. Skene (R.A.M.C.)

OTHER RANKS.

8464	C.S.M.	J.R. Turner.
3648	L/C	P.E. Richardson.
1462	Pte	H. Etheridge.
3526	Sgt	W. Essex.
52247	Cpl	D.D. Blyth.
11869	Cpl	F.J. Porter.
3317	L/C	P. Oberman.
21464	L/C	F. Severn.
9373	Pte	J.D. Wadsworth.
14097	L/C	J. Birch.
9470	Pte	F. Ainsworth.

....
Commanding 12th, Batt. ROYAL FUSILIERS.

To Headquarters,
	17th Infantry Brigade.

	Herewith list of Officers and Other Ranks I should like to bring before you for Distinguished Conduct during recent operations.
	I should like them put forward in the following order :-

1. 2nd Lt. A.F.Watson.
2. 2nd Lt. A.Hope
3. Act/Capt.D.G.Gibson.
4. Capt.A.L.H.Skene. (R.A.M.C.)
5. 2nd Lt S.G.Brealy.

1. 8464 C.S.M. J.R. Turner.   D.C.M.
2. 3648 L/C P.E. Richardson.   "
3. 1462 Pte H.Etheridge.   "

1. 3526 Sgt W.Essex.   M.M.
2. 52247 Cpl D.D.Blyth.   "
3. 11869 Cpl F.J.Porter.   "
4. 3317 L/C P. Oberman.   "
5. 21464 L/C F. Severn.   "
6. 9373 Pte J.D.Wadsworth.   "
7. 14097 L/C J. Birch.   "
8. 9470 Pte F. Ainsworth.   "

	Commanding 12th.Batt. Royal Fusiliers.

12th BATTALION ROYAL FUSILIERS.   COPY NO. 8

Operation Order No 1 by Lt.Col.H.M.HOPE-JOHNSTONE. M.C.

24/7/17

Map Ref. 1/10,000
ZILLEBEKE TRENCH MAP
Sector 28 N.W. 4 and
N.E. 3 (part of).

1. 17th Infantry Brigade will be the left Attacking Brigade of the 24th Division. The 21st Infantry Brigade (30th Division) will be on the left and the 73rd Infantry Brigade on the right of the 17th Infantry Brigade.

2. The attack of the 17th Infantry Brigade will be carried out on a one Battalion front.
    (a) First Attacking Battalion (1st Royal Fusiliers) will take the first objective (BLUE LINE) from J.20.c.20.50 to J.25.b.75.47.
    (b) Second Attacking Battalion (12th Battalion Royal Fusiliers) will take the second objective (BLACK LINE) from JAVA TRENCH at J.26.a.45.55 along JAVA TRENCH to J.20.d.0.0, thence to tramline at J.20.d.60.40 then running north to J.20.b.60.05.
    (c) Third Attacking Battalion (3rd Rifle Brigade) will take the third objective (GREEN LINE) from J.20.d.0.0. to J.20.d.60.05 to J.21.c.20.30 TOWER HAMLETS to J.21.a.55.50.
    (d) 8th Buffs will be in reserve.

   From ZERO hour plus 83 minutes the Battalion on the left of No 1 Company will be the 19th MANCHESTERS, and the Battalion on the right of No 3 Company will be the 2nd LEINSTERS.

   The attack will commence about dawn.

3. The Battalion will attack on a three Company front with one Company in Battalion support as follows:-
    No 1 Company on the left whose objective is 200 yards in advance of JAR TRENCH from J.20.b.60.05 to tramline at J.20.d.60.40 inclusive (about 350 yards).
    No 2 Company in the centre whose objective on the left is 200 yards in advance of JAR TRENCH from tramline at J.20.d.60.40 to JAVA TRENCH at J.20.d.0.0. thence to J.20.c.95.10, (about 300 yards).
    No 3 Company on the right whose objective is JAVA TRENCH from a point 100 yards N.E. of where JAVA AVENUE meets JAVA TRENCH at J.20.c.95.10 thence to J.26.a.45.50 inclusive (about 350 yards). This Company will cover the advance of the 3rd RIFLE BRIGADE and protect the right flank.
    No 4 Company in support will move about 200 yards in rear of No 1 Company. This Company will establish strong points at:-
        (a) J.26.a.50.80. (S.P.NO 10).
        (b) J.20.c.80.40. (S.P.NO 8).
    This Company will also be prepared to assist the 21st Infantry Brigade on the left.

- 2 -

4. Each of the three assaulting Companies will attack with two Platoons in the front line forming one wave of two lines with one Platoon in support forming the second wave in one line who will act as moppers up. Moppers up to pay special attention to JAR TRENCH.

5. Up to as near the BLACK LINE as possible the advance will be carried out in artillery formation.

6. (a) On Y/Z night the Battalion will occupy assembly positions near RUDKIN HOUSE:-
    No 1 Company RUM TRENCH.
    No 2 Company HALIFAX STREET.
    No 3 Company HALIFAX STREET.
    No 4 Company THE BELT;
Battalion Headquarters will be in CANADA STREET TUNNEL.
(b) Companies will advance from assembly positions in artillery formation in sufficient time for the assaulting Companies to arrive 200 yards in rear of the 1st Royal Fusiliers about HEDGE STREET TUNNEL by ZERO hour. No 3 Company's right resting on "F" Sap at I.30.b.00.35. No 1 Company's left resting on ST.PETER'S STREET at I.24.d.50.10.
1st ROYAL FUSILIERS dispositions:-
    A right   C left.
    B   D
(c) At ZERO plus 5 minutes Companies will advance keeping about 200 yards in rear of the 1st ROYAL FUSILIERS.
(d) At ZERO hour plus 60 minutes Nos 1, 2, & 3 Companies will pass through the 1st ROYAL FUSILIERS on the BLUE LINE (500 yards front) and form up under the protective barrage which will be 200 yards in front of the BLUE LINE.
No 4 Company will be 200 yards in rear of No 1 Company.
(e) At ZERO plus 83 minutes the protective barrage lifts and advances at the rate of 100 yards in 4 minutes to the line J.26.a.45.55 along JAVA TRENCH to J.20.d.0.0. then to J.20.d.80.40. to J.20.b.60.05 (BLACK LINE 900 yards front).
No 4 Company will commence making strong points at:-
    J.26.a.30.75
    J.20.c.80.40.
Leading Platoons in advancing will keep as close to the barrage as possible and take care to conform to the movements of the barrage on their own particular front.
(f) At ZERO plus 1 hour 47 minutes the barrage lifts off the BLACK LINE and forms a protective barrage 200 yards in front and Nos 1, 2, & 3 Companies assault and capture the BLACK LINE which they will consolidate. Companies will push forward fighting patrols to mop up dug outs and cover consolidation of BLACK LINE. No 3 Company will proceed with the work of consolidating strong points at:-
    J.26.a.80.95. (S.P.No 9).
    J.26.a.45.55. (S.P.NO 11).
(g) At ZERO plus 6 hours 28 minutes when the 3rd RIFLE BRIGADE pass through the 12th ROYAL FUSILIERS to capture the GREEN LINE No 2 Company will take up positions in JAR TRENCH getting ready for further operations.

(h) No 4 Company will remain in strong points at:-
    J.26.a.30.15 and
    J.29.c.80.40.
and be prepared for a further operation.

(h) contd. O.C. NO 4 Company will send out patrols as far as possible to discover the best means of advance to the RED LINE between the points J.27.a.30.50 and J.27.a.40.75. The patrols will move between the tramlines running from:- J.20.d.65.35 to J.27.a.40.75 and the communication trench running from J.20.d.10.10 to J.27.a.05.55 inclusive.

7. Disposition of the Battalion after the capture of the GREEN LINE:-

    No 1 Company consolidating the line J.20.b.60.05 J.20.d.60.40.
    No 2 Company in JAR TRENCH from J.20.c.90.05 tp J.20.d.15.30.
    No 3 Company in JAVA TRENCH in depth from J.26.a.45.50 to J.20.c.90.05.
    No 4 Company about strong points J.26.a.50.80 (strong point No 10) and J.20.c.80.40 (strong point No 2).

8. MACHINE GUNS. Two machine guns in JAVA TRENCH with No 3 Company one machine gun at strong point J.20.c.80.40.

SECRET. M259 24T.

12th.(S) Battalion THE ROYAL FUSILIERS.

17/24

W A R   D I A R Y.   No. 24

for the Month of AUGUST 1917.

M Collisson 2/Lt.
................Asst. Adjt. for Lt.Colonel.
1/8/17.   Commanding 12th.Batt. Royal Fusiliers.

Army Form C. 2118.

WAR DIARY
or
INTELLIGENCE SUMMARY.

(Erase heading not required.)

13th Royal Fusiliers

Place	Date	Hour	Summary of Events and Information	Remarks and references to Appendices
Canada St Tunnel	Aug 1st /17	WET	The Batt were in Canada St Tunnel. Batt Hd Qrs were in the forward area. Major J.H.S. Lementen East Surrey Regt took over Command of the Batt. at 5.30 a.m. Batt Hd Qrs moved into Canada St Tunnels about 11.0 p.m.	
to	Aug 2nd /17	WET	Batt moved from Canada St Tunnel to Ecluse tunnel about 4.0 P.M.	
Ecluse tunnel	Aug 3rd /17	WET	Batt moved back to Micmac Camp in the evening about 6.15 P.M. having spent the day in Ecluse Tunnel.	

J. R. Day
13th Bn Royal Fusiliers
Commanding 13th Bn Royal Fusiliers

Army Form C. 2118.

WAR DIARY
or
INTELLIGENCE SUMMARY.
(Erase heading not required.)

1st Bn Royal Fusiliers

Place	Date	Hour	Summary of Events and Information	Remarks and references to Appendices
Murcar Camp	Aug 4/17		Unsettled weather brightened up towards evening but had Baths. Spent remainder of day in cleaning up.	
do	Aug 5/17		Fair. Companies paraded under Company arrangements. Major T.H.S. Swanston left to command the 9th East Surrey Regt. Capt. R. Sanghin took over command of the Batt. 105 O.R. joined the Batt.	
do	Aug 6/17		Fine. Major E.L. Wynne left the Batt. & proceeded to England. Companies were at the disposal of Company Commanders.	

J.R. Day, Major.
Comndg 1st Bn Royal Fusiliers

Army Form C. 2118.

13th Bn Royal Fusiliers

WAR DIARY
or
INTELLIGENCE SUMMARY.
(Erase heading not required.)

Instructions regarding War Diaries and Intelligence Summaries are contained in F.S. Regs., Part II. and the Staff Manual respectively. Title pages will be prepared in manuscript.

Place	Date	Hour	Summary of Events and Information	Remarks and references to Appendices
Larch Wood Tunnels	7/8/17	11.45	H.Q. Coy. & Nos 3 & 4 Coy. stored at LARCH WOOD Tunnels 12 midnight.	
			No 1. Coy. at CANADA ST Tunnels	
			No 2 Coy at ECLUSE TRENCH	
			Situation Normal Wind S.W.	
	8/8/17	9.10 A.M	Enemy shelled CANADA ST intermittently from 11 A.M to 4 P.M.	
			Heavy enemy barrage on CANADA ST ARMAGH WOOD & few Ca. shells were also fired on AIRCRAFT	
	9/8/17	5 A.M.	Our planes in considerable numbers over enemy lines. Few enterprise active.	
		10 P.M	Wireless on LARCH WOOD we. Lot. (unused) 1.0.R.	
	10/8/17	10.30 AM	Enemy shelled I.30 Central & I.29 C. Central? PRINCE'S WOOD & CANNON ST	
		11 A.M	7 Minenwerfer fell on E. of CHELUVELT	
		8.30 PM	Enemy shelled I.29 & I.C. & LARCH WOOD	
	10/8/17	2 A.M	Rifle at I.29.B.	

J.R. Daye Col
Commg 13th Bn R.M.R.

Army Form C. 2118.

WAR DIARY
or
INTELLIGENCE SUMMARY.   1st Bn. Royal Fusiliers

(Erase heading not required.)

Instructions regarding War Diaries and Intelligence Summaries are contained in F.S. Regs., Part II. and the Staff Manual respectively. Title pages will be prepared in manuscript.

Place	Date	Hour	Summary of Events and Information	Remarks and references to Appendices
LARCH WOOD TUNNELS	9/8/17	4.20am	Intense bombardment commenced by our Artillery all along our front.	
		5.5.am	Our barrage ceased on victors	
		6.Am	Our aeroplanes very active 9 in considerable numbers wind S.E.	
	10/8/17	7am	Enemy shelled following pts. J.29.a.0.9 to Channel Coppice.	
		8.30pm	Heavy gunfire on our front S.O.S. sent up by enemy & ourselves. Gunfire became normal	
		10.P.M.	AIRCRAFT.	
		8.00P.M.	Enemy aeroplane brought down in flames & fell by Cerio Crawl Tunnel. Wind S.W.	
			During our occupation of the line from the night of the 9/8 Aug to the afternoon of the 11th Aug when we were relieved by the Middlesex Regt. our casualties were - Wounded 1 O.R. We were relieved by 13th Middlesex Regt. & proceeded to Micmac Camp.	
MICMAC CAMP	11/8/17 12/8/17 13/8/17			

J.R.D. cofl Col.
Commanding 1st Bn R.F.

Army Form C. 2118.

WAR DIARY
or
INTELLIGENCE SUMMARY.
(Erase heading not required.)

12th Bn Royal Fusiliers

Place	Date	Hour	Summary of Events and Information	Remarks and references to Appendices
M/C M/C STH CAMP.	14/6/17	—	Showery. 2/Lt F.R. Day joined Batt'n from 8 & 9/th Norfolks and assumed command. Major J.C. Hartley joined Batt'n from 8 R.F. Kings Liverpools attached (England) assumed the duties of 2nd i/c.	
"	15/8/17	—	Showery. Batt'n moved to Camp "H" Dickebusch.	
CAMP H DICKIE BUSCH	16/8/17	—	FINE.	
do	17/8/17	—	FINE.	
do	18/8/17	—	FINE.	
do	19/8/17	—	FINE. Batt'n relieved 9th East Surreys in centre subsection. Bn H.Q. were at CANADA St Tunnels. Nos 2 & 3 Coys in FRONT LINE. No 1 in SUPPORT. No 4 in reserve. 2nd Lt. H.J. Keele } joined Battalion from R.R.F. 2nd Lt. W.H. Dean }	

J.R. Day Lt. Col.
Commanding 12th Bn R. Fus.

A.5834 Wt. W4972/M687 750,000 8/16 D.D. & L. Ltd. Forms/C.2118/13.

Army Form C. 2118.

WAR DIARY
or
INTELLIGENCE SUMMARY.

(Erase heading not required.)

12 R. Bn. Royal Fusiliers

Place	Date	Hour	Summary of Events and Information	Remarks and references to Appendices
CANADA ST TUNNELS	19/8/17	11 A.M. & 6 P.M.	Artillery. Enemy shells HERMAN WOOD & CANADA ST (rear) Sunken Battery positions. 1 N.C.O. & 1 O.R. wounded.	
	20/8/17		Patrols. 12 midnight & 4 A.M. (20/8/17) shelling increased considerably.	
		3.10 A.M.	Ga. & Fahrenheim shells were fired on our front line.	
			Men rested lay at LOWER STAR POST at J.25.D.2.9. Ref. sheet 28.	
	do		Several were seen at dawn & appears to be wiring. They were dispersed by L.G. fire.	
			Enemy planes very bad over our line at 7.30 P.M.	
			Spanish Line. Enemy quiet. at 10.30 & 1.30 A.M. we shelled with gas enemy's LOWER STAR POST	
	21/8/17	10.25 A.M.	Enemy artillery active. shot over heavy barrage on our support line.	
		7 P.M.	Enemy planes fraysed own behind our line in France.	
		11.30 P.M.	2 Lewis gunners wounded at J.25.B.30.45. & seen at J.25.B.20.15. dispersed by L.G. fire.	
			2/Lt E. MEATON wounded (remained duty).	
	22/8/17	1.12 A.M.	2 Lewis Lewis that direction gave reminder up at CHATEAU POST gave useful	
			information. Rely relayed to 17th R.I.R.	
			Enemy observed in wood at J.31.B.90.80. Sniper were seen at LOWER STAR POST working.	
		7 P.M.	3 Scouts seen advancing from J.31.D.90.88.	
			2 O.R. wounded.	

Signed
D.D.Kelly Col.
Commdg. 12th R.F.R. Fus.

Army Form C. 2118.

WAR DIARY
or
INTELLIGENCE SUMMARY.
(Erase heading not required.)

12th Bn Bryce Tralies

Place	Date	Hour	Summary of Events and Information	Remarks and references to Appendices
CANADA 55 TUNNELS	24/4/17	7 p.m.	On our left we heard an intense barrage. The enemy replied by shelling our support line for half an hour.	
		7.30 p.m.	Enemy flying very low over our lines. Enemy movement nil.	
		8.30 p.m.	Enemy sent up S.O.S. along his front. Front barrage on our support line. Enemy patrols & Lewis Gun seen.	
do	25/4/17	6.30 a.m.	18 Huns seen walking from a support at J.25.D.35.90. & a M.G emplacement at J.25.D.35.95. They were fired on by our artillery. We were unable to tell if any were hit. We saw no man in trenches our lines, but they were seen once.	
do		7 a.m.	2nd Bn LEINSTERS relieved our Bn. & we proceeded to MICMAC CAMP next of R.DAY LT. Col. featuring appearance in DeGoytte. 1.N.Cs killed & two wounded (Capt. D.E. Echo admitted to hospital)	
MICMAC CAMP 5TH	26/4/17		Heavy	
do	27/4/17		Fine	

J R Daly Lt Col
Comdg 12/24 R. Ins.

Army Form C. 2118.

WAR DIARY
or
INTELLIGENCE SUMMARY.

(Erase heading not required.)

1/1 Bn Royal Fusiliers

Instructions regarding War Diaries and Intelligence Summaries are contained in F. S. Regs., Part II. and the Staff Manual respectively. Title pages will be prepared in manuscript.

Place	Date	Hour	Summary of Events and Information	Remarks and references to Appendices
Micmac Camp 5TH	26/8/17		Line working. 2nd Lt. W.J. FRANCIS, 2nd Lt. B. PIZARO, 2nd Lt. R.J. ANGOOD, 2nd Lt. W.J. GROOT, 2nd Lt. L.G. PENSTON 2nd Lt. C.E. ANKETELL joined Batty.	
-do-	27/8/17		Heavy rain. Batty. moved to Camp H. DICKEBUSCH. Tents over accommodation from 9th R.W. Kents.	
Dickebusch Camp H	28/8/17		Rest & Refit	
-do-	29/8/17		Heavy demonstration raid by PT & B.F. Instructed S.Army as DICKEBUSCH attended by all officers. Platoon Sgts. Lay (Gunmaker) reconnected the centre sub-sector	
-do-	30/8/17		Rest	
-do-	31/8/17		Showery. Battalion relieves the 9th Bn East Surreys in the line (Centre Inf-Section) Details move to Micmac in Rele details Camp.	

J.R. Day
Lt Col
Comm'g 1/1 Bn R.Fus.

CONFIDENTIAL.

To Headquarters,
    17th. Infantry Brigade.

25 T

W A R   D I A R Y   No. 25.

For the Month of SEPTEMBER 1917.

                    MCollison 2/Lt
                    Asst. Adjt.
              ....for Lt. Colonel.
1/10/17.   Commanding 12th. Battalion Royal Fusiliers.

Army Form C. 2118.

WAR DIARY
or
INTELLIGENCE SUMMARY.
(Erase heading not required.)

12th Royal Fusiliers

Place	Date	Hour	Summary of Events and Information	Remarks and references to Appendices
31/8/17 CANNON ST TUNNELS	31/8/17		Bn relieved the 9 R.E. Surreys on the morning of the 31st by which Bn was complete by 9.30 a.m. Nos 1 & 4 Coys in front line. No 3 in Support & No 2 in Cannon St Tunnels with H.Qrs. Enemy artillery active during morning. Enemy aircraft very active.	Enclosed in last month's diary
	1/9/17 2.30am		2 patrols went out & movements of working parties were observed. Artillery active all day. Enemy L.T.M. shelled our front line posts. Enemy fire very low at dawn & dusk.	
	2/9/17		Enemy shelled our support line & Cannon St Tunnels. Our artillery retaliated. Enemy trench mortars again active on front line.	
		3 p.m.	Movement. Enemy seen moving about at J.28.0.75.35.	
ASCOT CAMP	2/9/17		Bn was relieved by 1/6 Cheshires & proceed to Ascot Camp (Westoutre)	
H C N N C	3/9/17		Bn moved to Micmac Camp.	
	4/9/17		Line	

J.R. D al, Lt Col
12th Bn Royal Fusiliers

Commdg 12th Bn Royal Fusiliers.

Army Form C. 2118.

WAR DIARY
or
INTELLIGENCE SUMMARY.
(Erase heading not required.)

12th Bn. Royal Fusiliers

January 12th Bn Royal Fusiliers

Place	Date	Hour	Summary of Events and Information	Remarks and references to Appendices
MIC MAC CAMP	5/9/17		Weather fine. Coys paraded under Coy arrangements.	
"	6/9/17	11.30 PM	Weather fine. Regt. Guard Mount. attended the Bn. in the afternoon. the Regimental team played the 13th R.F. a Soccer 7 a side 3-2.	
I Camp Dickebusch	7/9/17		Bn. Moved to I Camp Dickebusch	
"	8/9/17		Weather fine.	
"	9/9/17		Coy Commanders & I.O. reconnoitred the line weather fine.	
"	10/9/17		Weather fine.	
"	11/9/17		Line Regt. moved up to the trenches STIRLING CASTLE area & relieved the 1st NORTH STAFFORDS. Details moved back to Details Camp Chippawa. A few Gas shells fell round no 2 Coys area during the night. otherwise very quiet.	
[Trenches]	12/9/17		Line. Everything quiet. A lot of it E shell around No 3 Coys area. the MENIN RD. several 6.A. flew low over our lines 2nd Lt S. G. Bedford joined up. Lewis. LT T.D. STEWART wounded on a 3 in Ewart Gap Knee. MILLS m.m.	

Army Form C. 2118.

WAR DIARY
or
INTELLIGENCE SUMMARY.
(Erase heading not required.)

12th Bn Royal Fusiliers

Place	Date	Hour	Summary of Events and Information	Remarks and references to Appendices
Hersche	13/9/17		Line. Eno shells fired on No 2 Coy & BHQrs, 6 Artillery active all day. 6 O.R's joined the Bat from 175th Tunnelling Coy	
	14/9/17		Dull. Small attack delivered by the 9th London Rgt on our left, unsuccessful, lot of shells N.E. fell round Batt H.Qrs. No 3 Coy shelled fairly heavily, also the ruined Rd. 2/Lt N Osborn returned from leave.	
	15/9/17		Line. Enemy T.Ms & trench Mortars were fired on us at 8am & 10-0 a.m. on ? Mm, very reply heavily, heavily the 2 Coy area was shelled heavily. Batt relieved in the trenches by [ ] for the a & moved back to Camp F Dickybush. (relief was completed & message-sent to Bde at time). Extract from London Gazette 15/9/17. Lt. E.F. Watterhad R.M. Pegasus to be Temporary Capt. Capt R.E. Fonteyn	

J.R. Day
Capt
Comdg 12th Bn Royal Fusiliers

Army Form C. 2118.

WAR DIARY
or
INTELLIGENCE SUMMARY.
(Erase heading not required.)

12th Bn. Royal Fusiliers

Place	Date	Hour	Summary of Events and Information	Remarks and references to Appendices
Camp D Dehuysch	16/9/17		Fine. Batt. entrained at ALLEBAST CORNER for OUTERSTEENE and situated N. of the village. Batt. played Brigade at Base Ball and won by three runs.	
Outersteene	17/9/17		Dull. Brigade Commanders met all Batt. Commanders at Bing Hqrs at 12-30 P.M. 2/Lt R. Keay returned from a course. Lt. B. Home-Gall returned from a course. Capt. A. Eastwood promoted Capt. A. Eastwood, Capt. L. H. Shear-Revine in a months time to England. Capt. L. H. Shear-Revine promised to go to England before appointment Lt. H. C. Martin Rawie joined the Batt.	
"	18/9/17		Fine. Conference held at Bing Hqrs at 11 am for O.C. Batts.	
Nort Bar Bailleul Ypres	19/9/17		Fine. Batt. inspected by G.O.C. 24th Division. 2/Lt Ja... Evans – Denrath – 2/Lt. R Cornish admitted to hospital.	

J. R. Bail. Lt Col.
Commandg 12th Royal Fusiliers

Army Form C. 2118.

WAR DIARY
OF
INTELLIGENCE SUMMARY.

(Erase heading not required.)

12th Bn Royal Fusiliers

Instructions regarding War Diaries and Intelligence Summaries are contained in F.S. Regs., Part II. and the Staff Manual respectively. Title pages will be prepared in manuscript.

Place	Date	Hour	Summary of Events and Information	Remarks and references to Appendices
Ostrohove	1/9/17		Advance party left for new area.	
	2/9/17		Train 3/4 R.F. Cutter period the Batt. arriving there about 5.30 pm. Batt entrained for Bapaume detraining at Lauentier about 9 miles 3RD SEPTEMBER from YPRES) & proceeded to Dickie march to TALBOT WOOD Camp. (near YPRES) 3RD	
Talbot Wood Camp			arriving from Ostrohove. 2/Lt 2 Small arms school LE TOUQUET & the troops returned from same course.	
	23/9/17		21464 2/Lt Smith & Coy awarded the Military medal.	
	27/9/17		2/Lt Ledman 6.4.8 pm.	
	28/9/17		Fine. 4 OR's attached to 17th M.G. Coy.	
	29/9/17		Fine. Batt marched to Haut Allaines, came under the orders of 13.9.G 73rd Brigade. 4 OR attd 17th LTM Battery. Very hot. Batt moved to VADENCOURT by lorries & occupied Trenches, dugouts & tents marked by 11th Suffolks.	

(signed) J.R. Guy Major
Commg 12th Royal Fusiliers

Army Form C. 2118.

WAR DIARY
or
INTELLIGENCE SUMMARY.
(Erase heading not required.)

12th Bn. Royal Fusiliers

Place	Date	Hour	Summary of Events and Information	Remarks and references to Appendices
Halloy-[?]	25/9/17		Transport Lines & 2nd storms etc. remained at Bryas. 2/Lt W.J. Francis & 2-6-O.R. attached to 104 Fd Coy R.E.	
"	26/9/17		Fine	
"	27/9/17		Still 2/Lt W.T. [?] & 15 O.R. attached to 3rd Corps Tramway Coy. Draft of 6 O.R. joined the Batt.	
"	28/9/17		2/Lt G.D. Quinn & 2/Lt G.T. Boyer joint the Batt. & temporarily attached to No 4 Coy. 2/Lt S.G. Bewley M.C. rejd from leave.	
"	29/9/17		Fine. 2/Lt E.J. Moody joined Batt from Hospital. 2/Lt H.B. Randall proceeded to Corps Reinforcement Camp.	

J.R. Duffus Maj
Comdg 12th Royal Fusiliers

Army Form C. 2118.

WAR DIARY
or
INTELLIGENCE SUMMARY.

(Erase heading not required.)

13th Bn. Royal Fusiliers

Instructions regarding War Diaries and Intelligence
Summaries are contained in F. S. Regs., Part II.
and the Staff Manual respectively. Title pages
will be prepared in manuscript.

Place	Date	Hour	Summary of Events and Information	Remarks and references to Appendices
Tadmor	13/9/17		Draft of 2 O.R. joined the Bat. Capt a.f. Dalan. M.P. proceeded to III Corps Army Sig. School.	

J.R. Day 76ee
Lt. Royal Fusiliers
Commdg 13. Royal Fusiliers.

To Headquarters,
   17th. Infantry Brigade.

CONFIDENTIAL

W A R   D I A R Y. No. 26.

For the Month of O C T O B E R. 1917.

                              M Collisson 2/Lt.
                              Asst. Adjt.
          .... for Lt. Colonel.
2/11/17. Commanding 12th. Bn. Royal Fusiliers.

WAR DIARY or INTELLIGENCE SUMMARY

Army Form C. 2118.

12th Bn. Royal Fusiliers

Place	Date	Hour	Summary of Events and Information	Remarks and references to Appendices
Tadcaster	Oct 1st 1917		Day Commanders to arrange for daily instruction for Coops. recon. 822a of map reading & compass reading.	App 05
6?	Oct 2		Capt R.O.L. Ogilvie (Paris) joined the Batt. returned	
R.T.A.			Lt Marten J.C. R.A.M.C. despatched to England under 9 M.S. authority	
	Oct 3		2/Lt S.A. Mears-Donald rejoined Batt from Hospital	
			2/Lt J.C. Mitchell reported reported Batt. from 2 Army Grenade & T.M. school.	
	Oct 4		Lt Col J.R. Doy proceeded on leave to England. Major J.C. Hardy Lt Col YR Reg? Assumed command of the Batt. during absence of Lt Col J.R. Doy.	
			2/Lt C.O. & D.R.S. named pending the following officers to ???? the Rank of Lieutenant.	
			2/Lt E. Hughes M.C. 2/Lt ? ast ??? M.C. 2/Lt F.J. Deakin 2/Lt R.C. Butters 12th Bn. Royal Fusiliers.	

Commg 12th Bn. Royal Fusiliers

Army Form C. 2118.

WAR DIARY
or
INTELLIGENCE SUMMARY.
(Erase heading not required.)

2/4th Battn Royal Fusiliers

Place	Date	Hour	Summary of Events and Information	Remarks and references to Appendices
VADENCOURT	Oct 5th		No 4 Coy moved to MOREVAL TRENCH at 11.30 p.m. and returned to their quarters at 8 a.m. next morning VADEN COURT TRENCHES	
	Oct 6th		No 4 Coy returned from MOREVAL TRENCH to VADENCOURT 8 A.M. Operation orders issued for relief of 3rd Rifle Brigade in the line	APP. I
Trenches At Sub Sector from LONGUENOIR RIVR to R.Q.34.c.60.80.	Oct 7th		13 Battn relieved 3rd Rifle Brigade in the line with the Trench on our Right and No 1st Battn Royal Fusiliers on our left. Night passed quietly & patrols reported no signs of the enemy in NoMan's Land	
	Oct 8th		Enemy shelled the vicinity of LONE TREE POST at M.2.a.2.5.85 also at 6.2.73 8.w. and TUMULUS M.1.c.80.50. between 7 A.M. and 6.30 p.m. (intermittantly) 3 R.Q. A small patrol of our men driven in by the enemy and No 9105 Sgt. Conway G. was wounded, about	
	Oct 9th		Patrol report nothing out-of-the-ordinary of the Enemy. The TUMULUS was shelled during the day. Also LONE TREE POST and SALT TRENCH [about] M.1.c.80.80 sheet 62.73 S.W.B.2.a. M.2c and 5.9." One prisoner captured by daylight post in SOMERVILLE WOOD at M.1.c.50.80. == Q.32.c.10.60. sheet 62.73 NW.	

F.R. Daly Lt Col
Chdg 12/4 R.F.

Army Form C. 2118.

WAR DIARY
or
INTELLIGENCE SUMMARY.
(Erase heading not required.)

12th Bn. Royal Fusiliers

Instructions regarding War Diaries and Intelligence Summaries are contained in F. S. Regs., Part II. and the Staff Manual respectively. Title pages will be prepared in manuscript.

Place	Date	Hour	Summary of Events and Information	Remarks and references to Appendices
A.1 Salt Sector	Oct. 11th		Everything quiet, no sign of enemy seen by our Patrols. The TUMULUS & SALT TRENCH were shelled at regular intervals all day. 2 direct hits were obtained on SALT TRENCH, nothing to report.	
	Oct. 12th		Very quiet all day, nothing to report. About midday enemy fired 12 4.2" shell on LONETREE POST again at 3 P.M., non-casualties caused & no direct hits. Patrols encountered no enemy & found no signs of them.	
	Oct. 13		From 12.10 P.M. to 1.15 P.M. a considerable enemy bombardment in an area extending from SALT TRENCH to 100 yds S. of junction of WATLING ST. & SALT TRENCH. Bombardment although intense in trenches in vicinity & subsequently occurred. Shells used were 4.2" 5.9" & 8". REDWOOD & FORT ARRY also received a little attention during the afternoon but this was mostly shrapnel.	to be

J.R. Day

Comm'g 12th Bn. Royal Fusiliers

WAR DIARY
or
INTELLIGENCE SUMMARY

Army Form C. 2118.

1st Bn. Royal Fusiliers

Place	Date	Hour	Summary of Events and Information	Remarks and references to Appendices
Fauquisart	Oct 14		Enemy shelled SALE TRENCH & vicinity intermittently all day; no damage was done. A patrol of 2 officers went out all day in no-mans-land. Signs of enemy were everywhere. Important identifications were secured from dead Germans found interred. Two enemy Aeroplanes flew low over our lines to a height of about 50 ams. Batt. were relieved by the 3rd Rifle Brigade, relief was completed at 7-10 p.m. & moved back to BERNES.	Appendix II
Bernes	Oct 16		Battalion cleaned up after tour in the line.	
	Oct 17		Lecture given on "Discipline" by Major 24th Division in Theatre BERNES. All officers attended.	
	Oct 18		Letter of appreciation received from Lieut. L.S. Bols C.B. D.S.O. (late G.O.C. 24th Division). Lecture scheme carried out under Brigade arrangements.	Appendix 3

J.R. Day Lt Col
Comm'g 1/2th Royal Fusiliers

Army Form C. 2118.

WAR DIARY
or
INTELLIGENCE SUMMARY.
(Erase heading not required.)

12th Bn Royal Fusiliers

Place	Date	Hour	Summary of Events and Information	Remarks and references to Appendices
Berles	Oct 19		A draft of 5 OR joined Battalion.	
	Oct 20		Had Platoon & Section training	
	Oct 21		ditto	
	Oct 22		Lecture given by Medical Officer to the Battalion. Subject "Gas".	
	Oct 23		Battalion relieved the 3rd Rifle Brigade in A1 Sub Sector. Enemy very quiet.	See Operation Offensive A/
	Oct 24		Enemy was very quiet, a few shells fell round the TUMULSS.	
	Oct 25		Draft of 3 O.R. joined Battalion	

J R Day
Lieut Col
Commt 12th Bn Royal Fusiliers

Army Form C. 2118.

WAR DIARY
or
INTELLIGENCE SUMMARY.
(Erase heading not required.)

13th Bn Royal Fusiliers

Place	Date	Hour	Summary of Events and Information	Remarks and references to Appendices
A1 Subsector	Oct 25		Between 11.30 am & 4.30 pm the enemy shelled SALT TRENCH & the TUMULUS intermittently, very quiet otherwise. MG's fairly active.	
	Oct 26		Enemy Artillery quiet, just a few light shells fell in vicinity of TUMULUS. Enemy MG's were firing between 7pm to 11pm into SOMERVILLE WOOD. At 11.15 am enemy put up Golden Rain & Red rockets along Brigade Front.	
	Oct 27		Parts of B & D Coy joined Battalion. Patrols under 2/Lt HILLS reached ELEVEN TREES at B.2.C.60.60. Sheet 62BNW searched for an Enemy M.G. which was supposed to be firing from there. No trace of enemy was found. The enemy fired a few shells at [?] in vicinity of MUSTARD QUARRY at M.7.A.50.70. Sheet 62B SW into DRAGOON POST during the night. At B.3.1.C.90.30. Sheet 62B NW Casualties. nil O.R.	
	Oct 28		Enemy Artillery very active between 11.45 am to 12.30 am. several direct hits in trench. Calibre of shells 4.2 & 5.9. Our enemy Artillery fired several shells round TUMULUS, the enemy were very active all the morning. 1. O.R. accidentally wounded. Refr 1 O.R. Jones J. Batts.	

Cmmd 13 Bn Royal Fusiliers

Army Form C. 2118.

WAR DIARY
or
INTELLIGENCE SUMMARY.
(Erase heading not required.)

13th Royal Fusiliers

Place	Date	Hour	Summary of Events and Information	Remarks and references to Appendices
A.1. Sub-sect.	Oct. 29.		D. About 5:30 a.m. an enemy patrol attacked Day Post in SOMERVILLE WOOD, strength about 30, on withdrawing left with a loss of one enemy Officer, an identification was obtained showing that the 26th R.I.R. were in front of this sector. The B. Coy O' congratulated 2/Lt. J. J. 130 R&H & L/Cpl. Thompson for their good work in this sector. Between 3 pm & 6 pm enemy fired several shells in vicinity of Left Company's machine gun. Otherwise quiet.	
ditto	Oct. 30th		Strafe 1 O.R. joined Battalion. Patrols were sent out to try & get enemy very quiet. Further hit of enemy patrol under Lt. Moor Denerich no further were found	
ditto	Oct. 31st		Batt. relieved in the line. Enemy attitude quiet. Batt'n Strength. Officers 44. O.R. 782	A.T.

J.R. Day
Lt. Col.
Comm'g 13th Bn. Royal Fusiliers

OPERATION ORDERS.
by
Major J. C. HARTLEY.
Commanding 12th. Battalion Royal Fusiliers.   6/10/17.

Appendix I

1. The Battalion will relieve the 3rd Rifle Brigade in A.1 Sub-Sector on the night of the 7/8th October 1917.
No. 1 Company to Right Sub-Sector - No. 4 Company Centre Sub-Sector.
No. 3 Company to Left Sub-Sector. - No. 2 Company from Le VERGUIER to COOKER TRENCH.
Battalion Headquarters to COOKER'S QUARRY.

2. Two guides per Company will be at COOKERS QUARRY at 6-30 p.m., and the relief will be carried out in the following order :-
LEFT No. 3 Company, CENTRE No. 4 Company, RIGHT No. 1 Company.

3. DRESS :- Full Marching Order, Steel Helmets to be worn and Caps to be carried.

4. ORDER OF MARCH.
Companies will march by half platoons at 70 paces interval.
2nd in Command's of Companies and C.S.Ms will proceed in advance at 5-30 p.m. to take over Trench Stores, Dug-outs and assist in dispositions etc, the remainder of the Battalion will move off independently to meet their respective guides as stated above.

5. TRANSPORT.
The Transport Officer will forward Company Rations as under on the 7th inst.:-
Headquarters and No. 2 Company to COOKERS QUARRY.
No. 1 Company to MUSTARD QUARRY.
No. 4 Company to TWIN CRATERS.
No. 3 Company to HODSON POST No. 2.
O.C. Companies will arrange guides for same at Road Junction, COOKERS QUARRY at 7-30 p.m.
The Transport Officer will maintain 1 Water Cart (full) at COOKERS QUARRY and 1 to fill up Tanks and dixies at TWIN CRATERS nightly.
Blankets will be tied up by Sections and labelled clearly to be at Gate No. 4 Company and Battalion H.Qrs by 6 p.m.
Officers Valises will also be packed and put in the same place by 6 p.m.
No. 2 Company will take their blankets with them into COOKERS TRENCH.
No. 2 Company's Officers valises will be sent down by the return Ration Limber.

6. WORK IN HAND, TRENCH STORES ETC.
All trench stores will be carefully taken over and a copy sent to Orderly Room on the morning of the 8th.
Work in hand, Proposed Tactical Dispositions, Routes and Defence Schemes will be carefully taken over. O.C. Companies are responsible that the DEFENCE SCHEME is thoroughly explained to all ranks.

7. INTELLIGENCE.
Sgt Conway G., L/C Robbins No. 1 Company, will be attached to 2/LIEUT. J.A.MEARS-DEVENISH, who will act as Intelligence Officer during this tour.   Each Company will detail 2 Observers to take over the O.P. at BERTHINCOURT.   These men will report to 2/LT.J.A.MEARS-DEVENISH at 9-30 am tomorrow the 7th inst.

8. PATROLS.
No. 1 Company will find the same standing patrols as hitherto on the RIGHT SUB-SECTOR.   No. 3 Company will find the patrol commencing at dusk and be relieved at midnight by No. 2 Company.   No. 2 Company will move a platoon consisting of 2 Officers 50 men including a Lewis Gun Section up to HODSON'S POST No.2.   The Officer in charge will report to O.C. No. 3 Company.

Cotinued.:-

9. **LEWIS GUNNERS and SIGNALLERS.**
Lewis Gunners and Signallers will parade for relief under Company arrangements at 5 p.m. O.C. Companies will detail an Officer to make reconnaissance of all Lewis Gun Positions in their Company Area and to guide teams. This relief will commence from the RIGHT No. 2 Company will detail 1 Lewis Gun Team to be attached to No. 1 Coy.

10. **ATTACHMENT.**
The following Officers will be attached to No. 1 Company for duty during this tour :- 2/LIEUT. B. PEZARO and 2/LIEUT. W.J.BURCH.

11. **COMPLETION OF RELIEF.**
Completion of Relief will be wired to Battalion Headquarters by the Code Word " TALLY - HO ".

12. **WINTER TIME.**
Winter Time will be taken into use at 1 a.m. on 7th instant. Clocks and Watches will be put back one hour at that time accordingly.

sd. A. HOPE. 2nd Lieut.
Acting Adjutant 12th. Battalion Royal Fusiliers.

Copies issued to :-
　No.1.　C.O. 12th. Royal Fusiliers.
　No.2.　C.O. 3rd Rifle Brigade.
　No.3.　Adjutant.
　No.4.　O.C. No. 1 Company.
　No.5.　O.C. No. 2 Company.
　No.6.　O.C. No. 3 Company.
　No.7.　O.C. No. 4 Company.
　No.8.　L.G.O.
　No.9.　S.O.
　No.10.　Transport Officer.
　No.11.　Quartermaster.
　No.12.　I.O.
　No.13.　War Diary.
　No.14.　File.

Copy No......10......   OPERATION ORDERS.
                ---- by ----
              Major J. C. HARTLEY.
    Commanding 12th. Battalion The Royal Fusiliers.   15/10/17.

Appendix II

1. The Battalion will be relieved tonight by the 3rd Bn. Rifle Brigade.
   The relief will commence from the Left :-
        "A" Coy 3rd R.B. will relieve No. 3 Company.
        "C" "   "   "   "   No. 4   "
        "B" "   "   "   "   No. 1   "
        "D" "   "   "   "   No. 2   "
   Relief will commence at 5.p.m.

   Patrols for the 15/16th will arrive at 4.p.m.

   All details as to Patrols, Dispositions, Aeroplane Maps, Log Books
   completed to date etc, will be carefully handed over.
   Trench Stores will be carefully handed over and a receipt obtained.

   O.C. Companies will pay particular attention to the cleanliness of
   their lines on handing over.

   O.C. No. 2 Company will consider his relief complete on the handing
   over of Cooker's Trench to the first half of "D" Coy, 3rd Rifle Brigade.

   On completion of relief Companies will march out by Sections at 150 yds
   interval, closing up to half platoons at 100 yds interval on reaching
   VENDELLES and thence to HERMES.

   TEAS to be served at 4 .pm.

   Company Quarter Master Sergeants will arrange to meet Companies on
   arrival at HERMES and guide Companies to billets and have tea ready
   on arrival.

2. TRANSPORT.
   O.C. Transport will detail, limber complete, one each for Nos 1.3 & 4
   Companies, 2 limbers for No. 2 Company, 2 extra limbers, Mess Cart,
   Maltese Cart for Battn H.Qrs.
   These will arrive at VADENCOURT at 4-45 p.m. and thence be forwarded
   to Companies under Battalion arrangements.

3. COMPLETION OF RELIEF.
   Completion of relief will be wired to Battalion Headquarters by Code
   Word " BUSKUM".

                                    sd. N. COLLISS R. 2nd. Lieut.
                          Asst/Adjutant 12th. Batt. Royal Fusiliers.

Copies issued as follows :-

Copy No.1 ---- C.O. 12th. Batt. Royal Fusiliers.
  " No.2 ---- C.O. 3rd. Batt. Rifle Brigade.
  " No.3 ---- O.C. No. 1 Company.
     No.4 ---- O.C. No. 2   "

     No.5 ---- O.C. No. 3   "
  " No.6 ---- O.C. No. 4   "
  " No.7 ---- Transport Officer.
     No.8 ---- Quartermaster.
  " No.9 ---- Headquarter Coy Offr.
  " No.10 -- War Diary.
  " No.11 -- File.

Appendix III

APPRECIATION.
****

an attack 8rd

The following is a letter received from Major General L.J.BOLS. C.B.,D.S.O. (late G.O.C.24th.Division) :-

My hasty departure prevented me from wishing your
" gallant fellows goodbye.
" I would like to thank those under your command for all the
" great work they have done during the past 4 months.
" I appreciate very deeply the honour of having had under
" my command so fine a Battalion during these strenuous times.
" May good fortune go with them always.

****

OPERATION ORDERS.
==== by ====
Lt. Colonel. F. R. DAY.
Commanding 12th. Battalion Royal Fusiliers.   22/10/17.

1. The Battalion will relieve the 3rd Batt. The Rifle Brigade as follows:-
   No. 4 Coy. 12th. R.F. will relieve "D" Coy. 3rd. R.Bde.
   No. 1 Coy.   "   "   "   "   "   "C" Coy.   "   "
   No. 3 Coy.   "   "   "   "   "   "B" Coy.   "   "
   No. 2 Coy.   "   "   "   "   "   "A" Coy.   "   "
   Headquarters "   "   "   "   Headquarters   "

   They will parade at 4-15 p.m. in the above order (with exception of No. 2 Company which will move up as detailed below) and will march with 5 minutes interval between Companies and leave VADENCOURT by Platoons with 1 minute interval.
   Officers requiring Guides will make the necessary arrangements with the corresponding Companies of the 3rd. R.Bde during the morning when visiting their respective positions.
   C.S.Ms and Gas N.C.Os should be sent up before to take over Trench Stores.

2. The Companies will hold the Front as under :-
   RIGHT FRONT COMPANY................No. 1 Company.
   LEFT FRONT COMPANY.................No. 4 Company.
   SUPPORT COMPANY....................No. 3 Company.
   RESERVE COMPANY....................No. 2 Company.
   The Reserve Company will proceed by Platoons to VADENCOURT tomorrow morning and have dinners there. After dinners they will proceed by Sections to the Reserve Line.
   The following men will be attached to No. 2 Company for their dinners and will relieve the 3rd R.Bde at dusk :-
   No. 4 Company.......... 6 men to work under the R.E. at DRAGOON POST. This party to report there at 6 p.m.
   No. 3 Company.......... 1 N.C.O. and 6 men for NORTHERN SOMERVILLE WOOD POST, and 1 N.C.O. & 6 men for SOUTHERN SOMERVILLE WOOD POST.
   1 Lewis Gun, 1 N.C.O. & 5 men infront of LONE TREE POST.
   These parties will take over at dusk.

3. Blankets will be rolled in bundles by sections, (so that they can be sent up if necessary) and stacked at the Q.M.Stores by 8-30 a.m. tomorrow morning.

                    sd. A. SIMKINS. Captain.
            Adjutant 12th. Battalion Royal Fusiliers.

Copies issued to :-

   No. 1   O.C. 12th. Roy. Fus.
   No. 2   O.C. 3rd. R. Bde.
   No. 3   O.C. No. 1 Company.
   No. 4   O.C. No. 2 Company.
   No. 5   O.C. No. 3 Company.
   No. 6   O.C. No. 4 Company.
   No. 7   O.C. H.Qrs. Company.
   No. 8   War Diary.

RELIEF ORDERS.
*** by ***
Lt. Colonel F. R. DAY.
Commanding 12th. Battalion Royal Fusiliers.   30/10/17.

1. The Battalion will be relieved by the 3rd. Bn. Rifle Brigade tomorrow evening 31st inst and will proceed to VADENCOURT and be in Bde Buppers.

2. All movement will be by platoons at 200 yds interval.

3. All trench stores, work in hand and proposed, details of working parties, will be carefully handed over and explained to incoming Unit.

4. No. 4 Company, after relief will proceed to BOB TRENCH between MILL POST (inclusive) and L.34.a.9.7. Coy H.Qrs at MILL POST.

5. Nos 1.2 & 3 Coys will each send down 1 Officer to report to MAJOR HARTLEY at Battn H.Qrs by 10 a.m. for the purpose of takingm over their Company Areas at VADENCOURT.

6. The Transport Officer will arrange to send :-
1 limber per Coy for L.Gs and Mess Kit. - also Mess Cart and limbers for Batt H.Qrs Kits and Orderly Room Boxes. - Maltese Cart for Medical Stores.
All Limbers Etc, to be at VADENCOURT at 5-30 p.m. and will proceed thence with 200 yds interval between each vehicle.

7. Completion of relief will be personally reported by Coy Commdrs at Batt. H.Qrs.

Sd. A.SIMKINS. Captain.
Adjutant 12th. Battalion Royal Fusiliers.

DEFENCE OF SOMERVILLE WOOD.

On enemy being discovered in SOMERVILLE WOOD by Patrols or Posts the following procedure will be adopted:-

(a) If a Patrol is out one red Very light will be sent up by the Unit discovering the enemy. This will be the signal for No 9 Machine Gun to open on SOMERVILLE WOOD. This signal will be taken up by DRAGOON & LONE TREE POSTS and repeated every half minute until complied with.

[margin: E. of WATLING ST.]
[margin: at No 6 Post]

(b) In event of no Patrol being out the above procedure will be adopted with the addition that "Trap Barrage" will also be telephoned to Battalion Headquarters immediately. This will be repeated at once to A/106 R.F.A.

In the event of (a) No 9 gun will not fire beyond the Eastern end of SOMERVILLE WOOD.

In the event of (b) all available Machine Guns will open on SOMERVILLE WOOD simultaneously with artillery, and No 9 will also sweep East of SOMERVILLE WOOD and cease with the artillery.

In the event of the enemy being located West of WATLING STREET the Trench Mortars will open fire under orders of O.C. DRAGOON POST.

These orders to come into operation from DAWN 31st OCTOBER 1917.

Show

J.R. Day
................Lieut. Colonel
30/10/17.   Commanding 12th Battalion Royal Fusiliers.

SECRET

G.2/36

12" R.F.

Reference above -

(a) This light should only be sent up by the Patrol in 'NO MANS LAND' and when they have occupied positions to intercept the enemy's retreat.

(a) What happens when this is done - from the Infantry point of view?
All this is unaimed fire, and very few casualties are likely to be caused. This, if used, should be kept up until our Infantry is out and attack

Will you please amend accordingly

W. Mackenzie
Capt.
BM. 17th I.B.

30/10/17

To Headquarters - 17th Infantry Brigade.

REPORT ON ENEMY RAID ON SOMERVILLE WOOD.

At about 5.30 a.m. on the morning of the 29th October 1917, about 20 minutes after the night posts had been withdrawn from the Wood and the day posts of 1 N.C.O. and 14 men established at about G.32.C.6.3. a party of about 30 to 40 of the enemy suddenly appeared from E. by S. They had presumably approached via DOGS LEG and under cover between the Bank and SOMERVILLE WOOD, some of them came through the WOOD and surprised our advanced riflemen.

The enemy Officer in charge fired 5 rounds and wounded one of our men, the Officer was then shot by L/Cpl. THOMPSON.

The remainder of the post engaged the rest of the enemy patrol who withdrew apparently discouraged by the loss of their Officer whom they left. Several traces of blood through the Wood found by our Patrol pointed to the fact that others of the enemy were either killed or wounded.

They secured nonidentification from our Post.

On the alarm being given, 2/Lieut. W.J. BURCH immediately took out a Patrol to ascertain what had occurred and recapture any of our men who might have been taken prisoner, but the enemy made good his escape.

Machine Gun fire and rifle fire was meanwhile opened from the direction of FILLER REDOUBT and SQUARE COPSE. This was subsequently dealt with by the Artillery.

Our casualties were 1 killed and 4 wounded.

The body of the dead enemy Officer will be brought down tonight for identification.

I have not re-established this post pending your authority, as I do not consider that it serves any useful purpose, and only gives the enemy an opportunity of obtaining identification and the ground

- 2 -

in its vicinity can be kept under enemy machine gun fire with direct observation by day.

No enemy were observed North of the WOOD by the Lewis Gun post at approximately M.32.C.2.6.

A Patrol has been sent out via FISHER CRATER to ascertain whether there are any bodies of dead enemy lying in No Mans Land.

........................Lieut. Colonel.
Commanding 12th Battalion Royal Fusiliers.

29/10/17.

To Adjt. 12th R.F.

Report on German Raid

At 5.30 a.m. about 20 minutes after the night posts had been relieved in SOMERVILLE WOOD a party of 35-40 BOSCHES attacked our day posts. They worked round via DOG'S LEG on our right got through the wire and surprised our advanced riflemen.

The officer in charge fired 5 rounds and wounded one of our men

The officer was then killed by L/C THOMPSON who shot him through the head. Meanwhile The remainder of the post had been engaged by the rest of the Boche patrol with rifles and bombs. Our casualties were 3 more men wounded and one killed. Although they outnumbered our men by 3-1. they retired hurriedly apparently discouraged by the loss of the officer.

They secured no identification from our casualties and did not stop to remove the identifications from their own dead officer. They took back several of their own wounded with them.

2nd Lt. W.J. BURCH immediately took out a party to search for the BOSCHES but they had made good their retreat.

Stretcher bearers who went out to bring in our wounded were heavily engaged by M.G. fire from VILLA REDOUBT and snipers apparently in SQUARE COPSE. By the C.O's orders the posts were withdrawn without further

Casualties, and all the wounded were safely brought in.

Special recommendation is due to No 62182 A/C Thompson J who was in command of the post and No 16345 P.G. Simmons J who brought back a helpless case under heavy MG and rifle fire

29-10-17   R.C. Cutter Lt.
                              OC No 1 Coy

On the enemy being discovered in Somerville Wood by Patrols or Post the following procedure will be adopted.

(a) If a patrol is out one red very light will be sent up by the unit discovering the enemy. This will be the signal for No 9 M.G. at No 6 Post to open on Som Wood sweeping the whole wood. This signal will be taken up repeated by Lone Tree & Dragoon Post & repeated every half minute till complied with.

~~the signal will not be initiated~~

Report on ~~German~~ Enemy raid on Somerville Wood

At about 5.30 a.m. on the morning of 29th Oct 17, about 20 minutes after the night Posts had been withdrawn from the wood and the day post [1 N.C.O. + 14 men] established at about G.32.c.6.3. a party of 30-40 of the enemy suddenly appeared from the

E. by S. They had presumeably approached via

D.0.G.sh.9 + under cover between the tank and wood. Some of them came through the wood [Somerville] + surprised our advanced riflemen.

The enemy officer &c fired 5 rounds + wounded one of our men. The officer was then ~~killed~~ shot by L/Cpl Thompson.

The remainder of the ~~patrol~~ post engaged the rest of the patrol who withdrew, apparently discouraged by the loss of their officer whom they left ~~found by the~~ our patrol. ~~Point~~ ~~had an~~ [found] Traces of blood through the wood ~~lead to~~ ~~the~~ ~~suppose~~ that others of the enemy were [to this fact] either killed or wounded.

They secured no identification from our post

~~On~~ on the alarm being given 2 Lt J.T. Burch immediately took out a patrol to ascertain what had occurred & recapture any of our men who might have been taken prisoner; but the enemy made good his escape.

Machine Gun fire & rifle fire was meanwhile opened from (the direction of) Filler redoubt & Square Copse; this was subsequently dealt with by the artillery.

Our casualties were 1 killed & 4 wounded.

I have not reestablished this post pending your authority, as I do not consider that it serves any useful purpose and only gives the enemy an opportunity of obtaining identification and the ground in its vicinity can be kept under enemy M.G. fire with direct observation by day.

No enemy were observed N of the wood by the L.G Post at approx M 32 c. 2. 6.

CONFIDENTIAL**********

WAR DIARY
****

of

12th.(S) Battalion ROYAL FUSILIERS.

From..1/11/1917...... To..30/11/1917............

(Volume No.27)

WAR DIARY
or
INTELLIGENCE SUMMARY.

Army Form C. 2118.

2/4 Bn. Royal Fusiliers

Place	Date	Hour	Summary of Events and Information	Remarks and references to Appendices
VADENCOURT (in support)	Nov 1		2 Lt. G.T. KEELE appointed Transport officer vice Capt C.V. WATTENBACH to duty.	
SHEET 62cSE R.17a.	Nov 2		No. 52112 L/C THOMPSON J.W. awarded R.M. by G.O.C. Bde (good work on 29th ult).	
		16.345	Pte SIMMONS J.J. presents to a second command of the 4/2nd R. Fusiliers	
	Nov 3		Weather good but working parties for 32nd R. Rifle Bde etc as in the line	
	Nov 4		Working parties were again supplied by us to help 32nd R. Bde.	
	Nov 5		11077 Pte WHATLEY J.C. joined Batty.	
	Nov 6		Enemy put a few small rifle shots into VADENCOURT & Lt E MOODY was slightly wounded	
	Nov 7		Enemy 77 aircraft guns fired at 100 of our planes & a shell which failed to burst in the air soon seen in road in VADENCOURT & badly wounded the center	
In the line	Nov 8		4th Bn relieved the 32nd 2/4 R Bde in the line (Bn LIVERPOOL). Relief of officer 1.30pm our unit out from BARRIER POST at 1.30am to FISHER CENTER Maps Sheets 7 SOMERVILLE WOOD. The enemy seen.	Appendix 1
SHEET 62 SW.	Nov 9		Artillery on both sides very quiet. Rebelay in B.R.Q. 9/11/17. Given authority to wear caps of the usual style by wearing officers of this Bn. Major in LONDON GAZETTE. Capt SIMKINS A.A. Major. Lieut COTTER R.O. Capt.	

J R D af Lieut Colonel
Command 2/4 Bn Royal Fus.

Army Form C. 2118.

WAR DIARY
or
INTELLIGENCE SUMMARY.
(Erase heading not required.)

12th Bn Royal Fusiliers

Instructions regarding War Diaries and Intelligence Summaries are contained in F. S. Regs., Part II. and the Staff Manual respectively. Title pages will be prepared in manuscript.

Place	Date	Hour	Summary of Events and Information	Remarks and references to Appendices
In the Field	Nov 10		Enemy fired a few shells on trench front during the day. At 9 P.M. the enemy fire in bursts burst on enemy positions with H. Gas Shells until 9.30 P.M. Secondly any retaliation by enemy. Lt Col F.R. Day & Capt R.C. Cotter dealt with effort of front down on our right.	
	Nov 11		Good visibility all day. Artillery were engaged in ranging from our observation post. Enemy artillery very quiet all day.	
Sheet 62B N.W. G.33.A.	Nov 12		Foggy. Quiet during day. No ambulances went on unaccompanied. Wire trench could be carried out. Our patrol went out at 1.30 A.M. to west of Squire Copse. They had talking at L.G Hills. A few men went close up. Enemy sentry challenged & threw but could not throw in the top shots were fired & one of our men was slightly wounded.	
Sheet 62 S.W. M.2.D.60&40	Nov 13		Foggy. Patrol again went out to Fisher Crater. The enemy developed splendid gun fire E. of Fisher center. Reflectors were immediately put on and in consequence the patrol returned to trench on our right work & road at 5.35 P.M. An enemy front line E. of Pontrat with 20 men (24 of prisoners were captured) who belonged to the 24th R.P.R. 32 BN. All of the enemy were killed. We had no casualties. No (6 R.F. Argood wounded in action (Feb) & 19R (Feb)	
Sheet 62 N.W. G.32.C.D.	Nov 14		Enemy artillery during day active at 8 P.M. the enemy sent over into No Man's Land (Somerville Wood) in 10 min. Verst 5.9 & 8 inch Shells until 1.30 A.M. He probably thought our patrol would be out.	

J.R. Day Lieut. Colonel.
Command 12 Bn Royal Fusiliers

Army Form C. 2118.

WAR DIARY
or
INTELLIGENCE SUMMARY.
(Erase heading not required.)

12th Bn Royal Fusiliers

Place	Date	Hour	Summary of Events and Information	Remarks and references to Appendices
B. Hebuterne G.33.C.	Nov 14	—	Our Patrol eventually went out at 2 am and proceeded to ELEVEN TREES where a German was heard shouting "English". Patrol did not follow him up, as it may have been a ruse. A.M.G. in ambulance would allow the line of trees. Lieut. J.D. Stewart invalided sick to England.	
SHEET 57.D S.W. 6.3 to 6.6 N.W.	Nov 15		Visibility poor. Quiet during day. Our Patrol left BARRIER POST at 11 pm and Patrolled own wire from ANGLE BANK to L'OMIGNON RIVER. None of the enemy wire encountered. 1 O.R. wounded.	
	Nov 16		Foggy. Quiet during day. The Battalion was relieved in the line by the 3rd Batt. RIFLE BRIGADE and moved into Divisional Reserve at BERNES.	
BERNES	Nov 17		The following letter of appreciation (re patrol work of 2nd Lieut. L.G. Hills and 2nd Lieut J.A. Mears-Devenish) received from G.O.C. 24th Div. (Major-General A.C. Daly):— "2nd Lieut. Hills of the 12th ROYAL FUSILIERS splendid work of this time in NO MAN'S LAND, and has been doing exceptionally good reconnaissance & patrol work ever since the Division first came into this sort of the line — He has gained valuable information several times. Another officer who always accompanies 2nd Lieut Hills, is 2nd Lieut Mears-Devenish also of the 12th ROYAL FUSILIERS.	

SIGNED A.C. DALY Major General
Comm'g 24th Division

J R ffrench
Lieut Colonel
Commanding 12th Bn Roy Fus

Army Form C. 2118.

WAR DIARY
or
INTELLIGENCE SUMMARY.

(Erase heading not required.)

Instructions regarding War Diaries and Intelligence Summaries are contained in F. S. Regs., Part II and the Staff Manual respectively. Title pages will be prepared in manuscript.

4th Bn. Royal Fusiliers

Place	Date	Hour	Summary of Events and Information	Remarks and references to Appendices
BERNES	Nov 18		The Battalion supplied all the Divisional working parties.	
	Nov 19		Section and Platoon Training. An association football match between a representative side of the 17th & 18th and the FRENCH DIVISION first O.R. was played the same night. The former won by 2 goals to one.	
	Nov 20		Battalion supplied the Divisional working parties.	
	Nov 21		Carried out rifle & platoon training with the coy. Ptn. Offrs. & N.C.Os. & working party to be carried on employed.	
	Nov 22		Majority of Battalion again employed on working parties. Scouts and Lewis Gunners fired on range at HANCOURT.	
	Nov 23		Section and Platoon Training. Lecture to Officers on "Discipline".	Appendix II
In the Line	Nov 24		The Battalion relieved the 3rd Batt'y Rifle Brigade. Situation very quiet. Heavy rainfall.	
Sheet 62° NW	Nov 25		Our Patrol of 2 Officers, 20 O.R. & 1 Lewis Gun left DRAGOON POST at 1.30 a.m and interfered with ANGLE BANKS, FISHER CRATER and returned by BARRIER POST at 4.30 a.m. No enemy encountered. ST HELENE occupied. Enemy attitude quiet during day.	
G.31.d. Sheet 62° SW M 2	Nov. 26		Our Patrol under 2nd Lieut J.A. HEAPS - DEVENISH left DRAGOON POST, SHEET 62° N.W. G.31d.8.0.60. at 1.30 a.m and proceeded via ANGLE BANKS, MAX WOOD, FISHER CRATER and returned by BARRIER POST Sheet 62° SW. M.2.c.30.w at 5.30 a.m. No enemy met on from MAXTBANK M.2.B. ST HELENE TRENCH M.3. now occupied. The Patrol noted Visibility very good. Enemy attitude quiet.	

J.R. Dey
Lieut Colonel
Commanding 4/2 Ro Fus. Rg.

Army Form C. 2118.

WAR DIARY
or
INTELLIGENCE SUMMARY.
(Erase heading not required.)

12th Bn. Royal Fusiliers

Place	Date	Hour	Summary of Events and Information	Remarks and references to Appendices
In the Line	Nov 27		Our Patrol under 2nd Lieut. L.G. HILLS left BARRIER POST, Sheet 62B M2 c 20.20. and proceeded by FISHER CRATER, MAX BANK, SOMERVILLE WOOD and returned by DRAGON POST Sheet 62 B N.W. G 31 D 80.60, at 4-30 a.m. The enemy encountered snow fell early this morning followed by heavy snowfall. A daylight patrol under Lieut A.H. LEE. M.C. consisting of himself and one officer left RIVER POST Sheet 62B SW M6 a 60.20 and proceeded along the RIVER D'OMIGNON to M 3 d 80.20. The Patrol reports that there is only one bridge over the river, and that this bridge is impassable. Lieut LEE was congratulated for his good work, both by the Brig. General and the Divisional General. Enemy Patrols quiet.	
	Nov 28		Our Patrol under 2nd Lieut J.A. MEARS-DEVENISH left RIVER POST 62B SW M 8 b 60.20 at 1.30 a.m. and proceeded via FISHER CRATER, DOG'S LEG, SOMERVILLE WOOD and returned at 4.35 a.m. by DRAGON POST 62 B N.W. 31 d 80.60. No enemy were encountered. Enemy attitude Quiet.	
	Nov 29		Owing to extremely brilliant moon a reconnoitring party only consisting of 3 Officers & 3 O.R. under 2nd Lieut J.A. HILLS. left BARRIER POST Sheet 62B SW M2.C. 20.20. and proceeded via FISHER CRATER, SOMERVILLE WOOD, SQUARE COPSE were reconnoitred and an enemy hut at G 38 a 45 ⋅r was located. Enemy shelled ridge immediately in rear of COOKER'S QUARRY. 62 S.E R 11.c 8.9.9. Artillery attitude Quiet.	

dn 18 Co. Oakeleigh Inf. to R.F.C.↓ ₍Observer₎ J.R. DEW Lieut. Colonel.
Command 12 ??? Bn. Royal Fusiliers

Army Form C. 2118.

WAR DIARY
or
INTELLIGENCE SUMMARY.

(Erase heading not required.)

12th Bn. Royal Fusiliers

Place	Date	Hour	Summary of Events and Information	Remarks and references to Appendices
In the line	30th July		Patrol, under 2nd Lieut. L.G. HILLS left BARRIER POST 62B S.W. 2.c.2.0.0. at 2 a.m. and proceeded to ANGLE BANKS, SOMERVILLE WOOD, and returned by LONE TREE POST at 5 a.m. No enemy was encountered. Enemy attitude quiet.	

J.R. Duff
Lieut. Colonel.
Command 12th Bn. Royal Fusiliers

Appendix I

OPERATION ORDERS.
**** by ****
Lt. Colonel F.R. DAY.
Commanding 12th.Batt. Royal Fusiliers.   8/11/17.

1. The Battalion will relieve the 3rd Batt. The Rifle Brigade in the line today the 8th instant.

2. Companies will be situated as follows :-
   No. 1 Company.................HODSONS POST.
   No. 2 Company.................MUSTARD QUARRY.
   No. 3 Company.................SALT TRENCH.
   No. 4 Company.................COOKERS TRENCH.

3. All movement will be by Sections at 100 yds interval.
   No.4 Company will move off at 2 p.m. No.1 Company will move off at 4-30 p.m. followed by Nos 2 & 3 Coys at intervals stated above.

4. No.2 Company will arrange to send 1.N.C.O. & 4 O.R. to relieve International Post and L.G.Post at BERTHAUCOURT. They will report to H.Qrs COOKERS QUARRY by 4 p.m.

5. 1 limber for Nos 1.2 & 3 Coys. will be at Company H.Qrs at 4-30 p.m. a representative from each Company will accompany limbers.

6. No.4 Company will arrange to carry their L.Gs etc to COOKERS TRENCH.

7. All Trench Stores, Work in hand and proposed will be carefully taken over.

8. Completion of relief will be notified to Battn H.Qrs by wiring Company Commander's name.

sd. R.C.CUTTER. Lieut.
Adjutant 12th.Batt. Royal Fusiliers.

Copy No...11...

APPENDIX II

OPERATION ORDERS.
issued by
Lt. Colonel F. R. DAY.
Commanding 10th. Battalion Royal Fusiliers.   23/11/17.

1. The Battalion will relieve the 3rd Battn. The Rifle Brigade in the Line tomorrow the 24th instant.

2. The Companies will be situated as follows :-
   No. 1 Company........................COOKERS TRENCH.
   No. 2 Company........................SALT TRENCH.
   No. 3 Company........................HODSONS POST.
   No. 4 Company........................MUSTARD QUARRY.

3. Companies will proceed by platoons at 200 yards interval in the following order :- Nos 1, 2, 3, 4 and H.Q. Coy.
   No. 1 Company will move off at 2-15 p.m.

4. 1 limber will go with each Company to carry the Lewis Guns, Mess Kit and dixies etc.
   The usual transport for Battalion H.Qrs.

5. No. 4 Company will arrange for the reliefs for International Post and the Berthaucourt L.G.Post to be there at 4 p.m.

6. All Trench Stores, Work in hand and proposed will be carefully taken over.

7. Completion of relief will be notified to Battalion Headquarters by wiring the code word "TROGAN".

                                          sgd. R.C.CUTTER. Captain.
                           Adjutant 10th. Battalion Royal Fusiliers.

Copies issued to :-

Copy No.1 to Commanding Officer 10th. Royal Fusiliers.
     2   Commanding Officer 3rd Battalion The Rifle Brigade.
     3   O.C. No. 1 Company.
     4   O.C. No. 2 Company.
     5   O.C. No. 3 Company.
     6   O.C. No. 4 Company.
     7   O.C. Headqr Company.
     8   R.S.M.
     9   Transport Officer.
    10   Quartermaster.
    11   War Diary.
    12.   File.

Army Form C. 2118.

WAR DIARY
or
INTELLIGENCE SUMMARY.

(Erase heading not required.)

C O N F I D E N T I A L.
****

(Unit). 12th. (S) Battalion ROYAL FUSILIERS.

W A R   D I A R Y for the Month of DECEMBER 1917.

..................Lt. Colonel.
Commanding 12th.(S) Battalion Royal Fusiliers.

28 T

Army Form C. 2118.

WAR DIARY
or
INTELLIGENCE SUMMARY.
(Erase heading not required.)

Instructions regarding War Diaries and Intelligence Summaries are contained in F. S. Regs., Part II. and the Staff Manual respectively. Title pages will be prepared in manuscript.

Place	Date	Hour	Summary of Events and Information	Remarks and references to Appendices
L.H. Cne.	1/8/17		Our patrol under 2/Lt Mears Devenish left River Post (Shelt 62 B.5.v) M8a 20.10 at 2 A.M. & proceeded via Fisher Crater, Duff's EG, Somerville Wood & returned by Brewer Post. M.8.c.x.0.80. No enemy seen.	appdx 1
	2/8/17		Patrol under 2/Lt A.G.Hills left River Post M8a 20.10 (Shelt 62 B.5.v) and proceeded via Fisher Crater, Max Banks, Somerville Wood & returned by Long Tree. M.24.30.30. No enemy encountered. Patrol fired at letts from Ziwel (Claud) Country 32 Div.	
	3/8/17		Patrol under 2/Lt Mears Devenish left River Post M8a 20.10 & proceeded via Fisher Crater, Max Banks & Wood & returned by Long Tree. No enemy were encountered. The Battalion were relieved in the line by the 9/2-9/4 Pick Bde. & moved into Divisional Reserve at Berne's.	
Bernes.	4/8/17		Both were at stations to the Battalion & Companies absorbed up.	
	5/8/17		Coy. Platoon & Section Training	
	6/8/17		Coy. Platoon & Section Training	
	7/8/17		Coy. Platoon & Section Training (by Commanders reconnoitred the support line held by the 2 Airmouth Fandor.	
	8/8/17		No.1 & No.4 Coy relieved the 8.2 (Airmouth) Fandor & took over 9 took in support. No were situated at George Copse (Shelt 62 o N.6) L.1.c.50.65.	
	9/8/17		Nos 2 & 3 Coys carried out Platoon & Section Training.	
	10/8/17		Nos 1 & 4 Coys were relieved in the line by the 8 Buffs, & returned to Bernes.	
	11/8/17		Nos 1 & 4 Coys were allotted Bathes — dressed up parades. Remainder carried out Coy Platoon Training.	
	12/8/17		Coy. Platoon & Section Training during the morning. Games in afternoon	

J.R. Day Lt. Col.
Commdg. 12th Royal Fusiliers

Army Form C. 2118.

WAR DIARY
or
INTELLIGENCE SUMMARY.
(Erase heading not required.)

Instructions regarding War Diaries and Intelligence Summaries are contained in F. S. Regs., Part II. and the Staff Manual respectively. Title pages will be prepared in manuscript.

Place	Date	Hour	Summary of Events and Information	Remarks and references to Appendices
BERNES	13/9/17.		School volume carried out by Coy Commanders.	
"	14/9/17.		Coy & platoon training	
"	15/9/17.		School volume carried out by Companies	
"	16/9/17.		Officers notes class went out with Company Commanders	
"	17/9/17.		Coy officers (by Companies) reconnoitred TEMPLEUX QUARRIES (sheet 62c N.E.)	
"	18/9/17.		Bn Hqrs relieved 9th Sussex Regt at TEMPLEUX QUARRIES (sheet 62c N.E.).	Appendix I.
"	19/9/17.		Front line by them reconnoitred.	
Pk. noire	20/9/17.		In cable situation. Nos 1, 2 & 4 Coys in front line. No 3 Coy in support. In the morning arm the Bath moved up to front line relieving the 2/Lr LEINSTERS. A patrol of 1 NCO & Keller (on patrol) taking advantage of the foggy weather succeeded in surprising and got at R.C.I.D. 15.15. ——	Appendix II
Tr mx Quarries	21/9/17.		a fro 7 pm shells were fired at to road at G.D. 1.9. No enemy seen.	
"	22/9/17.		Enemy artillery active all day. Shells were fired at G.D. 1.9 about 9 P.M. Otherwise quiet all day.	
"	23/9/17.		CHEBINI, MHINOFF & ENFILADE TRENCHES. Enemy planes also were active.	
Pk noire	24/9/17.		Bn H.Q was relieved in the line by the 3rd Rifle Bde (on forenoon) to TEMPLEUX QUARRIES (Bn moving)	Appendix IV
"	25/9/17.		Enemy artillery quiet. (Letter from Majors General Enemy. 17 th Sep 1917)	Appendix V
"	26/9/17.		Enemy planes were active all day. One or two short bursts of artillery in neighbourhood of to Quarries.	

J.R. Duff. Lt.Col.
Commg. 1st Bn Royal Fusiliers

A5834 Wt. W4973/M687 750,000 8/16 D. D. & L. Ltd. Forms/C.2118/13

Army Form C. 2118.

WAR DIARY
or
INTELLIGENCE SUMMARY.
(Erase heading not required.)

Instructions regarding War Diaries and Intelligence Summaries are contained in F. S. Regs., Part II. and the Staff Manual respectively. Title pages will be prepared in manuscript.

Place	Date	Hour	Summary of Events and Information	Remarks and references to Appendices
M. name	27/12/17		The Bn. was relieved by the 9th Sussex Regt. & proceeded to BERNES.	Appendix "W"
	28/12/17		A party (consisting of 5 officers & 200 O.R.'s) proceeded to JEANCOURT (by 3ME) under instructions of O.C. 52d Squadron to put out wire in front of new line of defence. Remainder of Bn. cleaned up & had baths.	
BERNES	29/12/17		Working party of 5 officers & 200 O.R.'s proceeded to JEANCOURT that night wire in front of new line of defence.	
	30/12/17		Working party under 52d Field Squadron proceeded to JEANCOURT to work on new line of defence.	
	31/12/17		A Concert was arranged for the Battalion men of the Battalion in Y.M.C.A. Hut at BERNES.	

J. R. Day Lt. Col.
Commg. 12th Bn. Royal Fusiliers

R.C.8.   APPENDIX II

Operation Order No 75
by
Lt Col. F.R. Day Commanding
12th Battalion Royal Fusiliers

The Battalion will relieve the 2nd Bn LEINSTERS and 13th Bn MIDDLESEX Regt in the line tonight as under:-

(1) C Coy 2nd LEINSTERS on the right relieved by No 1 Coy.

(2) D Coy 2nd LEINSTERS centre relieved by No 4 Coy.

(3) D Coy 13th MIDDLESEX left relieved by No 2 Coy.

(4) B Coy 2nd LEINSTERS. Support relieved by No 3 Coy.

(5) A Coy 2nd LEINSTERS Reserve relieved by A Coy Rifle Brigade

Guides
.   Guides for Nos 1 and 4 Coys will be at L.10.a. at 3.45 p.m.

Guides for Bn H.Q., No 3 Coy and A Coy 3rd RIFLE Bde will be at TEMPLEUX QUARRIES at 3.30 p.m.

Guides for No 2 Coy will be in accordance with arrangements made by O.C. No 2 Coy.

All movement will be by Sections at 100 yds interval.

Spare Kits will be dumped at present location of Coys and two men will be left in charge of each Coy dump. These will be brought forward to Bn. H.Qrs in limbers.

Each coy will on arrival send back a guide to Bn H.Qrs. to direct carrying parties to their respective coy H.Qrs.

Coys. will move in the following order:-
    Right.
    Centre
    Left
    Support
    Reserve
    H.Q.

Code word from 12 noon 19th —

12 noon 20th is "FIG".

Gum boots will not be taken into the line.

Lists of Trench Stores taken over will be sent down to Bn. H.Q.

Completion of Relief will be reported to Bn H.Q. by wiring Company Commanders name.

The Battalion will stand to every morning from 6 A.M. — 8 A.M.

Front Line Coys will arrange to patrol their own fronts from right to left once before midnight and once between 4 and 6 AM.

Strength of Patrol about 1 and 6.

O.C. Coys will make the necessary arrangements that these patrols do not meet in NO MANS LAND.

Posts in the Front Line which cannot be visited by daylight will be relieved every 12 hours.

Captin.
Adjutant 12. Bn Royal Fusiliers.

19-12-17.

APPENDIX III

Report on Minor operation on
Post of 12th Bn. R.F. which took place
at 2.35 a.m. on 20.12.17.

At about 2.35 a.m. this morning
the enemy strength about 20
raided the post of 1 N.C.O + 6 men
at A.25.d. 15.15
Their method of procedure was as
follows:—

"A" party about 15 strong crawled
up a disused trench from approx
A.25.d.15.25. and got round on the
W. of the post.

"B" party lay up in the trench
running from 15.25 - 20.25 (A.25.D)
When "A" were in position & made
their push on the post B party
opened fire with rifle grenades & bombs
on the posts on either flank.
The post was also bombed and all
the garrison wounded by either
hand or rifle grenades.
Fire was opened by the post attacked
& the posts on either flank.
One of the garrison of the post is
missing
A strong patrol was at once
sent out but none of the

enemy were discovered.
The whole affair did not last
more than 2-3 minutes.
There was no artillery fire.
The damaged trench has now been
blocked & eight broken gaps at L.6.8.65.92.

J.R. Day Lt Col
Comdg 11th Batt. Royal Fusiliers

20.12.17

Appendix IV   RCC No 11

O.O No 76   by Lt Col F R Day
Commanding 12th Bn. Royal Fusiliers

The Bn. will be relieved in the line by the 3rd Rifle Brigade tomorrow afternoon. as under

Time and place ~~and two of~~ for ^and number of same guides ~~will be notified~~ later.

On completion of relief the Bn will be located as under :-

No 1, 4 Coys and Bn H Q at
TEMPLEUX QUARRIES

No 2 Coy at L.10 a. in accommodation vacated by 3rd Rifle Bde.

No 3 Coy ~~attached~~ under O.C. 3rd Rifle Bde as reserve Coy. They

will take over accommodation vacated
by A Coy. 3rd Rifle Bde.
(Nos 1 & 4 Coys & H.Q.

Limbers for Lewis guns and spare kits
will be at Butt Q after dusk.

Limbers for No 2 Coy will be at
No 2 Coy dump.

On arrival at new locality the ~~Bn will~~
~~each~~ Coy will send representatives of
each platoon to reconnoitre the
following battle positions which will be
occupied in case of alarm.

1) No 2 Coy. HARGICOURT TRENCH N of
TEMPLEUX – HARGICOURT Rd.

2) One platoon No 1 Coy in TEMPLEUX
SWITCH (M.G. emplacements) in

F. 27.

3). H.Q., No 4 Coy. and No 1 Coy less 1 platoon mobile reserve in TEMPLEUX Quarries under orders of B.G.C.

Companies concerned will report to Orderly Room when these positions have been reconnoitred.

Completion of Relief will be wired to Bn H.Q. by Code Word "Rabbits"

22-12-17

R.C. Cutler. Capt. Adjt
12th Reg mo

No 1 Coy by B Coy.

No 4 Coy by D Coy.

No 2 Coy by A Coy.

No 3 Coy by C Coy.

4 guides per coy from No 1, 4 and 3 Coys will be at road junction L 5. d. 20. 80 at 4 p.m.

Guides from No 2 Coy will not be required.

No 3 Coy will be up at dusk.

4) O.C.s Coys will send one guide for each guard found by them to report to Bn HQ by 2 p.m.

7) Relief complete will be reported by wiring the code word BOW. OC 3 Coy will report to OC 3rd Rifle Bde. and report to Bn HQ on their arrival at BERNES

Issued to OC 1 Coy
           OC 2 "
           OC 3 "
           OC 4 "
           Royal Sussex
           Rifle Bde
           TO DW
           HQ Coy "

Appendix VI

Operation order No 77 by Lt Col.
A. L. Day commanding 12th Royal Fusiliers

1) The Bn will be relieved tomorrow by the 9th Royal Sussex, relief to be complete by 3.30 pm

2) On relief the Bn will proceed to BERNES

3) All Trench stores aeroplane maps guards and working parties will be carefully handed over to the incoming unit

4) Route via Templeux Roisel. All movement to be by platoons at 200 yds intervals.

6) All blankets stores etc will be ready for Transport by 2 pm. Transport

00.17

26.12.17

APPENDIX 1.

Mon Général

Je vous remercie bien vivement des souhaits que vous exprimez pour L'Infanterie de la 5me Division, et pour les camarades de L'Armée Française.

Nous sommes profondément touchés, mes Officiers et moi, des sentiments de camaraderie que vous nous témoignez, et qui sont entièrement réciproques.

Nous n'oublierons jamais l'accueil si cordial que vous nous avez fait. Je souhaite de tout coeur de me retrouver bientôt en contact avec les vaillantes troupes Britanniques, et il me serait plus particulièrement agréable que ce soit avec la belle at glorieuse 17me Brigade d'Infanterie que le contact soit repris.

Veuillez agréer, mon Général, l'expression de ma respectueuse et affectueuse camaraderie. Je vous adresse, mon Général, pour vous, pour vos Officiers, pour votre Brigade, au nom de mes Officiers, et au mien nos meilleurs souhaits.

    sd. L. MARTENET
  Colonel Cde. L'Infanterie de la 5me Division.

APPENDIX V.

To :- 17th Infantry Brigade.

In sending you all my best wishes for Christmas and the best of Good luck in the New Year, I would like to convey to all ranks of the 17th Brigade my unbounded admiration for all the splendid work they have done throughout the Year.

It has been a very hard year, and great demands have been made on all of you, and the magnificent way in which those demands have been met and accomplished, not only in your many battles, but also during all the most trying times you have been holding the Line, is worthy of the highest traditions of the British Army, and could not have been equalled.

You have established a record which I am confident, no matter what may be in front of us, you will always uphold. Remember that the great traditions of the 17th Brigade, left to us by those gallant men who died to make them, must ever be in our safe keeping, and above all we must ever preserve the memory of those great men who gladly gave their lives for the greatest cause in Christendom and for the Honour of their Regiments and Brigade.

The capture of LIEVIN in April - the Battle of MESSINES in June- followed within a week by the Attack on the strongly fortified Enemy positions East of BATTLE WOOD- holding the Sector East of YPRES until the end of June - the Third Battle of YPRES on July 31st - holding the YPRES Sector until September 16th - and holding the Line from September to the present time. is a fine record, and in looking back on 1917 it will always be to me a record of fine work well done - and I thank you from my heart for your great efforts.

I have never yet heard a grumble- never had to deal with a serious case of Lack of Discipline - and the loyal support which has been given me by all ranks has made my period of Command an easy one. To have had the Honour to Command such men as these will ever be the proudest period of my life.

This high standard could never have been achieved without that spirit of Camaraderie and mutual confidence which pervades all Ranks. With this spirit we will start the New Year, full of Hope for the future, and assured of Victory.

24/12/17

Brig. General.
Commanding 17th Infantry Brigade.

Army Form C. 2118.

WAR DIARY
or
INTELLIGENCE SUMMARY.
(Erase heading not required.)

CONFIDENTIAL.
****

(Unit) 12th. (S) Battalion THE ROYAL FUSILIERS.

WAR DIARY for the month of JANUARY. 1918.

A R Day................Lt. Colonel.
Commanding 12th. Battalion The Royal Fusiliers.

Army Form C. 2118.

WAR DIARY
or
INTELLIGENCE SUMMARY.

(Erase heading not required.)

1st Bn. The Royal Fusiliers

Place	Date	Hour	Summary of Events and Information	Remarks and references to Appendices
BEENES	1/1/18		Company & platoon Training. Extract from London Gazette 1/1/18 Major R. Sinclair award the D.S.O. (Military Cross)	
	2/1/18		Bn. (Battalion parade) to Vanignes Q.19.B.D. (Sheet 62c) in inclement weather.	
VANIGNES (on R.8)	3/1/18		Coy. Training. Musketry & baths	
	4/1/18		Interior Eng. Training & Musketry under Coy arrangement	
	5/1/18		Practise Ceremonial parade. Service in afternoon.	
	6/1/18		Sunday	
	7/1/18		Bayonet assault & forest (scramble) course by Coys under Bn.	
	8/1/18		Battalion paraded to Ceremonial support at Beenes (Sheet 62c)	
	9/1/18		Coy & platoon Training	
	10/1/18		Coy Training under Coy arrangement	
	11/1/18		Coy & platoon Training under Coy arrangements.	
	12/1/18		Bn. paraded to Templeux Quennots. (Bn. move) relieved the 1/24th London in Coy in the quarries. Bn (C) at L.10A (Sheet 62N.E.) & 1 Coy in reserve to the 3rd R.Bs in the line.	
	13/1/18		Enemy shelled Lestrey positions around TEMPLEUX	
	14/1/18		All quiet during the day	

J.R. Day
Captain 1st R. Fusrs

Army Form C. 2118.

WAR DIARY
or
INTELLIGENCE SUMMARY. 1/2nd Bn. The Royal Fusiliers
(Erase heading not required.)

Instructions regarding War Diaries and Intelligence Summaries are contained in F. S. Regs., Part II. and the Staff Manual respectively. Title pages will be prepared in manuscript.

Place	Date	Hour	Summary of Events and Information	Remarks and references to Appendices
B.H.Q. near	15/1/16		Enemy activity below normal. No 2 Coy. in reserve to 8 R.B.'s moved up to Osborne Res. 4th + Coy. at L 10.A (what 62.H.E) proceeded to Sing Quarry.	
Cité Calonne	16/1/16		The B.H. relieved the 3 R.B.'s in the line (centre subsector) No.4 Coy. left by No.1. Coy. No 3 right No 2 in support a Coy of 8 R.B.'s in reserve.	
	17/1/16		Considerable amount of enemy movement observed from O.P. Artillery quiet	
	18/1/16		Enemy artillery inactive all day. M.G.'s were active during night	
	19/1/16		Enemy artillery quiet. Our own artillery very active.	
	20/1/16		The B.H. were relieved in the centre subsector by the 4th Northants. 9th R.B. proceeded to Templeux where they entrained for Vraignies (Div. reserve)	
	21/1/16		The B.H. claims up generally. Road baths	
Vraignies	22/1/16		Bathing + working parties	
(L 25 E.2.)	23/1/16		Working parties found for work on R.F.C. aerodrome	
	24/1/16		Working party sent to Estrées to work for 35th Flying Squadron	
	25/1/16		Working party found working party at Treuilly to dig a new line of defence.	
	26/1/16		B.H. continued work on new line of defence at Poch 114	

Orders received for disbandment of the B.H.
J.R. D ay
Lt. Col. Comdg 2 R.F.

Army Form C. 2118.

WAR DIARY
or
INTELLIGENCE SUMMARY.
(Erase heading not required.)

2nd Bn. The Royal Fusiliers

Instructions regarding War Diaries and Intelligence Summaries are contained in F.S. Regs., Part II. and the Staff Manual respectively. Title pages will be prepared in manuscript.

Place	Date	Hour	Summary of Events and Information	Remarks and references to Appendices
VRAIGNES	28/1/8		Working party (continued) work on new line of defence at POEUILLY. The recurring repairs of HQ (RE) were cont. along with the consummation effort.	
"	29/1/16		Working party at POEUILLY supplying new line of defence. Enemy planes dropped bombs during the early part of the night in the neighbourhood of VRAIGNES	
"	30/1/16		Working party commenced support line of new line of defence at POEUILLY	
"	31/1/16		Working party continued work on support line at POEUILLY	
			" " " "	
			" " " "	

J.R. Day. Lt. Colonel.
Commg. 2nd Bn. Royal Fusiliers.

25th January, 1918.

Dear Colonel Day,

The Commander-in-Chief has asked me to express his great sympathy to you and your Battalion on being broken up. It is a hard necessity.

I do not think I can convey his sentiments to you better than he does himself, and I am therefore sending you a copy of his letter.

In these feelings I join, and I cannot say how much I feel for you and your men in having to break such fine bonds of comradeship, and after creating so many grand traditions.

Yrs truly,

[*Not for publication or communication to the Press*].

Care must be taken that the information contained herein does not fall into the hands of the enemy.

GENERAL HEADQUARTERS,
BRITISH ARMIES IN FRANCE.
20 January, 1918.

No.

My dear Gough.

The situation with regard to man-power has rendered it impossible to maintain all the units now in the field, and in consequence the Army Council have issued orders that a large number of battalions must be broken up. I wish, through you, to convey to the Commanders and all ranks of the battalions about to be disbanded my great regret that this step should have been found necessary.

I know how deeply officers and men will feel the severance of the ties binding them to the units in which they have served and fought with such splendid gallantry and success and with which they had hoped eventually to return home after the great struggle had been won and their task achieved. But I know also that since this reorganization has to be it will be accepted with the loyalty and devotion with which every trial has been met by British officers and men throughout the war.

Please convey to the officers and other ranks concerned, with my deep appreciation of their services in the past, my confidence that they will accept this disappointment in the right spirit and will give to their new units to which they are transferred the same devotion and esprit-de-corps that they gave to those they have been with until now.

Very truly
D. Haig.

Gen. Sir H. de la P. GOUGH,
K.C.B., K.C.V.O.,
Commanding Fifth Army.

17th Inf. Bde. A/15

H.Q. 2nd Draft

Herewith War Diary of 17th Inf Bde
for February — up till the date of
disbandment.

(Signed) C. Westmacott Lt Col
7/3/16   late Comdg 17 Bde

CONFIDENTIAL.

To Headquarters,
 17th. Infantry Brigade.

  Attached please find WAR DIARY for the period of Feb.1st to 13th. 1918 (inclusive).

          M.Allison
         Actg. Adjt. for Lt.Col.
        Commdg. 12th.Bn.The Royal Fusiliers.

16/2/18.

Army Form C. 2118.

WAR DIARY
or
INTELLIGENCE SUMMARY.
(Erase heading not required.)

CONFIDENTIAL

Unit. 12th.Batt The Royal Fusiliers.

W A R D I A R Y for the Month

of FEBRUARY 1918.

[signature]

Actg Adjt. for Lt.Col
Commanding 12th.Bn.Royal Fusiliers.

WAR DIARY or INTELLIGENCE SUMMARY

Army Form C. 2118.

Instructions regarding War Diaries and Intelligence Summaries are contained in F.S. Regs., Part II. and the Staff Manual respectively. Title pages will be prepared in manuscript.

(Erase heading not required.)

Place	Date	Hour	Summary of Events and Information	Remarks and references to Appendices
VERIGNIES	1/2/18		We found working party for digging an advanced line at POSOITY. (about 60°N E)	
"	2/2/18		2/Lt. MEARS DEVENISH and Ptes. OWEN J, WHITNELL A.H. were awarded the Croix de Guerre. (Belgian)	
"	3/2/18		A draft of 10 Officers & 200 O.R's of this Battalion were posted to the 10th 2nd Bn Royal Fusiliers. (37th Divn) remainder went to POSOITY to continue work on trench.	
"	4/2/18		A draft of 10 Officers and 200 O.R's of the Battalion left this afternoon to join the 17th Bn Royal Fusiliers at HANCOURT. (about 60°N.E) 7th Div Command.	Attached 4 & 5 & 111
"	5/2/18		The remaining details taken over by Lt. Col. R. Huey (Commandant Entrainment. Letters received from Commanders of 10th & 17th Royal Fusiliers. Nothing by.	
"	6/2/18			
"	7/2/18		Yesterday the Regt. were to be keenness & close accommodation accepted by us. Nothing by.	
"	8/2/18			
"	9/2/18		3 Officers & 8 men proceeded as a draft to the 10th Bn Royal Fusiliers.	
"	10/2/18		Remaining details nothing by.	
"	11/2/18		" " " "	

K. Tintin Major
Commanding 12th Batt Royal Fusiliers

Army Form C. 2118.

WAR DIARY
or
INTELLIGENCE SUMMARY.
(Erase heading not required.)

Instructions regarding War Diaries and Intelligence Summaries are contained in F. S. Regs., Part II. and the Staff Manual respectively. Title pages will be prepared in manuscript.

Place	Date	Hour	Summary of Events and Information	Remarks and references to Appendices
VRAIGNES.	12/9/18		Draft of 11 Officers & 220 O.R of this Battalion proceeded to join 11th Batt. Royal Fusiliers.	
	19/9/18		Major A. Simkins M.C. - Lt. M. Calthsson & 7 Warrant Officers proceeded to 7th Corps Reinforcement Camp HAUTE ALLAINES to await re-posting to new Units.	

A. Simkins Major
Commanding 12th Batt: Royal Fusiliers.

Appendix I. War Diary. Officers /

Re Disbanding of Battalions

Received from 17th Lieut./ Mk. Sqn.

1) To be then asked to reduce all Brigades to 3 Battalions and to keep them up to War Establishment

2) Orders have been issued that the 12th & 13th Bns Royal Fusiliers are to be disbanded and the officers & men will be distributed to other Battalions of their own regiments.

Appendix III

SPECIAL DIVISIONAL ROUTINE ORDER
** by **
Major General A.C. DALY, C.B.
Commanding 24th. Division.

3rd FEBRUARY 1918.

(3382).

On the occasion of the disbandment of the 8th Battn: The Buffs (East Kent Regiment) and the 12th Battn: The Royal Fusiliers (City of London Regiment), the Divisional Commander desires to express his high appreciation of the valuable services performed by these two fine battalions, and his sincere regret at losing them.

He sympathises deeply with their Commanding Officers and all ranks in these battalions in their feelings of sorrow and regret at having to sever their connection with old comrades and friends, and to bring to a premature end the history and traditions built up by these two young but already veteran battalions.

He feels sure that all officers and men will rapidly assimilate that pride in their new battalions and that "esprit de corps" which has been such a large and important factor in the history and traditions of the British Army for centuries, and has played such an important part in the glorious achievements of every unit.

He wishes Colonel F.R. DAY and Colonel F.C.R. STUDD and all Officers and men of the 8th Bn: The Buffs and 12th Bn: Royal Fusiliers good luck and success.

E.P. Riddell

Lieut-Colonel,
A.A.& Q.M.G. 24th Division.

www.ingramcontent.com/pod-product-compliance
Lightning Source LLC
Chambersburg PA
CBHW080921230426

43668CB00014B/2169